S0-BDP-581

also by amy friedman

Kick the Dog and Shoot the Cat

Nothing Sacred: A Conversation with Feminism

Best Bedtime Stories

Tell Me a Story

The Spectacular Gift

DESPERADO'S WIFE

a memoir

amy friedman

Copyright © 2012 by Amy Friedman
All rights reserved

Epigraph from Chris Hedges, *The World As It Is: Dispatches on the Myth of Human Progress*, Nation Books, © 2011, Used by permission

Excerpts of *Desperado's Wife* originally appeared in
The *New York Times*, Modern Love, February 2009, *Kept Together by the Bars Between Us*
Salon.com, February 2011, *My Husband, the Convicted Murderer*
Spike Gillespie & Katherine Tanney's *Stricken: The 5,000 Stages of Grief*, Dalton Publishing, 2009
For information about permission to reproduce selections from this book, write to Amy Friedman, amy@amyfriedman.net

Cover Art and Design © 2012 Gary and Laura Dumm

Friedman, Amy
Desperado's Wife: a memoir / Amy Friedman – 2nd ed.

ISBN – 9781619272040

Desperado's Wife is a work of memoir. It reflects the author's present recollection and understanding of experiences over a period of many years. Some names, locations and identifying characteristics have been changed. Dialogue and events have been re-created from memory.

for sarah and cassandra

foreword

Men and women meet and sometimes fall in love—for all of the usual reasons. Prison romances are no different. People meet and often, to their surprise as much as the surprise of others, they fall in love. What is different in a prison romance is not the relationship but rather the enormously difficult environment and the ugly pressures put on the couple and their fledgling connection. The outside partner becomes suspect as though a criminal herself and is subjected to the unrelenting humiliation of searches and invasion of privacy. Often her community rejects her and she carries the mantle of a stigmatized, unwell person. At the same time she must struggle to develop her relationship in an artificial, sterile, public, hostile environment, with little opportunity to participate in the usual activities of courtship and of life together as a couple. Love becomes a cause for which she is compelled to fight very powerful systems—alone.

Amy Friedman has been there. A simple attraction and growing love forced her to combat employers, penitentiary officials, family and friends. Finally even her partner saw her as an adversary as he became slave to the heavy and oppressive suspiciousness that is the life blood of prison. She had to endlessly justify what in any other circumstance would be accepted at face value. Most difficult was to realize the inevitable cancer that these external pressures would create in her and the person she wanted to love.

As few others could, Amy explains it all in its simplicity and complexity.

With nearly 2.5 million Americans now in prison, there are millions of loved ones—wives and husbands, brothers and sisters, parents and friends—who will find strength and comfort in this story. For anyone interested in how relationships survive in trying environments, *Desperado's Wife* will be a revelation.

This is a story that needs to be heard.

Graham Stewart,
National Director, Ret.
The John Howard Society of Canada
Criminal Justice Advocacy Society

We are saved not by what we can do or accomplish but by our fealty to revolt, our steadfastness to the weak, the poor, the marginalized, and those who endure oppression. We must stand with them against the powerful. If we remain true to these moral imperatives, we win. And I am enough of an idealist to believe that the struggle to live the moral life is worth it.

Chris Hedges, *The World As It Is: Dispatches on the Myth of Human Progress*

part one

chapter one

I know the date I first walked into Maynard Penitentiary without looking it up because it was my father's birthday, April 24, and the year was 1992. Later the date seemed a portent, but that day I was thinking only of my work. One of my former writing students, a retired military man named Harry Windsor, urged me to visit some of the prisons that surrounded Kingston, Ontario, my adopted hometown. Harry was a member of The Citizens' Advisory Committee—a group of meddlesome if good-hearted citizens who visited prisons to "keep an eye on things." Harry primarily visited medium security Maynard, the hulking place that sat out on 640 acres between Highway 15 and the Rideau Canal, just off the road I drove to work every day.

I was a columnist at Kingston's daily newspaper. Outside of eastern Ontario *The Whig Standard* never sounded like much, but I think of *The Whig* of that era the way Burt Lancaster in *Atlantic City* described the ocean to Susan Sarandon as they strolled the beach: "You should have seen the Atlantic when it was the Atlantic…" *The Whig* was something people should have seen when it was *The Whig*. It was Canada's oldest daily that for 156 years, from its founding in 1835 until that very spring, was owned by just two families. Housed in a four story red brick building that overlooked Kingston's Market Square, the paper was literary and courageous, its owners community-spirited types who did idiosyncratic things like sending reporters to Bosnia to report on the war from the frontlines to allowing its columnists, like me, to write luxuriously long pieces.

For seven years I had reveled in writing that column, but earlier in 1992, Southam Syndicate purchased the paper, and our new boss, Lawrence O'Connor was friendly enough, and he seemed to like me—just that month he selected me to be the writer who would join him at a Celebrity Golf Tournament in Ottawa. Still, I must have sensed the possibility of losing the column when I suggested to my editor that I write a second one too—something for kids. My editor applauded the idea, and so the daily Bedtime Story was born—adaptations of myths, folktales and fairytales. By the time I visited that first prison, ten other Canadian papers had picked up *The Bedtime Story*, and I was working 70 hour weeks.

I was 39—I would turn 40 that summer, not young but I felt on the brink of becoming myself. I felt as if I had arrived as a writer, and I believed my place in the world would only get better—that I would somehow eventually have it all. I might never be rich and famous, but I was certain I would forever after be at least financially comfortable and intellectually admired. I assumed I would publish many more books—my first had just come out and I was in the middle of writing a second. I was confident life would always include adventure and good fortune, awards and rewards like the prestigious literary prize I'd recently won, the contract for a second book I'd just signed, and journeys like those I had taken with my long-time partner, Dean. I also thought that some kind of grand love—the kind my parents seemed to share—was in my future.

Dean was a professor, and he and I had shared his 100-acre sheep farm outside Kingston for the past seven years. I loved the turn-of-the-century farmhouse, our dog and cats, our flocks of sheep and our crazy horse. In those years Dean and I had traveled the world together, and he had taught me to take my writing seriously, to create and meet deadlines no matter what, even or especially when the muse was nowhere in sight. He'd also taught me how to birth lambs and fix pumps, lay insulation and construct walls, bleed pipes and lay roofing tile. We looked and sounded like the perfect couple—he was a decade older, wiser, quiet and confident; I was the young woman who kept him young, warmer and more outgoing. But no matter that we looked the part, not only weren't we perfect, we were barely a couple. We had stopped sleeping together, and he'd always kept me at half an arm's length. Despite his professed passion for me, he didn't care if I slept with other men, and so I did (and although he professed to always being, first, faithful to me and later celibate, when we did split up I learned that neither had ever been true). I had begun to notice he was drinking too much—shot after shot of expensive single malt Scotch. And we were forever arguing about the most mundane things (how best to toss a bale of hay) and the most profound (our relationship). He had two teenagers from a first marriage that had ended bitterly and left him vowing never ever to marry again. I liked his daughter—she was a sweet-tempered teenager, and we had always been nice to each other though never especially close, but his son, a more difficult child, and I often crossed swords. Dean and I had just returned from a trip. He had stayed home for a week before leaving for a few months to do research overseas. I was grateful for the solitude at home.

Secretly, so secretly I seldom let myself give it a thought, I had always wished some man would come along who would adore me the way my dad had always adored my mom. I suspect every one of us four kids had one version or another of this same wish, but all four of us had thus far failed to find that adoring and adored partner. My sister, Karen, three years younger than me, had recently divorced the man we'd all believed was the perfect husband. My brother, Peter's, marriage seemed okay but more a marriage of intellect than of heart, and my youngest sister, Rachel, in her early 30s, was not a romantic and was happy enough with her single status and talked of finding a sperm donor so she could have a child soon.

I talked a good game, taming occasional flare ups of a desire to have a child and to live in a monogamous, devoted marriage. Instead I professed to feel lucky that I wasn't burdened by the ties of a traditional marriage like my mother's and like those of so many of my friends. I talked about how glad I was not to be caught up with the demands of children (and I shied away from any kind of mothering of Dean's kids). I told myself I did have it all: The security of a nice home and endless travel opportunities combined with the freedom to meet who I wanted to meet, to love who I wanted to love, to write what I wanted to write, to go whenever and wherever I wanted to go.

That spring my freedom to go anywhere led me to prison.

Maynard Medium Security Institution was where Harry Windsor invited me to visit first, and I read its mission statement asserting that Maynard allowed its inmates "the freedom of an evening sitting room with television as a medium of entertainment, and where they could dine in association using regular eating utensils." The buildings were designed as four story barrack blocks around a central courtyard. I'd passed it on my daily drives to work, and occasionally I'd noticed people moving up and down its winding drive. When I drove by at night and saw it lit up by sodium lights in the dark countryside, I thought it looked like an alien spaceship, but everything I read about all of Canada's correctional facilities made them sound earthy, humane and focused on justice and rehabilitation in equal measure.

Harry said Maynard was roiling with racial tension and other difficulties the outside world had remained ignorant of, and that was why he wanted me to come see for myself and write a few columns about it. With Dean I had taken months'-long journeys to places like South Africa and Belfast and afterwards I'd written about conflict and racism. I'd also written about date rape and youth in trouble, about the group home for young offenders where I served on the board of directors. Like all those difficult, divisive, sometimes dark worlds, prison and its politics intrigued me, ignited my curiosity. I was glad Harry arranged the opportunity for me to visit.

That first day as I drove towards Maynard, I could hear the belching heaves that rise from down deep in rivers and lakes as ice breaks up. Kingston sits on the shore of Lake Ontario and the St. Lawrence Seaway, and my ride took me along the snaking Rideau Canal where I noticed grass pushing out of muddy, frost-laden earth and buds forming on bare black branches. I felt buoyed by the coming spring the way most people in that part of the world do; the world was coming back to life after long, frigid winter months. But inside prison it could just as easily have been December or July. Inside there was no weather.

As I walked through Maynard's dank, dim hallways, I began to imagine what I might write. I envisioned something powerful, poignant, descriptive and apt, and I also half-imagined the letters to the editor readers might write about my prison columns. I knew some readers who would be angry; I had fans, but I had enemies too because I tended toward a liberal viewpoint, toward seeing things from the point of view of those who seemed most victimized. I'd always had a soft spot for the fallible and powerless. I grew up rooting for the Cleveland Indians, fell for the weakest lambs and craziest horses on the farm, favored my most awkward students, leaned towards empathy for the Irish and the Palestinians and the black South Africans. When I read that Canada was second only to the United States in the numbers of those who were incarcerated, that prison populations continued to rise despite falling crime rates, I sensed that something was off. It seemed that our culture was addicted to punishment, and I had come to prison to see what that addiction had spawned. I believed if I could paint a powerful portrait of what actually went on inside—offering every point of view—I might just alter attitudes. It was a bold, perhaps naïve belief, but one I never lost.

Harry had arranged for me to meet two Lifers—Mark, a smooth-talking and handsome African-American in his 40s, and Luke, a white man in his early 30s, with a bulging gut, a flourishing beard and a genial smile. Within hours of talking with them I learned that prisoners do not talk about their crimes—essentially what mattered more was that they were doing their time for their crime, no sense talking about it. I already knew that most of those who were sentenced to Life had committed murder, so I assumed both men had killed someone, but we didn't talk about who or how or when or why. We talked about the food—passable; the guards—good and bad; the time—it felt endless; their visitors—manna; prison culture—complex. I also met Warden Claussen, a poker-faced man whose presence was starchly polite. Claussen was new to Ontario, transferred from his post in British Columbia to help liberalize Ontario's joints—or so Harry believed and told me. He explained that Ontario was considered by the Correctional Services National Headquarters to be a backward province when it came to corrections, tending towards corruption and punishment, and was not up to speed on rehabilitative measures.

Claussen had been warden for only a few weeks, and for that reason he explained he had invited his deputy warden, Louise Salem, to join our meeting; she would know more about Maynard than he, he told me. Salem reminded me of Nurse Ratched from *One Flew Over the Cuckoo's Nest*. Tall and straight-backed, she wore her graying blond hair in a tight, uneasy twist. Her voice and her face and handshake were stiff and cold. She did not smile or say one kind word, but I didn't hold her steely reserve against her; I simply reasoned that to survive in this hostile, dominantly male world, a woman needed to be hard.

And nearly everything did feel hostile—the clanging gates, the echoing halls, the lifeless air, the hard stares of those we passed in the halls. But Mark and Luke were remarkably talkative and friendly as they guided me from Sally Port, the entryway, on into the Visitors and Correspondence Room, the V&C, the high-ceilinged room with rows of hard-backed seats arranged like a bus station waiting room. At the far end two guards glared out at us from a glassed-in booth, then turned to stare at the visitors who shuffled in and out of the room, hugging the prisoners who came in the room to meet them. I barely glanced at the visitors. I wasn't interested in mere citizens.

I was interested in the guards and the inmates. I knew prison only from movies and television, and I wanted to know more than what I could read in material furnished by the Correctional Services of Canada. From the literature I knew that Maynard had been built to house 430 men but that month more than 500 were incarcerated. I knew that of the majority of prisoners—55%—were serving sentences of 40 months and over, that 11% had life sentences (which in Canada meant they could eventually be paroled but would serve a lifetime on parole), and that 34% were short-timers, serving fewer than 40 months. Maynard employed approximately 340 men and women as correctional officers (guards) and nurses and parole officers and psychologists and social workers and pharmacists and internal police.

But I wanted to know what all those numbers and those titles meant, and I wanted to know what people talked about and thought about and argued about. And most of all I wanted to know what happened to inmates and guards alike who lived each day and night inside such a physically depressing world. There was too little air inside, and the cells Luke and Mark showed me were the size of the small upstairs bathroom in our farmhouse. They were square with hard bunks, thin mattresses, everything concrete and steel. Every window in the place was tiny and barred and looked out either onto the dusty central courtyard or miles of empty fields surrounded by barbed wire and manned gun towers. Towards lunchtime Luke and Mark took me to Unit 5 where they lived. This unit, they explained, was built more like a dorm with hives surrounding a common area; inmates won the privilege of living in Unit 5 by displaying "good behavior," though they didn't exactly explain what good behavior was. They invited me to join them for lunch at a sticky table where they chowed down on greasy beef and fries lathered in gravy. I politely declined any food.

As they ate, Luke described the Inmate Committee to me. He was the co-chairman. He served along with another two men—his co-chairman and a treasurer. He explained that they had been elected by the 500 prisoners to meet regularly with administrators to discuss prisoners' complaints and desires. When I asked him why his co-chairman hadn't joined us, Luke shrugged and quickly said, "He couldn't make it," and just at that moment a strapping man strode into the room. "This is the Administrative Manager of Unit 5," Luke introduced me to Rick LaFlamme who smiled as broadly as Mark was smiling. When Luke told him I was from *The Whig*, Rick grinned even more broadly.

"Lawrence O'Connor's a good friend. In fact he's my golfing buddy," and he heartily shook my hand. "Glad to see the paper's interested in us."

I accepted the handshake and the three of us chatted about nothing important. I was brimming with pride about my use of the lingo I'd learned in those few hours—Sally Port and V&C and Unit Five and Lifer—words I hadn't known that morning were slipping easily off my tongue by afternoon.

I cringe at the memory of my desire to know insiders' secrets and my naiveté in thinking I understood anything at all—my cocky belief that because I wrote a newspaper column, I deserved (and would receive) the keys to every world I entered. For past columns I had taken control of a Cessna at a flying school, covered a criminal trial, had visited South African writers in their underground newspaper offices. That day

I figured I'd have the whole prison thing down in no time and afterwards would move on.

But after that lunch in Unit 5, everything happened so quickly, I struggle to conjure the interior life of the woman I was before.

At 2:00 it was time to leave, and Luke agreed to escort me to the exit. As we walked down the hallway, I assured him that I would return. He wanted me to visit some of the inmate groups—the Lifers' group, the Native Brotherhood, the Chinese group. I explained to him as I had to the warden and deputy warden, that before I published anything I planned to show each story to representatives from each of the groups—the administrators, the prisoners and the guards. Although I was interested in knowing how the Mission Statement with its emphasis on the "offender's responsibility" and its assertion that the court's sentence constituted punishment in itself played out in reality, and although I wanted to paint a picture of what prison life was truly like, I did not want to stir up trouble inside. These columns weren't meant to be exposés, I explained; rather, they would be portraits of a world too few people knew about.

As Luke and I walked I was aching for air, and a hundred yards from the last gate, a muscular, tattooed inmate in dark glasses approached us. Luke's eyes lit up. "Hey, Will," he said. "This is that reporter I wanted you to meet."

"Amy, this is my Inmate Committee Co-chairman, Will Dryden."

Will began to look me slowly up and down, and I instantly felt his wariness, and for the first time that day I felt judged, and that pissed me off. Like all the other inmates, Will wore a stiff, pea green jumpsuit that flattered no one, but I immediately noticed his looks—muscular arms, narrow waist, broad shoulders. It was only later that I realized his eyeglasses were supposed to alter with the changing light, but even in that dark hallway, they were opaque. His graying hair was cut military short, though he always thought his hair was as blond as it had been before he was arrested at 31, seven years earlier; he never believed it had turned gray. Later his mother would tell me it had turned overnight. Later mine would too. But that was later.

That day Will was, simply, the only person who greeted me as if I were an enemy and it was only when, looking back, that I saw how the scene had unfolded like those classic movies I'd always loved—Bogey whispering to Bacall in The Big Sleep, "What's wrong with you?" and her throaty reply, "Nothing you can't fix." Or Vivien Leigh trading insults with Clark Gable in *Gone with the Wind* before falling into his arms. In that first moment he infuriated me, and he scared me. He gave off sexual, dangerous heat, but I was intent on pretending I felt no fear, and certainly not attraction. I tried to ignore that prickly feeling in my limbs, the trembling knees, and when he said in a voice so gravelly and deep I had to lean forward to catch the words, "I don't talk to journalists," I summoned my inner Katherine Hepburn, Rose to Bogey in *The African Queen* and haughtily shot back, "Nice to meet you too," and offered him my sweaty hand.

I'm sure he saw through the effort to sound braver and smarter than I was. He was accustomed to seeing through guises—an ability he may have been born with and certainly a skill honed in prison. He refused my handshake. "Every time a journalist walks inside, something bad goes down for the guys," he said. "You think anyone cares about prisoners? We're sitting ducks."

"So why even bother meeting me?" I charged.

"Because you're beautiful," he smiled a sideways half smile I could tell he had practiced. "We don't see a lot of beautiful women in here."

Damn his imitation Cary Grant. I had purposefully dressed conservatively in a long-sleeved top, a long skirt, in clothes that revealed as little skin as possible, and the comment embarrassed me. Besides, it was so damn corny. I'd noticed in a few earlier conversations with prisoners—brief and in passing—that prisoners tended to be a little corny. I reasoned it was because they didn't get out much. Maybe they watched too many sappy movies. Maybe they were just out of practice with social niceties. At any rate, my defenses rose.

"How do you expect anyone to know anything about what happens inside if none of you talks to outsiders?"

He smiled again, a bemused smile. "What do you care?"

The tension between us was a combination of attraction and competition, and I knew that right away, but I also felt as if in those few hours inside I had wedged open a door and I was damned if a mere prisoner was going to slam that door in my face, make me believe I couldn't write what I wanted to write. And I was damned, too, if a prisoner was going to woo me. That was absurd. Like most of my friends, I had fallen for bad boys in my life, but like most of my friends—and most everyone else—I believed that anyone who was in prison was well beyond the pale. The bad boys I'd known weren't that bad. Somehow men who went to prison were—what? They were losers. They couldn't get away with things. I'd always fallen for the men who did.

"Maybe I want to know what goes on inside. You ever think that?" I asked.

This time his smile revealed a dimple, and if I could have seen his eyes, I'd have seen he was teasing me—good naturedly. His voice softened, just a little. "You want to know about what goes on inside?" he asked.

"Didn't I just say that?" I said.

He leaned in closer. "Talk to the families. They never hurt a soul, and they know what prison's about."

Luke had been shifting foot to foot, and when he piped up, "True," I turned and noticed him again, and I could see he wasn't sure how to intervene, or if he should.

"There's a social on Saturday," Will said, pulling my attention back to him. "Kids and wives will be there. You should come. Talk to them."

I nodded. I looked at Luke who was nodding too. This was one of the best ideas anyone had offered that day, and the suggestion instantly softened my feelings towards Will. If he was someone who cared about families, he couldn't be all bad—he must have one of those soft centers, just like Bogey's characters always did.

Luke said he would arrange things. I looked at Will, trying to see through those glasses. "It's a deal," I said. This time when I offered my hand, he took it.

"So I'll see you there," he said. "You should talk to my daughters."

"Right," I said. I didn't give them another thought as I drove home inhaling the scent of ripening alfalfa fields along the way. But back home I began to think about those daughters and about the other visitors I'd seen over the years streaming out of Maynard's long roadway. Once in a while, on bitter cold days, or rainy days, I had thought about stopping to pick up one of the women waiting by the roadside for the bus into

Kingston, 10 miles away. They always looked sad, but always as my foot edged towards the brakes, I'd think: But she's probably smuggling drugs or knives. For years I had joined with others in town in swapping jokes about prisons and their inhabitants—they were "them," nothing like "us." I only vaguely knew the names of the ten institutions nearby, and though I knew tales of a few infamous prisoners—wrongly convicted men that Hurricane Carter championed and Stephen Reid who married the famous poet Susan Musgrave and wrote a book and became famous too—most of what I knew stemmed from rumors. I knew that much of Kingston's population earned a living as guards, administrators, and contractors in the prisons. I believed that in prison rapes and murders were daily, acceptable fare. I believed that prisoners and their loved ones were of a breed somehow different from mine.

But I never said such things out loud. I admired friends who tutored prisoners and an editor pal who visited prisoners' AA meetings. And I wanted to learn. I thought about how good I would feel when I'd unearthed prisons' secrets. I believed my dad's experience as a WW II POW was in part to blame for the darkest parts of my own nature and for my curiosity. I was certain that nobody with all that sadness in his past could feel as happy as Dad seemed to feel without some of that despair and terror seeping under his children's skin.

So it is true that I began visiting prison with the idea that imprisonment itself causes harm. Because of my dad, because of Kurt Vonnegut's *Slaughterhouse Five*, I went to prison largely to find out what happened to people who were locked inside cages for long stretches of time. Eventually I learned, in spades, that Will was right: Few people know better than do prisoners' loved ones what prison does to human beings.

chapter two

Sunday afternoon, the day of the family social, was sunny and warm, and as I was whisked past the long line of waiting families, I didn't stop to think about how they must feel. It never crossed my mind that my being above suspicion was as absurd as the idea that every one of those family members—from the old women to the tiniest babies—was considered capable of criminal behavior. I didn't stop to think that anyone else considered "official" could just as easily be guilty of smuggling in some kind of contraband. Back then I just thought "they" were different from me.

Luke met me on the other side of the Sally Port gate and escorted me into a cement-walled room where the Native Canadian Brotherhood had gathered. Their leader, Pete, was passionately kissing his girlfriend, long fingers caressing the thick black braid that hung to her slender waist, and embarrassed at intruding I turned to talk to someone else who began to tell me about his parents, dead by the time he was five, and his heroin addiction. Another man interrupted to introduce me to his three pudgy daughters with chocolate smeared faces who clambered over their dad as he talked about his sad childhood. I scribbled notes as others told me stories, and the day went on that way.

At some point I poked my head into the gymnasium that crammed with long tables spread with a feast and festooned with balloons. It looked like a school carnival except the women wore sexy dresses. At a table in the far corner I spotted Will sitting beside a pretty woman and surrounded by kids. For a moment I was disappointed to see there was a wife, but before I could spend too much time thinking about that, someone tapped my shoulder, and I ducked out of the room to talk.

That's all I remember of that day, a blur of tales and invitations to return to hear more.

Afterwards I drove to Kingston to eat supper at Chez Piggys, the chic restaurant owned by Zal Yanofsky who was, next to Peter Gzowski, my favorite famous Canadian. Once upon a time Zal had been the guitarist for the Lovin' Spoonful, also once married to one of Canada's famous actresses, Jackie Burroughs, whom I also knew. This is what I loved about Canada—after years of living in Manhattan and feeling swallowed by the big-ness of the city and its stars, Canada felt like a big small town, and since I was one of Kingston's literary lights, I knew many of the denizens. Zal, once famous for his cowboy hats and Davey Crockett gear and his ability to play anything on the guitar, was now just as well known for his restaurant in a converted piggery with sleek limestone walls. Whenever I was there I felt like singing, "Zal and Denny working for a penny," and Lovin' Spoonful songs would spin through my mind—*Do You Believe in Magic? Summer in the City*.... Everyone who was anyone in Kingston's artistic and intellectual elite hung out at The Pig, as we called it; the zaftig bartender, and the cool, leggy maitre d' greeted me by name. Everyone ate there—rich kids whose parents owned waterfront real estate, professors and sailors, reporters from *The Whig*, Dan Ackroyd with his body guards and biker pals. That is, everyone hung out at The Pig except the prison people who were more likely to go to the Toucan, the working class Irish pub that shared the courtyard space with The Pig.

There should be a demarcation line that marks that weekend as the moment my life altered from being a minor celebrity, hanging with Zal, schmoozing at The Pig, on the way to literary notice, from the rest of my life. There wasn't one moment when I understood this, and I certainly didn't back then, but for all my sophistication and worldliness, deep down I was still a little girl who wanted to be adored the way my father adored my mother. In my 20s I'd married a man who was kind and smart, but we never adored each other, and in the fifth year of our marriage, we parted ways. Dean, my current partner, had seemed even more perfect given all the freedom he offered me, but what I wanted was a man who looked at me the way my father looked at my mother, someone who would ache for me the way the heroes in my favorite movies and books ached for the women they loved. I wanted Heathcliff, Darcy and Rochester, Romeo. None of my romances had been passionate enough, and none had obstacles to surmount. Love had been too ordinary.

* * *

On the Monday morning after the social, I was in my office at *The Whig*, a makeshift, windowless space with a telephone and long table, off the second floor newsroom. A producer from Ottawa's CJOH TV had come to tape a show about The Bedtime Story, my kids' column. Jane McDonald was a feisty television journalist who had long been a devoted fan and friend. There we were, Jane with her short hair and quick wit interviewing me, her cameraman shooting, when the phone rang. Jane silently directed me to answer and kept the camera rolling.

"You didn't come to the social," a voice I recognized at once as Will's said.

Did I imagine he sounded angry? I'm sure I did, and I didn't want a murderer angry at me. Heat rose to my neck. I looked at Jane, wishing she would ask the cameraman to turn away. I didn't want to ask, so I said, "I was there, you just didn't see me." I smiled for the camera. "Can I phone you back? I'm a little busy right now."

"Sure," he said, and he reeled off a number. I wrote it on a scrap of paper and hung up. I was blushing as I whispered to Jane, "That was a prisoner I met. I'm writing about prisons now..."

"Cool," she said.

"He invited me to a social, and I went, but I didn't see him, and he called because he thinks I just didn't show."

"Touchy," she grinned. "Keep me in the loop on this one, okay? But I read your column, so I'm sure I'll hear the whole story..." And we continued with the shoot.

A few hours later, after Jane and the cameraman left, the office was quiet. It was after five, and most of the reporters were gone for the day. I picked up the phone and dialed the number Will had given me. The voice that answered wasn't Will's, and when I asked for him, the voice snarled back at me. "You can't call prisoners."

"Listen," I said sternly, "Will Dryden called and I promised I'd call back. I'm calling from *The Whig*. I'm a columnist. I'm sure you can make an exception."

"Like I said, you can't call prisoners." He hung up.

For a minute I didn't know what to do, and I felt sick at having let Will down, but I gathered my wits about me and called Harry Windsor. I hurriedly explained to him that it was important that everything I do having to do with the prisons I do with integrity and since I had promised this guy I would call, I had to find a way to get in touch with him. Harry promised to pull a few strings, and within the hour Will and I were connected by phone and I was explaining I had been there. "I saw you in the gym. With your wife."

"Ex-wife," he said.

Did I feel relief hearing that? I don't remember, though I do know I was giddy with the idea of this flirtation and certain that was all it would ever be. "I've written a first draft of the first column," I told him. I'd worked on it all day Sunday, and I was ready to show it around. I'd planned to take it inside later in the week.

"I'd like to read it," he said.

"Great, I'll bring it to you when I'm in. I'd like to hear your point of view."

That wasn't precisely true. I thought the story I had written would strike him as fluffy. It was personal, an introductory story about what I planned to be the first of a series of prison stories. It was about how important I thought it was to convey a sense of the place and the people I'd met, and I confessed that like most people, I had imagined penitentiaries as gray places full of shady characters but because I had never met any prisoners before that first day at Maynard, I couldn't know.

I wondered if Will wanted to read the column only because he was flirting or if he was actually interested in what I might have to say. And I wondered if I was flirting back with him. I tried to ignore that notion. No one in her right mind flirts with a man who has killed someone, and he was a Lifer, so he likely killed somebody, and I had no idea who that somebody was. I didn't particularly want to know either, but I did want to write stories that mattered, pieces that felt true. Pleasing people like Mark and Luke felt easy—they clearly loved attention, and they wanted me to think they were good guys, and interesting. Harder to appeal to a cool cynic like Will. "I'll be in tomorrow. I'll bring the article," I said. We agreed I'd ask for him in the V&C.

chapter three

It had never once occurred to me that I couldn't visit whomever I wanted to in prison, so I wasn't surprised when I asked to be admitted to the V&C to visit Will Dryden, and the guards buzzed me through the two gates. I followed the narrow pathway towards the visiting room where Jake Strike, one of the older, kinder guards, called up to the range for Will.

I sat waiting in one of the hard-backed chairs. The room was bleak, the kind of place I was usually in a hurry to leave. In one corner a large television sat on a high shelf, a shaggy rug covering a swath of floor beneath it. It was turned on, too soft to hear but loud enough to fill the room with static noticeable over the voices. In another corner stood five vending machines that sold Cheese Doodles and Smarties, stale sandwiches, watery coffee, cocoa and soft drinks. Each visitor was permitted to bring $10 in change into the visiting room so they could spend their money in those machines, and everyone in the room seemed to be chowing down on junk. The room was also veiled in a cloud of cigarette smoke, and though I smoked in those days, lighting a cigarette felt redundant. I felt as if I'd already smoked a pack just sitting there. A door on the south facing wall led to the small outdoor visiting area, scraggly grass and dirt, with picnic tables and a rusting swing set. People moved in and out, and each time the door opened, I could hear the creaking swings.

After ten minutes Will walked through the doors, and I watched him swagger towards me, confident and unsmiling. He had removed his dark glasses, so I could see his eyes—pale blue, both soft and piercing. And I could see he was handsome—a fact I hadn't wholly registered. At 5'10", he was thick and strong, and he had a blond goatee. He wore long sleeves that day—covering his tattoos, including the word Power down his right arm, and down the left the word Desperado, amidst a cluster of stars and other less-recognizable images. If I had been casting a movie and wanted a convict hero, I would have cast him—bigger and broader than Ed Harris but with that kind of gritty beauty, a gentleness that in an instant could turn hard. He briefly nodded as he took a chair across from me.

I leaned forward, handing him the pages. "Here it is…"

Without saying a word he began to read. As he did I studied the only tattoos I could see that day—red stars on his wrists. One of his arms, I noticed, looked smaller than the other, and later he would tell me he had busted a bicep years before while attempting to lift a car barehanded. He was that kind of macho, but it was a stunt he wished he could forget, one that he had pulled when he was drunk or high as he had so often been in his young days. "Just me being an idiot," he said. So often in the future, that line put an end to our conversations. He didn't like to remember the days that led him to prison. He preferred to think about the future.

But I didn't yet know that, and as he beamed in on the pages, I tried not to feel nervous. I stared at the grimy floors, the grim overhead fluorescents, the others in the room. I noticed a wiry, sandy-haired prisoner with a thick Maritime accent flitting from visitor to visitor. Mack. I knew his name because people kept calling him to come take their picture with the clunky old Polaroid he lugged around. Luke had told me that Mack lived in the hope that eventually the Innocence Project that had helped to win other innocent men and women their releases would take on his case. Despite the notion so many people had, not many prisoners professed their innocence, but Mack had for 15 years. For now he was the prison photographer, and stuck inside because of the Parole Catch 22. Parole Boards, as a rule, refuse to consider parole for those who do not express remorse for their crime, and those who are truly innocent cannot in good conscience express remorse for something they haven't done. In prison a "stand-up person" will not lie, and from what I had read about parole, experts seemed to agree it was so riddled with gamesmanship, political pressures and parole violations of a merely technical nature, it was rendered impotent.

I felt sorry for Mack, and I was curious to talk with him about his conundrum, but in that moment I was more interested in what Will was thinking and wondering what he would say if he hated the piece. I wanted not to care. Did it matter what one prisoner thought anyway? I wished I didn't care, but I was already hooked on his opinion and amazed by his stillness, the kind of stillness I eventually came to associate with so many prisoners. Most I came to know were either perfectly still much of the time—deadly serious and focused—or precisely the opposite—hopped up and jittery.

Finally he looked up and offered that sexy half-smile as he folded the pages in half. He cleared his throat. "It's good," he said, his voice so soft I had to lean forward to make sure I'd heard. "You're okay," he added.

I realized I'd been holding my breath.

As he went on, I understood that being "okay" meant that I had no intention of bringing harm to anyone at Maynard, and it also meant he would agree to talk to me. He was never an optimist, but I think still he might even for one moment have thought I might bring something good to the joint. And though he had faith in me, he wanted me to get one thing straight, fast.

He moved to sit beside me to tell me, almost under his breath about Mark. Mark had been assigned as one of my contacts inside because, as the producer of a television show called Con-Tact, one of things I planned to write about, he was a logical choice. The show was inmate-produced, run and directed, and though it was meant to air weekly, it aired irregularly on public television. It was, Mark and others told me, designed to teach the public about life inside from the prisoners' point of view.

"Con-Tact's bullshit," Will said, "and Mark's NG. No good. He works with The Man. He's a big-time rat." He went on to tell me that just like other rats Mark would say anything that would help him; it was the Rats who would tell The Man whatever The Man wanted to hear. In exchange, The Man offered goodies to the Rats.

Mostly those goodies were merely the absence of negatives. Rats had a freedom other prisoners didn't have—the freedom to start fights, take drugs, get drunk, all without risking a bad report being added to their records, a sudden transfer to a higher security joint, missing a parole hearing date. Goodies in that bleak little world might not look like much to outsiders, but to inmates they were everything—a chance for early release, a shot at passes outside, extra canteen money, more trailer visits with loved ones. All a prisoner had to do was sell his soul, Will explained, and those who did, like Mark, lived in single cells and were assured of having spotless records when it came time for the parole board to make their decisions about passes and release.

"Get it?" Will asked.

Mostly I did, though I had no reason to believe him more than anyone else except I had a gut feeling that John, as I studied him, was too slick, too smiley, too smooth.

I listened. I nodded, and I noticed Will's skin seemed to be almost ceramic, as if a smile would render a crack. He looked untouched, maybe untouchable.

"I think I understand," I said. "And thanks for taking the time to read the piece." This time it was he who extended a hand, and he held mine a beat too long and said, "You're beautiful."

I pulled my hand away. I felt immediately as if I'd done something wrong, but he quickly looked at the ground and mumbled, "Sorry, I was a bit of a player. Hard habit to break…" Then he added, "But your eyes are sad."

I hated that I was drawn to him. He was a player. That was clear, and who needs a player in her life? Not me, I told myself. "My eyes aren't sad," I said as coldly as I could muster, and as we walked towards the exit, I could feel my palms sweating; they were leaving stains on the pages I was gripping. Just ahead of us a couple had reached the exit before us, and they stopped for a long kiss. I turned away, but just then I heard someone wail "Yeeaah," and I turned again to see a child leaping onto Will's back. "Yeeaahhh," she wailed again, and she leaped back to the ground, and he smiled at her, really smiled. The warmth that flowed between them softened me, but the girl's father quickly pulled her away and looked sheepishly at Will. "Sorry man, she asked if she could play with you but I seen you're busy…" He turned and looked apologetically at me.

"It's okay," Will said, and he patted the girl's head.

To me he said, "Come back soon. We'll talk some more."

I told him I would, and shuffled out into the late afternoon, feeling equal parts relieved and undone.

chapter four

I don't recall if I was aware at that time of the David Milgaard case, though it had been on the nightly news and in every paper, so it would have been hard to avoid. The story went like this: After serving 22 years for a murder he didn't commit, after decades of his mother fighting for justice, on April 14, 1992 David Milgaard had finally been released from prison.

In 1969, when David was 16, he and two friends had taken a road trip across the prairies, and while they were in Saskatoon, a 20-year-old nursing student named Gail Miller was found dead on a snow bank. The night Miller was killed, Milgaard and his crew were stopping to pick up a friend, Albert Cadrain. Later Albert Cadrain, interested in the reward offered for information on Miller's death, testified he had seen Milgaard on the night of the murder wearing blood-stained clothing; he also claimed Milgaard was a secret Mafia member plotting to have witnesses assassinated. Police charged Milgaard with murder. Months into the trial, Cadrain's wild tales grew wilder. When he claimed to be the Son of God, he was admitted to a psychiatric hospital. But by then Milgaard's friends had testified against him though they later explained the police had told them they were under suspicion. On January 31, 1970, Milgaard was sentenced to a 25 to Life for first-degree murder.

Over the years, Milgaard had appealed his conviction many times, but a justice system unwilling to admit its guilt and a clunky, unyielding bureaucracy kept him locked up. Eighteen years into his sentence, he completed a formal application to reopen his case; it was three more years before a stay of proceedings against Milgaard was announced, but by the time he was released, he was addled by depression and drug addiction, and that story—like many similar ones I heard, fueled my interest in uncovering what actually happened in prison.

That story and Will's willingness to talk about prison led me back for a second visit in the V&C. This time we both were more relaxed, and we talked a little bit about the Milgaard case and Mack and some of the complaints he and the others on the Inmate Committee were trying to bring to the attention of the administration—some men who weren't being properly treated medically, others whose C.O.s (correctional officers) weren't doing their paperwork which resulted in missed parole hearings and transfers to lower security. But he also took time from our conversation to horse around with a few of the kids, and while he did I began to focus on his ability to arouse joy in that otherwise miserable room. He seemed like the high school football captain or class president, the big man on campus of 500 incarcerated, powerless men, and I began to lose my bearings, began to feel not like a grownup newspaper columnist doing research but like the high school girl who was dating the captain. Most of the men were deferential to him—apologizing when their kids interrupted us, asking Will if he thought their story was worthy of telling to me. In the hierarchy and in the gossip and longing and posing, prison didn't feel much different from high school, or for that matter, from the newsroom.

But he and I absolutely disagreed on one important point. He was adamant that every guard and administrator and most "straight Joes" (like me) were not to be trusted, were out to screw him and every other prisoner. I was equally adamant that it was vital to talk to everyone, that it was only in hearing peoples' sometimes competing versions of a story that I could discover anything close to the truth. I insisted he was wrong to think in terms of good guys and bad guys, black and white. The way I saw it, truth was a slippery thing and almost always existed somewhere between the lines. He thought there were simply, people who were full of shit and others who were the truth tellers, like him.

And so we argued. I chastised him for his disdain of everyone who wasn't a prisoner. That, I said, was just the flip side of those people who labeled every prisoner as the same kind of man. I urged him to give Claussen a chance. "Anticipating the worst of him will only bring out the worst. If you go to him on the attack, he'll go on the defensive. Think about how you almost snubbed me. If you don't stay open to possibilities, people will close themselves to you," I said.

He smirked and told me I was too naïve, that I just didn't get it. He said I'd find out what prison was really like if I hung around a while, but he said I probably wouldn't hang around. It was a challenge, definitely, and probably half-defensive, but was it a ploy to keep me intrigued? It may have been, but what was clear was that he didn't want me to disappear, and when the guards called the end to the visit, we stood up and walked towards the exit, and when we were almost there he said, "Can I call you?"

I wasn't sure I'd heard him correctly. I stopped and looked at him, waiting, giving myself time to let this idea sink in and process, and while I was quiet, he went on talking, apologizing, "It'll have to be collect, and every call costs 75 cents. Do you mind?"

"It's fine," I finally said, sure, but as I scribbled my number on a piece of paper to hand to him, I realized I had to draw the line. This could be a friendship but never more. "I live with my boyfriend," I told him. "You should know that."

"Who is he?" he asked. He didn't seem particularly disturbed by the fact that I had a boyfriend or that I lived with him—we were doing a dance, playing our parts to the hilt. He either couldn't show that he cared or he really didn't care; I either was flirting or I wasn't, but that didn't matter because he was in prison and Dean was a university professor. "He's a kind of a genius in his field," I said. "I hope you understand I enjoy talking to you but this will only ever be a friendship."

"Sure," he said. "But I see it in your eyes. Your boyfriend doesn't make you happy."

"Your imagination," I laughed, but I was angry too. He'd stepped over a line—become too intimate too fast. And as we said goodbye I was sure he wouldn't actually call or maybe he would but only if something happened inside that he thought would interest me. Or maybe I already knew he was trying to woo me and that he would certainly call, and maybe I hoped he would. Still, I was sure nothing could ever come of such a flirtation. Or maybe I hoped something would because at least this wasn't dull and flat and drained of life the way things were. At least

24

this was dramatic and dangerously enticing yet somehow safe. After all, he was inside.

* * *

I'd been home only a couple of hours when he called.

I was in my study, a room that faced north and was perpetually cold. Paint was peeling from the corners. I had a desk and a single chair, a computer tucked into the corner of this room farthest from Dean's newly renovated study with its freshly stained oak floors and double-paned glass windows. It was obvious whose creature comforts mattered in this house. Still, I loved my private corner that overlooked the apple orchard and the 100 acres of hayfield, that long, flat landscape that panned out to the horizon. And I loved my collie, Kell, who was most days and nights, my comfort and companion. Now she sat beneath my desk and listened as Will and I talked.

That evening I began to sense the danger of this connection. Even over the phone I could feel the electricity between us, and I couldn't hang up. I told myself (and half-convinced myself) that he was educating me about things I needed to know about prison if I was going to write anything meaningful about prison. I told myself that despite the attraction to him, I was being no more flirtatious with him than my mom had always been—flashing her beautiful smile, enticing desire in men but naively unaware of the sparks she ignited and thoroughly flirtatious and devoted to my dad. And I was like my mom in other ways. She taught high school government and her classes focused on understanding justice through individuals' stories. I'd been her student; in fact the only prisoners I'd ever met were the men and women she'd invited to our class to talk about their time inside. So as I talked to Will, and as I listened to his stories, I pretended I was only doing what my parents would be proud to see me doing—focusing on understanding those who were wholly different from me, those who endured deprivations I had never endured.

Some of that was true, of course; motives are seldom pure or simple. But it is also true that I was pushing boundaries, and I knew even then that some of the heat stemmed from my long-held desire to do just that. I had always wanted not to be just one more Jewish girl from the suburbs and the Ivy Leagues, and the people I emulated lived outside of comfort zones—the Daniel Ellsbergs and Bella Abzugs of this world, Janis Joplin, Adrienne Rich, Gloria Steinem, even Dean who besides enjoying all his creature comforts also steeped himself in a world that included manure and frigid nights in barns and studying, up close, the world's war zones. The part of me that secretly longed for a 50-plus years of happiness, adoration and devotion kind of marriage also refused ever to imagine living such an ordinary life. What truly scared me was that I might become that kind of normal.

So Will's appeal had two parts. I was attracted not only by his sexy swagger but by his offer of entry into a world for which I needed one of its denizens as an escort. After he warned me away from Mark, he continued to tell me about the people I was encountering, telling me who I ought to listen to and who I should ignore, and I believed him. I'm not sure why, but he never steered me wrong. He had killed someone—that I knew—but he'd shot another drug dealer when he was a dealer, a man who, he said, would have killed him if he'd pulled his gun first. But he wasn't a scam artist or a rat. If this had been the McCarthy era, he wouldn't have named names, and that, to me, meant a great deal. That felt important. In that first call we shared a few personal stories— he told me he was ashamed of the anguish and sorrow he had caused his three sisters and his mother. They were all professionals, upstanding citizens, hard workers, successful women. They didn't deserve to live under the shadow of his crime, he said.

When we at last hung up—we talked nearly an hour—I called Kate. In those days she was my closest confidante, almost a stand-in mother since mine lived so far away and lately hadn't been communicating much. I'd met Kate several years earlier, and she had always seemed heaven sent. In the 1930s and early '40s, she'd been a Hollywood starlet, and in the early '50s she wrote the movie *The Blob*, a movie that was the center of the first novel I wrote years before I met her. We met at the local hardware store, and right away we became fast friends. It was Kate who had, for the last many months, been insisting I break up with Dean and move to my own place. She hated the way he talked to me. One night when she came to supper, she pulled me aside and hissed,

"He talks to you like you're less than," she fumed. "Who the hell does he think he is?"

She answered the phone with the usual song in her voice. "Darling, hello…"

I think there must have been a quiver in my voice when I said I'd just met an interesting man.

"Good…" she began, but I stopped her. "He's in prison for murder," I laughed nervously.

In her usual unflappable way, Kate simply said, "Well, that's interesting," and then she told me a story—she was always telling stories. It turned out she'd had a friend back in her Hollywood days who had married a man in prison.

"Jesus, Kate, I'm not going to marry him," I said.

"Of course not," she said.

chapter five

The Talmud says that a child tells in the street what its mother and father say at home, and in our family my dad always insisted that we were the opposite of snobs. He grew up on the wrong side of the tracks with immigrant parents who ran a dry-cleaning business, while Mom's family, Russian immigrants, had made a great deal of money with a family business. My dad was dismissive of their airs, and he liked to repeat his father's saying, "No matter how much you have, you give it all back when you die." Dad talked about how Mom had made the right decision in resisting her mother's snobbish disapproval of him. He loved my mom not only because she was smart, beautiful and fun but because she didn't care about big houses or fancy cars. Like Dad she shunned gated communities and country clubs.

I was the eldest of four kids, and by the time was in second grade, we moved from a working class suburb of Cleveland to a street of brand new homes in lofty Shaker Heights—to that suburb's far eastern edge. Our block was empty but for our house and one other. One day when I was in third grade and walking home from school a bully—a kid from the next block—leapt out of a tangle of brush and ordered me to halt. He was dangling handcuffs. For a long time—mere minutes but they felt like hours—he refused to let me pass. Then he simply let me go, and by the time I reached our house, I was hysterical. My dad called his parents to discuss the matter with them. But he also insisted I stand up to my tormenter and prove this boy couldn't stop me from walking to and from school on my own. He insisted I not be afraid. I kept walking, and the bully, shocked I suppose, left me alone.

When I first talked to Will on the phone some of that well-learned bravado stirred. I was determined not to let him hear any fear in my voice; more than that, I was determined not to feel fear. But when we're kids we cannot imagine our future lives, and I never imagined myriad things. I never imagined that my vibrant, flirtatious, talkative mother would begin to fade—still in her early 60s—from early-onset Alzheimer's. In those months my parents were still hiding the fact from us kids, but I had begun to feel slightly abandoned; otherwise I might have confessed this attraction to her. And still, I never imagined, even as Will and I continued to talk, the next night and the next after that, that I would fall in love and marry him.

Our conversations began to feel, so oddly, like a balm to the loneliness I hadn't allowed myself to acknowledge. And those conversations became proof to me that I could talk to people that others feared, to people others didn't listen to or care about. I was the opposite of a snob.

* * *

It was Pete who had invited me to the Native Brotherhood Group Meeting at Maynard, so when I walked into the windowless cement room and saw Pete's arm slung over Will's shoulder, the shivers of mistrust that had laced our conversations turned me cold. Was Will watching everything I did? Was he after something other than conversation, other than romance? Was he playing me for something? Was he trying to con me into writing something that wasn't true—something he wanted to convince me and my readers was?

He gave me that flirtatious half-mile.

"What are you doing here?" I asked, but Pete quickly intervened. "I invited him. Will's an honorary member of our group..." and the other men in the room—Natives all—began to nod. "Not a lot of stand-up guys in this shithole," Pete added.

I still didn't trust him, or any of them. Maybe they were setting me up, somehow, but there was no one I could ask about that. By then I'd spent almost two weeks talking to prisoners of all ages and races and shapes and attitudes. I'd been listening to their gripes and grievances, to what they longed for and what they feared, so I understood they had plenty to fight for and fight against. Mack's innocence. Pete's never-ending stints in segregation. Untreated illnesses and addictions. Education programs closed. Fears about the prison's new policy to integrate sex offenders into the general population. I had seen Will in action, heard him passionately defending to administrators and guards alike those who seemed too meek or ill or tongue-tied to defend themselves. He was adamant that the Inmate Committee do something more than stump for more cigarettes in the canteen or better oatmeal in the dining hall. He wanted decent medical care, fewer strip searches of families, fewer arbitrary tossing of men into segregation cells.

Every inmate I talked to—I had stopped listening to Mark—told me that Will took no bullshit from anyone—not from the despised deputy warden, that woman who so reminded me of Nurse Ratched; not from Joe Book, the head of security who tossed guys in "the hole" and wrote up lies that he tucked into their files. Several of the men in the Native Brotherhood group and many of the Lifers told me it was Will who managed to calm them when their tempers flared, Will who talked guys down from drug highs and who insisted guys give up drugs and booze. Pete said if Will's skin weren't so white, he'd swear he was a brother—he understood the Natives that well, and Bing told me he stood up for the Chinese, too, and Mack said he buoyed the depressed, and the Filipinos, the Jamaicans, the Vietnamese, all of them told me how hard Will worked for them. The place was a virtual United Nations, and it was as divided as nation engaged in civil war, but Will moved easily from group to group. I was proud for having earned the trust of someone all these men admired. By the time I wrote my second column—this one about the Native Brotherhood Group—I was confident Will would like what I wrote. And I was beginning to feel almost at home inside Maynard.

The Native Brotherhood Society story was about the men—Pete and Puck and Gordy and Rory and Paul—who had grown up in cities where white people called them names, and worse. In that column I confessed that people had warned me not to romanticize prisoners but their stories had reminded me of a day when I was a counselor leading canoe trips in the Canadian boundary waters and two of my campers asked me to show them my horns. "Our parents told us Jews have horns," they'd said. Back then I'd wanted to teach those girls and their parents to banish their prejudice, but instead when their parents came at the end of camp to pick them up, I avoided them. I had no words to explain.

But now I was determined to say things out loud, and my empathy, I admitted, went to those men whose anger and mistrust and sadness had coiled inside and burst out in violence. Empathy, I wrote, was what offered hope.

"...there I sat surrounded by seven men whose lives are as different from mine as mine is from theirs, but I couldn't help but believe that some warmth grew up between us. I couldn't help believing in the strength of their comradeship. I couldn't help but feel some hope for all of us.

chapter six

During our second week of conversations Will began to tell me stories about his ex-wife, the mother of his three children. Whenever he mentioned Laura, he quietly seethed the way people so often do when talking about ex-spouses, and sometimes he blamed her for everything short of the murder itself—"If she hadn't wanted money so badly..." "If she hadn't pushed me to keep selling drugs..." Then he would catch himself laying the blame and backpedal, "I'm not saying it's her fault I'm in here..."

Blaming others wasn't what stand-up guys did. Stand-up guys didn't shirk responsibility. They never asked someone else to shoulder the burden of their lives. But I didn't ask many questions about Laura. I also never bothered trying to get straight the story of when and how he'd first begun dealing drugs. His father died when he was two years old, and his mother raised him and his three sisters working double shifts as a nurse. When he was in his junior year of high school, after living his whole life in this household of women, he began to hunger for a world of men. He was a good athlete, and his reputation as a tough guy on the hockey team—the goalie and unofficial enforcer—led somehow naturally to his joining a motorcycle gang. When he tried to leave that gang he left behind deep-seated ill-will amongst those who had once been "brothers." He began to work as a contractor, supplementing his income by dealing drugs, and he built himself and his new young family a beautiful house. When the marriage began to falter, he moved to Calgary where there was a housing boom. He said he planned to go straight there—to give up the drugs and the dealing and all the petty criminal acts he'd committed while part of the gang (crimes like walking out on large restaurant tabs and fiddling with his books). But Laura followed him to Calgary and got pregnant again, and they returned to Ontario where he somehow wound up in a drug turf war. That ended on a cool spring night in a showdown with another dealer whom he shot. He was arrested the next day and months later he was convicted of second degree murder that earned him a 13 to Life sentence. He had to serve at least 10 years before being eligible for day parole—days outside and nights in a halfway house. At year 13 he would be eligible for full parole which he would serve for the rest of his life. He was midway through year 7, and the two of us laughed over the fact that we had moved to the Kingston area in the same year.

The way he told his story made it sound like a Greek tragedy, replete with those inevitabilities that reverberate forever, but whenever I made lame attempts to understand if and when he had ever lived a truly straight life—without drugs or drink or crime—he dodged the details. If I pushed at all he simply eased his way onto another subject and admonished me for prying. But there was also this: We were talking on tapped phones and in visiting rooms; everything we said was watched and listened to and recorded. He couldn't tell me everything without risking misinterpretation by those prying ears—anything he said might be construed and become a wrench in his efforts to keep a clean record for the day he finally appeared before a parole board. Sometimes, when I asked a question, he would nod at the guards' booth or, if we were on the phone, he'd cough. "Everything we say can and will be used against me," he said.

I was also learning that part of being a stand-up guy was learning not to pry into private business. Most of the men didn't like to talk about their pasts at least in part because it was the past that had brought them to prison, and no one was glad to be there. I had read stories about people who claimed that it was prison that had saved them somehow, but in my many years of visiting and talking to dozens and dozens of men and women doing time, I never once heard anyone say such a thing. If they had gone straight—the way Will had—they'd done so not because prison helped them but because they decided to make that choice, and part of making wiser choices clearly came with growing older. And some people didn't make that choice; there was a thriving black market inside and drugs were plentiful, but I was enough of an outsider—and I kept myself that way for my sake and Will's— that I never learned who precisely was lugging in drugs. I only knew that it wasn't only prisoners' family and friends.

Will blamed drink and drugs for most of his woes—and most of everyone else's idiocy, which included their crimes. Now that he was clean, his body and mind were precious to him. He was obsessively careful about what he ate, and he constantly worked out. Although the food inside was heavy on the grease and carbs, and he tended to pack on pounds with ease, he pushed himself on the weights, and when he did gain weight, he upped his workout times and jogged miles around the prison yard. He had always been good looking—in pictures of his younger self I could see how easily he must always have attracted women. And he liked that about himself and wasn't shy about admitting it. His good looks were what he could count on when everything else failed him. I was drawn to him the way women always had been, and though he had a vanity about him, I wasn't without my own. I wasn't the slender Ingrid Bergman type my mother was but I'd always, with relative ease, attracted men.

* * *

My close friend Debi Wells had, for years, worked as a tutor in the prisons. When I told her I was visiting Maynard, she urged me to read Claire Culhane's books and articles. Claire was the country's foremost prisoners' rights activist, a brilliant woman who knew the system inside and out, Debi said. Debi wanted me to arm myself with information, with allies, with enough to protect me from harm. But by the time I was talking to her about prison, I was already done in. I resisted her suggestions. Another friend had, years before, coined the term *fuck struck* to describe that sexual attraction—usually before consummation—that blurs reason, that charged feeling that softens intelligence, obscures facts and creates an invisible armor that protects its subject from anything but the object of attraction. We hadn't kissed. We'd barely touched, but Will and I both wanted to. I felt it every time we talked—and the fact that I knew it was so damn wrong, so impossible, would never happen, seemed only to stir the flames. Quickly, and almost against my will, he had become one of the only people I would listen to. Those like Debi who warned me to be careful, to create distance, to feel suspicious or afraid or wary only stirred my rebellion against even those who, had I stepped back for a moment I would have realized, had my best interests at heart.

I'd been visiting prison for about a month, talking nightly on the phone to Will, wishing I could talk to my mom. I may have been nearing 40, but I felt out of my depth, and wanted the kind of guidance I'd never asked from her. I thought she might have wisdom to offer. She had, after all, fallen for a man from the wrong side of the tracks when she fell for Dad. She had rebelled against the conventions of the world she was accustomed to. Her parents had wanted her to marry a rich boy. In fact my dad had always joked about their wedding, about the fact that if he hadn't been the groom, my grandparents wouldn't have let him through the door to attend.

I called and asked her if she might consider coming to visit me. "Alone," I said, despite knowing my parents almost never left each other's side. I couldn't face letting my dad know about this attraction. Not yet. Mom was the gentler soul and the cooler personality. Besides, if I was Persephone innocently picking flowers in the field and Will was Hades, god of the underworld riding his horse-drawn chariot, ready to abduct me, I needed Demeter, the mother goddess, not one of the gods. I couldn't visit my parents in Ohio—if I did Mom would defer to Dad the way she almost always had. I reasoned that if we had some time alone, she might be able to tell me things that would help me make sense of this infatuation I finally was admitting to myself.

The first time I called and asked she told me she would think about it, then quickly handed the phone to my dad. I waited a few days and called again, but just like the first time she quickly fobbed me off to Dad. That time I was angry. What kind of Demeter didn't sense a daughter's cries for help? I had no idea then that she was losing her memory, and scared to death. Only much later did I learn that at just that moment she and Dad were first becoming aware of the fact that no matter how much they adored each other, this illness, early-onset Alzheimer's, was beyond curing with love. But because I didn't know about it—hadn't yet recognized that those brief memory lapses I had noticed signaled something more serious— I simply hated her. I hated them for being a fortress instead of a haven and decided I would carry on without them. I didn't need a cold, distracted mom, so I turned to Kate who listened to me when I told her how afraid I felt to be falling for a man who was so wrong.

"Don't be afraid, dear," Kate said. "Fear never helps. Besides, what's most important is that you find a place to call your own. I'm going to find you a home where you won't have to live beholden to anyone else."

* * *

One morning four weeks into my visits to prison, after the first three pieces I wrote had run, I walked into *The Whig*, and Josie at reception winked at me. She nodded towards my office, and I walked in to find bouquets everywhere. I pulled out the card tucked into the largest basket of flowers, and before I had even had a chance to read, Josie and Meghan and Alicia were peering into the room "Who're they from?" Josie asked.

I read out loud. "Thanks for the great stuff you're writing." I looked up at them. "It's from one of the guys inside. A guy I've been talking to."

"God," Josie drawled. "My husband never buys me flowers. He says they're a waste of money…and they are."

My father thought flowers were a sign of untrustworthiness. He associated them with his uncle who had always sent flowers but never came through for anyone and with my sister's ex-husband who frequently sent her flowers but left her for another woman.

But Alicia swooned. "I don't care if they're extravagant, he's a prince. Jeez, I wish someone sent me flowers like that."

They tossed questions at me. How had he done it? Didn't he have to make all his phone calls collect? Could prisoners use credit cards, and if they couldn't, how had he paid for them? Was he rich? Was this a bribe of some kind? Did he want me to write something I shouldn't be writing?

I couldn't answer any of the questions, but they swam in my brain until evening when he called and I could ask. "They feel like a bribe," I said.

"They're just a thank you. Seriously. Just to say thanks for caring about us…for paying attention…"

As for how he had done it, his mother had access to his bank account, and his daughter Sarah had helped. She was 14, living with her beloved "Granny." Earlier in the year Will's ex, Laura, had moved away from their hometown, but Sarah was finishing middle school and had wanted to stay.

"The two gals arranged it all," Will said, and when I told him it was too extravagant he laughed. "That's what my mother said, but I told her you were worth it," he said. "She'll see."

Until her retirement, Will's mom been a nurse at the local hospital and raised her four children on her own. Will's oldest sister and the younger twins were under three when his dad was killed in a car accident. Now it was Molly who usually brought Will's kids to prison to visit. He said she was the strength of the family, kind and smart and wickedly funny.

When Molly and I did meet a few weeks later, she was quick to let me know I was the best thing that had come into her life in a long time. She showered me with gratitude. Although she shunned extravagance, she had relented about the flowers because she was grateful, she said. She hadn't heard her son sound so happy in years as he sounded when he told her about our blossoming friendship

And it was those flowers that swept me right over the edge.

chapter seven

When I read Charles Bukowski's line—"I don't like jails. They don't have the right kind of bars," I think of the men I met in the Lifer's Group meeting. It's the kind of thing one of those men would have said and howled with laughter afterwards. But when I first met with the Lifers Group, I wasn't yet attuned to such subtleties, and I was nervous as I walked into that windowless room where 15 Lifers sat around a table waiting to talk to me. I thought about men serving life for murder the way most people do—that these were unpredictable, dangerous men who given a chance would kill again. But none of the Lifers I came to know over the years were particularly scary, and none of them were psychopaths. There are as many stories as there are people, and while even Maynard probably housed a psychopath or two, most of the murderers I met were men who had made one heinous mistake and were living with depression, regret, bitterness and sorrow. Most of them were men with broken families, broken dreams and broken hearts.

But I didn't understand that when I walked into their meeting room that day. Their quiet, in fact, surprised me. I suppose I had imagined people growling and angry, punch-drunk, and violent and tough. Instead they all stood politely and waited for me to take a seat before they took theirs. Men in prison opened doors, removed their hats and caps, never interrupted me, and whenever a woman walked into a room—so long as she wasn't wearing a uniform and a scowl—they stood. The Lifers were no different from all the other men I'd met.

Bernard Despon was chairing this meeting of their Lifer's group. "This is Amy from *The Whig*," he introduced me, and then he added, "She's a good girl." By then I understood that being a "good girl" was the ultimate compliment, a designation not easily earned. In calling me that, Bernard was signaling the others that I had been approved by men they trusted and admired, and when I heard the words, I knew that Will had talked about me to Bernard. Will wasn't there, but I could feel his presence anyway, and I thought if all these murderers thought I was okay, nothing bad could happen to me in this place.

That's how much I didn't understand prison.

Bernard told me he was serving a life sentence for first degree murder. That's the day I learned how sentencing worked. Those serving time for first degree murder, men like Bernard, were sentenced to 25 to Life and until that prisoner had served at least 2/3 of his sentence—18 years—he would not be eligible for consideration for parole (and consideration was all it was; there were no guarantees). But the Canadian system offered an additional option to those convicted of this harshest sentence (Canada has no death penalty). After serving 15 years, a Lifer could apply for something called a Judicial Review, a dollop of hope in the bleak trudge that was a life sentence; if his or her application was approved, he might receive a reduction in his minimum time. This was Bernard's 15th year, and he was in the process of applying for a Judicial Review. Those sentenced for second degree murder—men like Will— usually served slightly shorter times, with sentences ranging from a minimum of seven to a maximum of 25 years, always with parole for life.

"So, Amy, would you like to say something to the guys?" Bernard asked after he had called the meeting to order, and they had explained the way things worked.

I told them I only wanted to hear what they had to say. "Maybe you could just carry on with your meeting as if I'm not here," I said.

"Sounds good," Bernard said. And they began to talk. And talk. But their banter consisted mainly of jokes about the bleakness of their lives, revolving largely around the slim possibilities for winning parole. They called each other "losers," and teased each other about how unlikely it was that any Parole Board would stoop to consider springing such a band of bad boys, setting them loose on the innocents. The word "innocent" aroused their wry laughter. A lot of things did. But mostly they talked about the minutiae of their dreary daily lives, about whether they ought to serve hot dogs or ribs at their upcoming social and what kinds of cigarettes the canteen ought to supply. They bragged about how many pounds they had bench pressed that week; they argued about which copper was the biggest prick or whether the women guards ought to be allowed to supervise their strip searches. In the women's prisons, men had just been banned from supervising such searches; in the men's prisons any guard, male or female, could, and did, conduct strip searches.

The air in the room like most of the rooms in prison was thick with their cigarette smoke and dried sweat. Although they were polite and even obsequious—"Man, a columnist, that's cool…you must be smart as hell," they also were edgy and bored, almost from the start ready to be done with this meeting and back to the rest of their dull afternoon—or for some to a visit with a wife, a child, a friend. Bernard was different from most of the other prisoners I had met. He had a kind of gentleness I hadn't felt in anyone else. His eyeglasses were bottle thick, and still he squinted so I could tell he was nearly blind. He was short and slim, with muscular arms like all the men, but he had a pronounced limp and despite his muscles he seemed somehow frail.

Bernard told me he had served many of his 15 years in the SHU, the Special Handling Unit at Archaumbault—a super maximum prison in rural Quebec, a place even the Lifers feared. They all agreed—those who had been there and those who hadn't. It had a reputation as the place they sent "hard cases," and most men who went to Archaumbault and eventually returned to lower security joints came back physically and mentally destroyed. Bernard's description of the place made it sound like the definition of hell, but like so many other prison stories, tales of Archaumbault contained few specifics. Rather the men offered me vague images of endless drugs, senseless deaths, and a sea of caged human beings wallowing in relentless fury.

I immediately liked Bernard. I wasn't lit up by him the way I was by Will, but I felt relaxed and comfortable sitting beside him. He talked slowly and softly. He didn't challenge my opinions the way Will usually did. Will had told me that Bernard, Will's closest friend inside, had years earlier been a big wheel in the Satan's Choice Biker Gang. He'd shot another gang member and came to prison from cold, isolated Sudbury in northern Ontario with a hot reputation as a fierce and powerful man. I could see that prison had broken him, and I could see the others respected him—respect being the coin of the realm. In prison respect meant that some men feared him, some admired him, and no one messed with him. He was "stand-up." He would never rat anyone out. If you were dependable, so was he. Will had also told me Bernard tended to fall into dark depressions. He engaged in binge drinking of the stuff prisoners brewed inside—heady, bitter, hard and plentiful stuff. Will and Bernard both told me that it was Will who was forever trying to save Bernard from himself.

The other man I paid particular notice of was Big Bill—hard not to since he was 6'3, 300 pounds, and baby-faced. Will had told me Big Bill accidentally killed a man in a bar fight with a single punch. Maybe Will told me about his crime because it was such a ludicrously terrible way to wind up with a life sentence. But that day Big Bill wanted to talk about the barbecue for the upcoming Lifer's social. "Guys, burgers or ribs?" he kept asking. No one seemed able to decide. They argued back and forth about the virtues of each, and my attention drifted away. They sounded like ladies at a mah-jongg gathering, and I wanted them to talk about reinstating education in the prisons, about books they were reading or wished they could, about visiting, about loss. But as their laughter shifted nervously from corner to corner, I sensed their uneasiness at revealing the dullness of their days, something they became aware of because I was listening.

And I was struck by how perfectly normal they seemed—like guys I had known in school, guys I worked with at the paper. A line kept spinning through my mind—a line I'd heard often from criminal attorneys but one I suddenly understood. There but for the grace of God go I. There but for some grace and luck and happenstance.

Finally I decided I had to ask the question I'd been too shy to ask of anyone, including Will. "Can anyone talk about what it's like to kill someone?"

The room turned uncomfortably quiet. I saw in their startled faces that they didn't define themselves as killers. Although they each had a story they certainly ought to have been able to tell, they seemed unable to find a way into this conversation. Clearly asking directly wasn't the way. I saw the nervous tics and undercurrent of unhappiness shifting from one man to the next until someone muttered, "She thinks we're goofs."

A *goof*, Will had explained, was the worst possible epithet in prison. Goofs were the wholly untrustworthy people who would sell your soul for a soda or a day pass.

"Sorry," I said, "We can talk about whatever you want to talk about."

"Hey," someone said from across the room, "I did the crime, I'm doin' the time."

Bernard stood. I think he must have wanted to lower the temperature in the room. "Men, whaddya say we invite Amy to come to our social?" he asked.

A few men began to applaud and nod "yes," and soon they were all applauding, and thanks to Bernard they forgave me for asking the one question they didn't want to contemplate, the one question that haunted them, the question parole boards would ask, insisting on hearing of their deep remorse and skeptical of its existence.

Soon after that the meeting ended, I made my way back outside without seeing Will. I was disappointed, but I was now invited to the Lifer's Social, and I would see him there. When he called me next, I told him of the invitation.

I could feel his smile through the telephone line.

chapter eight

A few days before the upcoming social I was in my office at *The Whig* when the phone rang, and Josie told me Cal Costin was on the line. He was one of the Maynard administrators. "Amy, we love your columns," he said and then he coughed. "There's just one thing, though. A couple of guards complained about one of the inmates you're talking to, so I'm afraid I'll have to ask you to stop talking to Will Dryden. I'm sure you understand we don't want your visits to create any trouble."

His tone was cool and breezy. We had met and talked a few times, and he had seemed like a lot of the preppy, well-educated, nice looking men I had met in Kingston. At its core Kingston was a sharply segregated city. Wealthy whites lived south of Princess Street in fashionable limestone homes and most had second homes—cottages on one of the many lakes. North of Princess, in rickety brick or wooden homes lived the poor whites and a smattering of Natives and very few blacks. Many of the guards lived on the less tony side of town, but at the administrative level, there was a plethora of prep school types like Cal.

"I hope you understand," he repeated, but he also sounded distracted, as if I were just one more item on a list of things he had to take care of before taking off for his cottage for the weekend.

I hung up and thought about how foolish Cal was to think he could stop me from talking to whoever I wanted to. This was Canada. It was a free country. I worked for a newspaper, and I would and could talk to anyone I wanted to, and my boss would back me up on that. I figured Cal would wind up embarrassed for having inadvertently let slip that the one prisoner I could count on if I wanted to learn the truth was Will. He obviously wasn't a pawn in the game like Mark was. Clearly he wouldn't tell me only what administrators wanted me to know, wouldn't show me only what they wanted me to see. Cal was crazy if he thought I was naïve enough to stop talking to Will.

The clearest I can come to understanding my own emotional landscape in those days is in thinking about the way I felt whenever I looked at the photograph I always hung above my desk, a photo of me and my dad. It's a black and white photo, and I'm two years old, in my father's arms. We're both looking directly into the camera. We both look sunkissed, blond and tanned and shirtless, and he's smiling broadly, and we're cheek to cheek. Whenever I looked at the picture I could almost feel the way he loved me then. But somewhere along the way, the sweetness between us dissolved, and it was a long time before it returned. My dad was always kind and generous, but with me in those days he behaved more like the lawyer he was—argumentative, always certain, often passing judgment, far from adoring. I felt as if he found me wanting—not smart or savvy or pretty or successful enough, while Mom was smart and beautiful and dazzling. I wanted someone to adore me the way he adored her, the way he had once adored me.

But until Will, no man had ever heaped adoration on me. A lot of men had liked me; some had lusted after me. A few had even pined for a while. And I had been involved with other "bad boys"—the football player who relieved me of my virginity in high school; the barfly in Manhattan after college who collected women; the manic depressive painter in graduate school who liked to talk suicide. For a while in college I dated the nice Jewish pre-med with all the right credentials who turned out to have a colder heart than anyone I'd ever known, and I had learned that the guys who looked like good guys weren't necessarily that. Though the list of men I had dated was long and disparate, "good boys"—the premeds and the lawyers and the professor—had always let me down, and before Will none of the boys bothered to notice that my eyes were sad or told me they wanted to help take away my sadness. No one had seemed so full of that combination of confidence and longing, swagger and need, charm and desire as Will. Yes, he had killed someone, but from what I knew his had been a case of kill or be killed. And there was, of course, this one other thing.

Like a lot of men of his generation, my dad never talked much about his personal past. He especially wouldn't talk about his time as a prisoner of war. His silence implied that it wasn't the tough times that mattered. He had survived being a prisoner, and once he was free, he lived his life with more enthusiasm and passion than anyone I knew. The day he walked out of the prison camp he vowed he would treat each day—no, each minute—of his life as a precious gift. He had kept his vow in spades. Every sandwich he ate was terrific; every trip he took magnificent; every movie he saw, book he read, person he met, photograph, painting, song, story, day was fantastic. When there was a snowstorm outside, it was exciting. When the temperature was 90 degrees with 100 percent humidity, he laughed and said how great it was that days like this happened—to make us appreciate better weather.

I was already dreaming of the day Will would walk out of prison. I imagined that he would celebrate life the way Dad did. And if he did love me, and if I loved him well enough in return, he would celebrate our love the way Dad celebrated his love for Mom—by being at her side whenever she needed or wanted him there, by showering her with praise and attention, by guiding her and allowing her to guide him, by celebrating her achievements—whether it was a good pot roast she cooked, a good tennis shot, or a teaching award won.

I never told anyone that, of course. I knew if I told my dad that Will reminded me of him, he would feel nothing but hurt. My dad was also more honest and law-abiding than almost anyone I knew, and though he had served time as a prisoner, his crime had been to be an American soldier captured by Germans in the Ardennes. I knew even then, and know much more clearly now, how very different my father and Will are from each other, but back then all I could see in Will were the ways he reminded me of the first love of my life—he was handsome like my dad, blond and athletic like him, outgoing but shy, warm but distant, and a man who had endured imprisonment.

By the time Cal called, I had already imagined me and Will standing cheek to cheek. I was already in over my head, even if I didn't know I was. By the time Cal called, I wasn't making decisions with a cool and calculating head. And the day after he called I strutted right into Maynard's V&C and asked Jake Strike to call Will down from his range. Strike eyed me warily and said, "I think you're not supposed to talk to him." Word had gotten around, but either Cal trusted me to simply obey his rule and hadn't given any orders or Strike felt empathy.

When I said: "I just need to tell Will, that's only fair, don't you think?" Jake Strike buzzed me inside.

Like a lot of the older guards, Jake Strike had no interest in making anyone's life more difficult than it had to be. Five minutes later Will pushed open the door to the visiting room, and as he walked in, I watched his eyes dart around the room.

In prison no one's gaze settled in one place for more than a moment. "Prison eyes," they called this habit of never looking at anyone straight on. When people did lock eyes, it was like rams locking horns—the first to look away or blink lost the challenge. Prisoners were like gunfighters, squaring off with eyes instead of guns.

When he reached me, I leaned close as if he and I were co-conspirators, as if we had a pact we did not yet have. "You'll like this one," I said with the cockiness of someone who didn't get the way power worked in this place, or in this town, or in the world but thought she did. "Cal Costin says our talking has upset some guards. He doesn't want me talking to you."

Will's eyes darted around the room again. "And?"

"So now I know who's being straight with me about this place."

He shook his head. "Right. And you can't talk to me."

"Come on," I laughed. "How will they stop me?"

He curled a finger, beckoning me closer. "Amy, listen…"

When our faces were inches apart, a blush rushed up my neck, but attraction didn't preclude the fact that I was committed to fulfilling my professional mission, even if I couldn't precisely define what that mission was. But it wasn't all about Will. My commitment also welled up from my curiosity about what happened behind prison walls, and it welled up out of a desire to prove myself—to my editor, to the readers of the paper, hell, to the whole damn city.

"They'll stop you," Will whispered. "Remember, my Unit Manager and your boss are golfing buddies."

"But Lawrence likes me." I told him about the way Lawrence joked with me in the office and told me to keep up all the good work I was doing, about his invitation to join him at next month's Celebrity Golf

Tournament, and Will's voice softened, and a wry tone crept into his voice. "So, you an ace golfer?" he asked.

"Hardly," I said. "One of the guys in the newsroom had to teach me how to hold clubs…" and I began to describe the golf lesson the sports reporter had given me one night in the newsroom, and as I did, I could feel Will drawing inward. I wasn't sure what I had said that had upset him, but I thought it might have been that hearing stories of people outside having fun hurt too much.

"Sorry," I said. "I guess I shouldn't talk about that stuff…"

He scowled. "It's not like I've never been out in the world."

Now I'd insulted him. "I just meant that you can't…"

"Can't live?" he growled.

I was flooded with shame. Will saw himself as a guide, an instructor—to me and to all the guys inside, and to his children, and to anyone who would listen to him—and now, as he had for weeks, he looked for a way to instruct me in the ways of this world he knew so well. He loved being the man in the know, and like a lot of men inside he was prickly about his status, or lack of it.

And I understood. We weren't dissimilar that way. "I read three newspapers a day. I watch the news. I read books," he said. "The way I see it, I'll be out of here one of these days, so don't think I don't keep up with what's going on in the world. And whatever you do, don't go around feeling sorry for me…"

But I did feel sorry for him, and I didn't want him to know that, and now he had cornered me. "I don't know the ropes…I guess I'm nervous…"

His shoulders relaxed. Beginning with his eyes, his smile returned. "You're nervous because you like me."

He knew he had me under a spell. I thought I had him under one too. We both liked to seduce. Still, he was the better manipulator.

And he was in prison. I couldn't like him. Not *that* way.

"Sure I like you, but what I meant was that I don't know what it feels like to be in prison hearing about life outside…"

"Wish I could help you," he said coolly. "Too bad we can't talk."

"They can't stop me," I blustered.

"Sure they can, but you should still come to the Lifer's social. You'll like it—a whole gang of murderers at your beck and call..."

The rebel and the flirt in me were in high gear, but before I could reply I heard high heels clicking on linoleum and saw Will sit up straighter as Louise Salem, Deputy Warden, headed straight towards the door to the outside visiting yard. When she reached the door she stopped and called outside, "Everyone in." She repeated this a few times, rustling kids back inside, and when everyone was inside, she slammed the door and locked it. Then she turned to the room and announced in a booming voice, "There'll be no more yard for anyone." If she noticed me she wasn't letting on, but the blood rose to Will's face and he stood up and strode towards her and demanded in a voice as loud as hers, "What're you doing?"

He may have said "what're youse doing?" in that Ontario prison slang, *youse* instead of *you*, that made me cringe. But he was furious.

What could possibly inspire a decision to close the yard on such a beautiful day?

Salem said coldly, "It's a new rule. My rule."

Will and Luke and Tim Thomas, the Inmate Committee treasurer, met regularly with administration. Luke and Tim had told me that Will challenged administrators' decisions, but this time before Will said another word, Salem strode out of the room. When he came back to me and I asked him why she would impose such a patently ridiculous rule. "Because she can," he said. "Because they're freaked. Closing the yard is just one more way for her to let everyone know who's in charge. That everything is up to them, and there's nothing any of us can do or say that will ever change that."

He went on to explain that the administration was vehemently asserting their power these days because Maynard had just become the focus of a Correctional Services of Canada experiment. The powers that be had decided that Maynard would integrate sex offenders into the general population. In every other penitentiary, those men sentenced for sexual offenses were housed separately from other prisoners. In the wake of this experiment, prisoners were grumbling and worse, the Inmate Committee was trying to keep everyone cool while the administration was flexing its muscle.

Only later would I understand that, to staff and inmates at Maynard, the decision to integrate sex offenders meant that Maynard was poised for explosive trouble. Prisoners already living in crowded conditions, pent up and frequently high or drunk on a combination of intoxicants were being forced to accept into their ranges, their neighborhoods, the men they most abhorred and feared, and Will felt under pressure to tamp down the rage. I had no idea then how angry Salem was at Will's questioning her power, and I hadn't a clue that her fury would speed my journey down the rabbit hole. As it turned out, although I thought I was learning about how prison worked, I understood very, very little.

chapter nine

On the day of the social I gave up my self-imposed rule about dressing conservatively, professionally. I didn't admit it to myself, but I wanted to look pretty for Will, and I wore a yellow, scooped-neck, sleeveless dress, a sexy dress.

The moment I arrived it was clear I noticed that even that miserable joint had inhaled the force of spring's energy. The weedy brown grass in the yard was turning green, and instead of sweat and sadness, the air smelled of perfume and sizzling meat. Three enormous barbecues stood under a makeshift canopy, and big, strapping Lifers with aprons tied over their prison greens, were taking turns flipping burgers. Picnic tables laden with vats of potato salad and platters of fruit were lined up beside the barbecues, and in a far corner of the yard a boom box blared the Rolling Stones and Aretha, and the sun shone on all the pretty dresses. When the wind caught the edge of my dress, it swirled around my bare legs. When I half-closed my eyes I felt as if I weren't in prison at all, and when I told Bernard the scene reminded me of any picnic anywhere, he said, "That's the idea. The point is to try to spend a few hours like we're regular Joes."

I looked around for Will, and when I didn't see him I was disappointed. I pretended not to be and focused on listening to Bernard who was explaining the way socials worked. The men paid for everything out of their canteens, he said. We were standing near a group of people, and he turned to a few of the guys and said—not cruelly, Bernard was always kind—"Set her straight, fellas. Tell Amy. She thought The Man paid for good shit for us."

I felt as if I had no business standing among them, as if the despicable Man. Of course they paid for their own socials. I ought to have known that.

Big Bill, all 300 pounds of him, was standing beside a blonde who looked as if she could fit into his pocket. He whispered something to her, and she began to laugh so hard lemonade squirted out of her nose. "Don't, Billy, don't..." she squealed.

Big Bill pointed a beefy finger at the ground beneath the picnic tables. "All I said was someone's not thinkin'..."

Along with everyone else, I looked down at the spot where Big Bill was pointing and saw heavy-gauge wickets hammered into the ground; the picnic tables had 200-pound chains padlocked to them.

"So listen," he inhaled deeply, "they take these humongous chains, right? And they chain the tables to the ground, right? Why?"

"'Cause of the break," someone said.

Bernard explained that a couple of months earlier two inmates had tried to escape by piling picnic tables one on top of another and, using them as a ladder, they scaled the 30-foot fence and got away. They were caught the next day.

"Right," Big Bill said, "so they don't want us buildin' ladders, right?" he stifled a laugh that threatened to explode from his enormous body. "So now they stick a bunch a killers out here with these heavy chains ...I mean, someone's not thinkin'..."

Everyone began to howl with laughter, and I tried to join in, but murderers and heavy chains didn't strike me as funny. I wasn't afraid of these men, but I did feel stupid, an intruder, a spy who was prying into private lives. I felt like a naïve snob who didn't think this idea was funny, and I thought I ought to leave, but just as I turned, I felt someone's breath on my neck and heard Will's voice saying, "You'll get used to it."

So he had been there after all, and he had seen me withering, and he had come to my rescue. I wanted to throw my arms around him, but I just turned and smiled.

"We just need a little humor if we're going to survive this shit," he went on explaining the laughter, and before I could answer, he said, "You look pretty. Thanks," and he touched my shoulder.

It was the first time he had touched me, and though he took his hand away fast, my shoulder felt singed by his heat. But he couldn't know that I had dressed for him. I couldn't cross this line. "I didn't dress like this for you," I snapped.

"Maybe not but it still makes me feel good." He reached into his pocket and pulled out a CD. "I brought this for you," he said. "Hang on," and he strode across the yard toward the boombox. I watched him talking to the inmate/DJ who turned off Aretha and slipped Will's CD into the player. I heard a scratch and then the song: the Eagles singing, "You can't hide your lyin' eyes…"

I felt a dozen things at once. Moved and attracted and excited, and I hated myself for that. And his boldness infuriated me. How dare he think he knew anything about what my eyes said? How dare he presume anything about my life? He was a murderer. How dare he judge me or judge my current relationship? How dare he think I would let this flirtation go on? I hadn't told him much about my personal life. Dean was out of town still; I hadn't had to deal with what it meant that I was planning to move out and talking to another man every night and letting everything get out of hand while pretending it was all under control.

> …it breaks her heart to think her love is
> Only given to a man with hands as cold as ice…"

I had never described Dean as cold. I hadn't described Dean at all except to talk about how successful he was, how much he had helped me learn how to be a real writer.

> "On the other side of town a boy is waiting with fiery eyes
> and dreams no one could steal…"

I felt the heat scorching my shoulder, but I would never tell him that, cocky bastard.

He stood beside me, pale skin freckling under the sun making him look suddenly younger. Those words blared across the lawn, and I felt myself falling, and I knew this was madness. The last thing I needed as a love affair of any kind, and I certainly didn't need one with a murderer.

Besides, there were journalistic ethics to consider—I had crossed the line, though I hadn't meant to. My mind spun—why did I suddenly feel like I was in a mess I could never squirm out of? What was I supposed to do? I wanted to keep talking to him, but why? I wasn't allowed to talk to him, and why was that? Was there something about him that made him truly dangerous? Was that why Cal had warned me away? Or did Will have the goods on people who couldn't afford to have their dirty laundry aired to a newspaper columnist?

And there was this: I could not become one of *those* women. *Those* women who loved prisoners were such easy targets, and untrustworthy, and ridiculous. *Those* women were everything I was sure I was not. They were fools.

"I'm going to help the guys with cooking," he said, and he touched my shoulder again. "Catch you later…" He loped across the yard, leaving me stranded.

I looked around at all the wives and girlfriends in that prison yard. There was something untoward about coming here to be with a criminal—something dirty. I needed to be different from them. I was here because I wanted to find out who these people were, what made them tick, what prison did to them. I was here to listen to them, not to become one of them. I was here as an anthropologist, not a case study.

I chose Tina, Big Bill's girlfriend, because she was bubbly and sweet. Sidling closer to her I half-whispered, "Listen, I'm writing columns for the local paper about prison, and I wonder if I could interview you."

She looked at Big Bill who nodded. "She's okay," he said.

I soldiered on. "So what's it like? Visiting someone inside?"

Tina's laughter drifted away as she talked about how much it cost her to get here, how hard it was because of all the people she couldn't tell about her relationship. If she did tell she would be risking her job, so this big part of her life was also a big secret, and when she wasn't with him she missed him so much. She said she was more or less living for the day he got out. "It's weird being here," she nodded towards the guards who were hovering in every corner. "You know, the way they watch us all the time. I hate that. Who do they think they are?"

I thought: I'm watching too.

Connie was walking towards us. She was Bernard's new girlfriend. We'd met briefly in the visiting room one day, and I could see she and Bernard were wholly smitten with each other. She had bright blond hair down to her waist and big green eyes that gleamed with either tears or pleasure, I couldn't tell. "Did you hear about them?" Tina asked, "Bernard and Connie? How they got together?"

"A little," I said. But soon Connie had joined us and freely spilled out the story of how she'd known Bernard twenty years earlier, how she was just a teenager and had this big crush on him. "He was this famous outlaw in our town, and I wished I could meet him. He had this reputation, like, oh you know, like…"

"Butch Cassidy?" Tina suggested.

"Like that," she went on. A few months earlier a friend had asked Connie to keep her company on a trip to Maynard to visit her brother. She'd had no idea she would run into Bernard at Maynard, but the second she walked into the V&C she recognized him. He was there with his daughter, and somehow she worked up her nerve to walk over and talk to him. "And well…" she looked across the lawn at Bernard who was talking to some other guys, and as if he had felt her look, he turned and their gazes locked. "We just clicked. Just like that…"

Connie was giddy with this new love, and after she regaled me with stories of the pain and pleasure of visiting, Bernard walked over to gather her, and I watched the two of them walk away across the lawn, so close their bodies seemed attached. I thanked Tina and began to wander around, asking a question here, a question there—of mothers and fathers, daughters and sons, wives and kids. Everyone had the same complaints—the cost, the time, the dreariness of visiting rooms, the suspicion they lived under, the sadness in saying goodbye, the cruelty of separation, the longing for the day that prison door closed behind them for the last time.

As I listened, I batted away the awareness that I wanted Will to touch me again, and then, as if he had read my mind, he was behind me again. I turned and frowned at him. "I'm just trying to talk to some people privately if you don't mind…"

He raised his hands, mock innocence. "Whoa, sorry!" But as he backed away, one of the wives pulled him towards us. "Will's so good to all the guys. Hey, Will, where are those beautiful daughters of yours?"

"Couldn't make it today," he said, and I noticed a wave of sadness pass over his face.

"You should meet his girls," the woman went on. "They're so pretty. Aren't they pretty, Will?"

"Beautiful," he said and he looked right at me.

I had forgotten to ask him why they weren't here, but I didn't want to know any more than I already knew. I turned again and looked around and began to notice that couples were drifting into corners, seeking privacy to talk, to touch, to kiss. I began to feel stranded when he said, "Wanna sit?" and pointed to a picnic bench.

I was careful to leave some space between us. I folded my hands in my lap. "So, why aren't the kids here?" I asked.

"It's a long trip for my mom," he said. Whenever he talked about the children or his mother, his voice grew thick, and when I saw that he wasn't all independence and courage, that he couldn't take care of everyone even if he pretended he could, I began to feel almost maternal. Who took care of him? It wouldn't be me, I told myself, but my brain was whirling again, kicking up every side of every argument. It was his fault. If he'd wanted to live with his kids, he should have made different choices. I half-wanted to say that, but I couldn't say it. It sounded too cruel. That day especially when everyone seemed so joyful, kissing and hugging and laughing. I couldn't criticize him. Not there. Besides, if I did, he would hate me, and I didn't want him to hate me. I said, noncommittally, "It's too bad you don't see more of them. It must be hard on them, too."

He smiled. "You're thinking I should have made different choices."

I shifted farther away. The bastard could read my mind. "So? Why didn't you?"

"Long story," he said. "Or short story. I'm just a jerk…" he stood and said, "Think I'll go grab something to eat. Join me whenever…if you want…" and he was gone again.

I stayed on the bench, disappointed and relieved. A few minutes later I noticed some kids racing across the lawn towards the area that separated the Native's sweat lodge from the rest of the yard. They were just about to leap a thin rope to enter that sacred space, so I stood and began to walk fast towards them.

But before I could reach them, a female guard—one of the women with muscles as thick the prisoners' muscles and a downward curve to her lips—blocked their way. I watched as she touched the ringleader's arm. "Sorry, kids, you can't go in there."

As I walked closer, I searched in the crowd for Pete. I wanted him to see this hard-ass guard protecting his ground. I thought her gesture might make him feel hopeful. He was a lot like Will in his unwillingness to see only enemies in the guards, but here was a guard protecting inmates' sacred property.

"The sweat lodge is like a church," the guard explained to the kids. They grumbled and drifted back towards their parents. I approached her. "That was good of you," I said. I wanted her to know that while I wasn't part of her gang, I wasn't part of the inmates' gang either.

She raised her eyebrows and frowned. "Good?"

"Well, smart," I tried.

"Yeah, well listen, I'm still gonna report you." She nodded in Will's direction. I turned and saw him standing at the barbecues. "You're not supposed to talk to him."

"C'mon," I tried to sound jovial. "It's a social. Everyone talks to everyone. It's not a big deal. It's not like there's some kind of conspiracy."

"Uh huh," she said and strode away.

Will caught my glance and waved. "Over here, Friedman," he called.

I crossed the lawn, my heart knotted in anger at the guard for being so nasty in the face of my efforts to be friendly. I had been thinking about how I would defend her to Pete or Will, but maybe they were right after all; maybe all the guards were bastards.

It was only years later that I understood that that was the moment I crossed a barrier, the moment I chose sides.

When I reached him, Will took an apron and tied it around my waist. "You don't think you can get away with eating all our food without some work," he joked. He looked at one of the men at the grills. "Go on, man, be with your wife."

The fellow jogged away, and Will looked at me. "No one has enough time with their families. People like you who spend every night at home might not think being separated for a few weeks or months is a big deal, but put yourself in our shoes…Kids grow up fast, and we miss most of that …Parents grow old and die."

"So is this what you want me to learn?" I asked.

He reached to rub something off my nose. "This is what you want to learn. I don't need you to learn nothin.'"

"Anything," I corrected him.

"Anything." He paused and flipped a burger. "But I'd like to know more about you." I looked across the lawn and saw the female guard glaring at us. I nodded in her direction and said to Will, "She's going to report us."

He smiled. "You want me to leave you alone? That's cool. I don't want to hurt you." He turned away, but I reached out. This time I touched him. "Wait," I said. I needed to ask him one more thing. I needed to ask him why he was the one person I wasn't allowed to talk to? Who cared if I was attracted to him? Surely other women had been, and the guards and administrators weren't my parents or my friends. What did they care? "What's their problem with you?"

"I stand up for the guys," he said. "If you write about what really goes on in here—the stuff I'm going to tell you—they might have to change some things."

"But I'd figure it out on my own," I said. "Why just you?"

He shook his head. "They set you up to write what they want you to write."

I was no investigative reporter, but my column was popular, and sometimes I swayed opinion. "Still, why just you..?"

He shrugged. "They don't like me. I challenge them. They don't like that, and they'll fuck us whenever they can."

"That's paranoia. It's stupid to label all of them…"

"Stupid?"

"That's what people do with prisoners…label you as all alike …"

"Maybe we are."

"You're not. You told me yourself. You're not a rat. And listen, that guard over there just told the kids to stay off the Natives' sacred ground. That's something, isn't it?"

He rolled his eyes. "You think she cares about the sweat lodge?"

"Yes, I do," I said.

He snorted. I clenched my fist. "She doesn't give a shit. She just didn't want trouble from Pete and she knew she'd get it."

He was too unforgiving. "You're too hard," I said.

"And you're too naïve," he countered. He stepped closer. "And too soft," he said. "And you're lonely."

The day was growing late. Someone called for everyone to gather for pictures. I let him lead me to the group. I have the photograph which is why I know I let him put his arms around my waist, and I leaned back into him, and we both smiled. We both lit up. I see it in the picture. The pleasure, the lust. It was all out there for anyone and everyone to see.

And then? I remember watching him walk away, back to the range, in line behind all the other men. I remember being surrounded by all those women reaching for their men, taking in last, lingering kisses, crying, and calling goodbye. I must have wanted him to kiss me. But I wouldn't have let him, and he didn't. Not that day.

chapter ten

The next day at the office, before I'd even unpacked my bags, my editor sent for me. As I walked across the buzzing newsroom, I imagined Jack Morley must have something he wanted to say about my kids' column—it had taken off and was making the paper money. That surely was making him happy. Jack was a man of few words. He wasn't unfriendly, but he usually was all business, and I looked forward to hearing his praise. But the minute I saw his face I knew it wasn't praise he had in store for me. His bushy black eyebrows were frowning. Jack's everyday demeanor was dour, almost Nixon-like, and that day it was darker than usual. Although sunshine was pouring into his large, airy office, I felt as though I were walking into the eye of a storm.

"We got a letter," he said.

I must have looked puzzled.

"From Maynard. You're no longer allowed to visit."

I was sure I'd heard wrong. Who would have written to the paper? Why hadn't they come to me? And if the prison was complaining that I was talking to a prisoner they had warned me not to talk to, why would Jack assume I had done anything wrong? Wouldn't a seasoned journalist like Jack be suspicious of *them*? He knew my work. He knew me. He'd trusted me enough to give me a second column, and I couldn't fathom the idea that tough-minded, shoot-from-the-hip Jack didn't seem even to care about digging for truth. For heaven's sake, he'd sent a team of investigative reporters to Bosnia, was he going to cave to a local prison official? I could explain. I'd let a flirtation get out of hand. I would stop it. I leaned into his desk. "Who wrote the letter?" I asked.

"Can't tell you that. It's confidential."

"But Jack…" He never kowtowed to authority, and besides, he liked me because I didn't either. I thought we understood each other, at least a little. "Jack, please…"

He put up a hand. "No discussion. They want you out, you're out. And Amy, I don't have time for this. That's all." He waved me away.

Jack could be fierce and unyielding, and I wasn't the only person who was sometimes afraid of him. Still, I couldn't imagine what prison authorities could have said that had inspired this kind of response. Okay, I thought as I stepped out of his office, so I had talked to Will after a few guards complained, but I could explain that. And I was attracted to him, but I would keep that in check. I had to, and I would. I turned around, hoping to return to Jack's office and talk this out, but he had moved to the doorway. For a second we locked eyes, and then he turned and closed the door behind him.

Dizzy, I walked across the newsroom. Suddenly everyone there looked different—everyone looked hostile. Who could I explain this to? What would I say? That the prison was tossing me? Some reporter would want to know why, and I'd have to say I'd let Will touch me. I'd have to tell them I was flirting with a convicted murderer, but what did that matter? And if it did matter, wouldn't a real reporter want to know why? How could they accept the prison deciding to throw me out without asking for my side of this story? And what had they said? I had to know.

Years later, through the Privacy Commissioner's Act, I retrieved the letter the prison had sent to Jack, and I read between the lines the same way Jack must have. They described my behavior as having been inappropriate; sexual innuendo leapt off the page, and even all these years later I can feel both the fury and embarrassment I felt when I read those words. Even now I haven't forgiven those at the paper who could have asked me questions about what was going on. But that day I felt only frantic and abandoned and angry. Someone had to fix this, but I didn't know who to turn to. I drove home and waited for Will's phone call. Besides Kate, he was becoming the only person I talked to, and this time I didn't choose Kate first.

I tried not to cry as I told him about what had happened, and when I had finished, he was silent for minute before he said, "You could still come in if you add your name to my visiting list. They can't stop you from visiting prison if you're on my list," he said. "Unless of course you have a criminal record. You don't, do you?"

I didn't stop to ponder this idea of crossing the line altogether, of moving from my status as an official visitor, a writer seeking out everyone's stories, to becoming a woman visiting a specific man in prison. I was too upset, not thinking straight, and besides, I liked him. I liked talking to him. Damn them if they thought I'd just lie down and curl up and shut up. I drove to get the application papers the next day, filled them out and within 72 hours I had been accepted as one of Will's approved visitors.

I still fashioned myself the writer who would uncover the real story about how prisons worked. I pictured myself showing my writings to someone who would stand up for me and publish the prison stories. So I wasn't allowed to write about prison, but I would cross that bridge when I had to—and who knew, maybe Jack would cave. Maybe I would write something he couldn't resist. Maybe I would uncover some story that would make him proud of me for finding a way around the barrier prison officials had erected. That was the kind of thing Jack admired.

I'm sure my motives for signing onto Will's list were confused and complicated, and I paid no attention to the ways this rebellion might backfire on me or to the ways in which my position at the paper wasn't as secure as I'd imagined it was. I wasn't only naïve about prisons, I was naïve about what happened when a big press syndicate took over a newspaper and consolidated power in tighter and tighter circles. I wasn't sure who my enemies were, and I didn't understand how clearly divided sides were. I didn't fully realize that by ignoring orders and continuing to see Will, I had chosen a side.

* * *

Most people in Canada knew the stories of a few prisoners—David Milgaard, for one, Mark Lépine who had killed 14 women in Montreal in 1989, Guy Paul Morin, convicted in 1984 of the first degree murder of a little girl who after 10 long years was exonerated by DNA. But among the most notorious was Stephen Reid, the bank robber who, along with Paddy Mitchell and Lionel Wright, had pulled off some of

North America's most famous bank heists. The Stopwatch Gang, as they were known, committed more than one hundred robberies from Seattle to Miami. Before they were caught, they hauled off more than $15 million, and according to their victims, the men were always polite and considerate. When they weren't "out on jobs," they lived in a magnificent house in the Arizona mountains where neighbors thought they were music promoters. Even after their arrests, those neighbors had nothing but praise for the men.

In 1983, Susan Musgrave, a renowned Canadian poet and personality, was working as a writer-in-residence at the University of Waterloo. At the time she was a twice-divorced author of a dozen books beloved by readers and critics, and one day Musgrave received a manuscript from a man serving 20 years at Middle Harbor Penitentiary. That man was Stephen Reid, and the manuscript was his autobiographical novel, *Jackrabbit Parole*, published the same year Reid was released. He and Musgrave married, and Reid too had become a famous writer. Neither he nor Musgrave gave a damn what anyone thought about their love story. In the eyes of many, mine included, they were passionate, unswervingly honest, and daring—the ultimate love story.

I hadn't yet met Susan, but I knew their story, and during those first weeks of visiting Will, I began to romanticize us as the next Musgrave and Reid. From the get-go, he loved the fact that I was a writer. He talked about a dream he'd always had of writing books. He wanted my help. Many men and women, upon learning I was a writer, had told me they had a great story to tell. A lot of people said they planned to write those stories. Will was no different, but the difference was I wanted to believe him, and because of Musgrave and Reid, I did.

I was also drunk on the idea of helping him to remove the cloak of armor he seemed to be wearing—the protection that shielded him from feeling too close to anyone. Even years later whenever I looked at the photographs Mack took of the two of us in the visiting room that June, I see the pleasure we were taking in each other's company. He could make me laugh, hard. I evoked his smiles and his tenderness. I brought out the man who wanted to make something of his life instead of the man he could so often be—the proud and angry and belligerent warrior. I thought I had found a love like Mom and Dad's, like Susan and Stephen's, like all those whose devotion surmounted obstacles.

In those early weeks of June, I wasn't shy about telling people I was visiting a man in prison. I had almost forgotten I still had to find my own place and tell Dean we were finished. Maybe taking up with Will was part of what was helping me to make that break. But Dean was still overseas, and he never called or wrote, and I had started to pack. I was planning to move out before he returned. From my own home I would be able to tell him why. Otherwise I feared he might try to convince me to stay. I knew he didn't want me to leave, though I suspected he mostly liked the idea that I was there to look after the farm while he was on his long sojourns away.

Besides Kate, I wasn't talking to anyone at home about Will, but I did call Diane, my best friend who still lived in New York. She and I had been friends for years, and we'd also written a book together. She probably knew me better than I knew myself, and when I told her about Will, she laughed and said it sounded perfect. "You can be in a relationship and not in one," she said. "Perfect for you, but this one sounds a little crazier than usual." But instead of recognizing how right she might be, that the independence this arrangement offered me was right up my alley, I got mad and vowed not to listen to her or to anyone else who tried to offer advice.

Diane had probably nailed it. Will fulfilled my longing for high romance, and he was perfect for me because of my imperfections—my fear of being too normal. But I didn't think about that. I stayed caught up in the romance, falling in love with a boy from the wrong side of the tracks, caught up in dreaming of the day he might be free, caught up in the lyrics of *Desperado,* another of Will's favorite songs, inspiration for that tattoo—"You better let somebody love you before it's too late…"

Marriage never once crossed my mind.

chapter eleven

Making love, however, did cross my mind.

The Correctional Officer in charge of Will's case was a no-nonsense woman named Barbara Baker who had no interest in the petty games that some of her colleagues liked to play, wielding their power to make their charges' lives more miserable. Barbara, as she was called, was one in a long line of family who had worked for the Service, and the one time I met her at Maynard she gave off an air of "been-there, seen-that, let's just get on with what needs to be done." I never met Will's Living Unit Officer who, along with Barbara, was responsible for setting up his program, a program designed to prepare him for a transfer to a minimum security—or "camp" as the minimum joints were known. Charleston Institution was the camp that sat across a narrow road from Maynard, and the plan was for him to make it there within two years in order to prepare him to make his day parole in three. When I signed onto his visiting list, this "cascading" plan was well underway, and I was sure he would make his release on time. Once he was outside he could find out what kind of relationship we might create. We could find out. Out in "the real world" anything was possible.

I saw no way he could be deterred from earning parole given the support he had from his beloved and devoted and solidly middle-class mother, his beautiful children, and his three oh-so-respectable sisters— a doctor, a businesswoman, a nurse. Besides, unlike so many men inside, he was sober. He was smart. He had finished high school at least, and he read to educate himself. With my help he could learn to write. Visiting him in prison for through three years seemed feasible, in those years we could get to know each other—not just emotionally and intellectually but maybe even sexually. Once I had sorted things out in my life with Dean, I would be free to "date," if that was the term one used for a relationship with a man in prison.

I didn't immediately think about it in those terms, but in mid-June, two months since we'd met, he told me he loved me and wanted me to meet his mother and children. I suppose I was ready. I hadn't used the word "love," but I was thinking in longer and more serious terms. He told me his mother and kids would be coming, and he hoped I would join them for a visit. I said yes.

I arrived well after visiting hours began to give his family time alone with him, time to prepare to meet this woman he had told them he was falling for. I walked slowly toward them across the visiting room. I was happy to see how normal they looked and how happy they seemed with each other. They were huddling close, and despite the surroundings, they looked to me like any ordinary family spending time together anywhere. They were conservatively and neatly dressed. Sarah at 14 was pale and blond, a Lolita-like beauty, and Willie was 12, cocky and handsome with thick chestnut hair that fell over one eye. Will had told me 9-year-old Cassandra was taking summer school classes and wouldn't be there, but Molly, his mother was. She was small and slender, wearing a plaid wool beret that was perched at a rakish angle atop her short gray hair, and she had a radiant smile. As I approached them I saw Sarah slap her father's arm and begin to laugh uncontrollably. Their happiness struck my heart. Sarah's especially. She looked as if she loved her dad the way I loved mine, and I thought of my own difficulties with my dad's silence and distance; surely Sarah had to deal with the same. Willie was playing it cool—leaning back in his chair, keeping a straight face about whatever joke Will had just told them, but I could see laughter bubbling up inside.

Molly turned to look at me, and even from a distance I saw her eyes light up, and I fell in love with her more quickly even than I had fallen for Will. As I came nearer, they all stood. Sarah stepped behind her father.

"This is Amy," Will announced proudly, as if showing off an award he'd just won. "The woman I've been telling you about."

"So good to meet you," Molly said, offering her hand, and as we took our seats, I thanked Molly and Sarah for helping with the flowers. I could feel the kids studying me, but Molly dived right in, telling me how glad she was to finally meet the woman Will couldn't stop talking about. Her voice was quiet like so many small-town Ontario women's voices were—reflecting a too finely tuned self-deprecation. Molly reminded me of my farm neighbors and of so many of the women I'd heard on Peter Gzowski's CBC radio show, deeply modest but like those other women, provocative and practical and wise. "I dressed up for you," she winked, pointing at the hat. "Classy, don't you think?" And she laughed just like Will—dry and bemused.

They asked a dozen questions—where I was from, what working at the paper was like. Molly talked about how much she had enjoyed living with Sarah this past year but, now that she had finished middle school, Sarah would move to Ottawa to be with her mom and the rest of the kids.

Sarah couldn't look me in the eye, but she was sneaking glances at me, and all of a sudden out of the blue she said, "I don't wanna live with my mom."

"It'll be fine," Molly said, patting her hand.

"Shut up. Don't bad mouth Mom," Willie said. He cast me an angry look, but Molly changed the subject. She told me how much she admired writers, and I told her things I hadn't yet told Will—that I would be leaving the next week for a three-week stay at an artist's colony where I planned to finish a book that was due to a publisher in July. I hadn't figured out how to tell him I was leaving town, and as I told her, I couldn't look at him. I couldn't tell him because I had begun to feel sorry for him, locked up in here, and I didn't want to see his disappointment when I told him I wouldn't be able to see him for a while.

"I'm sure writing a book takes a great deal of concentration," Molly said.

If he was disappointed at learning the news, he didn't show it. Instead he simply jumped in to sing my praises again. "She teaches writing, too. At the local college."

"Wonderful," Molly said, and she looked at her son. "She's quite a woman."

"Just like you," Will said to his mother. "Mom's a nurse. She supported us kids all on her own..."

"Which means you and I are equally underpaid," she said, embarrassed by her son's boast. She deflected the flattery by turning it into a laugh line.

"And underappreciated," I offered, but she was already on to another subject. I could see she was thinking about something.

"I'm so glad spring is here," she said. "It's so much easier to visit when the weather's good. We'll come visit while Amy's away, and there's the trailer visit in July…" And then she turned to me. "Amy, why don't you join us for the trailer visit? That way we all would have an opportunity to get to know each other better. I know Will would like that…"

I knew from interviewing prisoners and their families and the warden and the guards that nearly every prison in Canada had trailers on their grounds, behind fences and walls. These were designed for Private Family Visits as they were formally called, 72 hours during which those inmates who had earned the privilege could spend time with their loved ones. Will hadn't mentioned that he had an upcoming trailer visit, as they were known vernacularly. I did know, though, that most inmates considered these visits as the one thing that kept them sane. Girlfriends and wives had told me they were vital, most especially for the children who shared so little reasonably normal time with their fathers. Molly's offer threw me off guard, but it also touched me. I had been wondering about how Will and I might find some private time—time not hemmed in by bells signaling the end of visits, time not surrounded by so many others—and this notion of hers was thrilling, both delicious and safe. As I wanted to sleep with Will, I wasn't sure about sharing a trailer alone since some part of me still wondered if this romance or crush or whatever it was wasn't sheer madness. I still thought he must be capable of doing me harm. But sharing the trailer with his family sounded mature and not crazily romantic. Sex could wait. Or maybe it wouldn't have to. Those trailers had bedrooms. On one of my "official" visits I had toured one, escorted by a guard.

"If you do want to come, we'll need the warden's approval," Will said. Correctional Services Canada was guided by Correctional Directives, and among the many hundreds, one of these restricted trailer visits to family members and/or friends who had been on an inmate's visiting list for over one year. Like so many directives, this one was malleable. Any warden could override the one-year waiting requirement.

I understood why such a rule existed. I saw the sense in imposing protection for guileless young women from men renowned for guile, and although every trailer was equipped with a panic button and the men were called to the door for "Count" every few hours, I wasn't opposed to the idea of caution. We weren't young, and I wasn't in need of any protection, particularly not with his mom and the children in tow—and they'd shared numerous trailer visits over the years. I was confident Warden Claussen would let us have the visit. While he clearly didn't want me inside as a columnist writing stories that might cause him problems, I couldn't imagine he would have any qualms about my spending private time with Will. We hadn't spoken since I had been officially ousted, but prior to that we had had a decent rapport. I was sure he held nothing against me.

Other people, however, were reacting oddly. In the newsroom especially a lot of people who had been my friends—not close but friendly for years—were beginning to look at me with a combination of uneasiness and pity. A few I chose to tell seemed to have spread the word to others at work, and some were outright hostile about my signing on to a visiting list just to keep going to prison. Other things were troubling me, too, mostly that I hadn't told Dean of my plans to leave him. In the past whenever I'd broached the subject of breaking up, he'd responded with anger. I feared I was making a mistake I'd live to regret and I feared hurting him. I knew he was more sensitive than he let on, and he liked things to be the way he wanted them. He liked my being there, half-belonging to him, even if we were not lovers. Kate had helped me to see that if I was going to make a break from him, I would have to do it without his acceptance, much less his blessing.

I was beginning to have dreams about our trailer visit, but the dreams weren't about sex. I dreamed that I knew Will's whole story. In a private space, he would tell me the things he couldn't tell me in that crowded, noisy visiting room where guards were forever calling out warnings, and other couples sat too near. I wanted to get straight the story of Laura and his marriage to her, and I wanted to hear about the murder and the court case about which I'd heard only refrains. "The day they arrested me, the cops celebrated. One in the ground and one put away for life." He told me Russell Davis, his friend and minister, had told him that on the day Will was arrested and Russell came to see him. When Will told me that, he laughed a dry, unhappy laugh. Will firmly believed that in this world there were two clearly opposing sides—the cops and the guards, or coppers as he called them, pitted against outlaws and renegades. Those two sides, he was certain, had little in common and would never get along. They meant each other harm.

I had a sense—only the vaguest sense—that in the weeks leading up to the murder, Will had been falling apart, in part from too much drinking, in part from sorrow at being separated from his kids because of his crumbling marriage. He told me he once belonged to the Outlaws Motorcycle Gang and that when he left there was a kind of war between he and his former "brothers" who were still in the gang. I didn't understand much about gangs and loyalty other than what I knew from movies like *Scarface* and *The Godfather* and *Mean Streets*, and what I knew from brief newspaper reports about gang wars. I'd read Hunter S. Thompson's *Gonzo Journalism*, his tale of hanging out with the Hells Angels, I read that in 1977 the Canadian Biker gang Satan's Choice joined the Outlaws' franchise and police categorized them as an organized crime syndicate. Two years later there would be a well-publicized biker war in Quebec, started when a jeep wired with a remote-controlled bomb exploded and killed a member of the Rock Machine and an innocent 11-year-old boy, followed the next month by the shooting of a Hells Angel member at a shopping ball; bombs went off around the province during his funeral, and in 1997 new legislation was passed that stiffened penalties for those convicted of crimes who were shown to be members of such organizations.

What I didn't understand was how a man like Will, brought up in such a straight and traditionally middle class family had chosen to lead a criminal life. I wanted to know more about his drug use and his drinking, the steps that led him onto the path that had proved his undoing. But his stories came to me in unfinished versions, interrupted by the end of visits or by the sound of clicking on the phone or by his sudden awareness that nothing we said or wrote was private. I hoped in a trailer visit he would fill in the blanks in his stories and help me to understand who he was and who he might still become.

The trailers were shabby places surrounded by fences and locked gates. They had flimsy walls, cheap furniture, floors pock-marked from spilled food and cigarette ashes, rickety tables and sofas that were too narrow and hard, but the promise of privacy overcame any uneasiness I felt about the actual place. Never mind that windows were grimy with years of rain splatter and soot or that the view out those windows was only of the postage-stamp sized yard. Never mind that when I first saw one I thought it looked like something out of a Hitchcock film, the kind of place I'd never want to spend a night—much less a romantic one. And never mind that all these years later when I recall the time I spent with Will in prison trailers, I feel sweaty and claustrophobic.

Will and I put in our request to his Correctional Officer, Barbara Baker, asking her to fill out the paperwork to request from the warden that I be permitted to join the family in their July trailer visit. Many of the women I had talked to about trailers when I was still "official" and still asking questions had spoken of the ache they felt awaiting those visits. In the visiting room if anyone's behavior became too intimate—a hand slipping inside a blouse, a leg lifted from the floor—a voice boomed over the loudspeaker, "Hands on the table, feet on the floor, let's watch it, people!" True on occasion a couple managed to sneak in a quick sexual liaison. At socials someone would guard a door while the couple sneaked into a closet or an empty room to fuck. (Fuck was the only word that could describe those furtive encounters.) There could be no tenderness, nothing romantic about those desperate and nervous and horny trysts. At that first family social, I had noticed a couple, hair tousled, brows sweaty, slipping out of a little room, and I'd looked around and seen guards everywhere, lurking in doorways, looming in towers. Some guards didn't care about these bleak assignations. Half the guys inside never were permitted conjugal visits, and even those who did could have them withdrawn for the slightest infraction.

Will was 31 when he first went to prison, and that year he was 38. By the time of our first private visit he would be turning 39, and in all those years he hadn't had a trailer visit with a woman. He and I had gotten good at kissing. We ended every visit with long, thirsty kisses that substituted for everything else, but often I left our visits reeling. After I said goodbye and walked outside, shuffling the half mile from Sally Port to parking lot, I felt woozy, intoxicated by a brew of pleasure and sadness that was like nothing I had ever known. I don't remember ever feeling that kind of longing.

* * *

I had had many love affairs—many brief, some with married men, some while drunk or high, some while I was married to someone, and some when I was achingly lonely—and though I sometimes still feel embarrassed admitting those affairs, it is also true that I was the product of a particular time and place—a time when women suddenly had the freedom to have sex without losing our reputation or winding up pregnant. A time when having sex was seen as taking back our power. And most of those affairs were fun or comforting or comfortable, and some were marvelously romantic and many ended in long-lasting friendships. One thing I did know about myself: Whenever I had stayed for any length of time at an artist colony, I not only wrote twice as much as I could ever write at home, but I was also inspired to seduce or be seduced by one of my fellow artists—wacked out painters and low key sculptors, wild-eyed composers and egomaniacal poets, southerners and foreigners, the famous and the nobodies. And now I was going to be at The Virginia Center for the Arts for three weeks.

My relationship with Will had become something I actually had to call a "relationship." I had confessed to Will the truth about Dean—that I was going to leave, that Kate was helping me look for a new place to live on my own. I was still half-pretending to myself that this "thing" with Will was only a bizarre and brief affair, something that would make a good story but would never last, something that wasn't exactly dirty but that couldn't properly continue unless and until he lived outside, and until then, we would see. But he sensed that I was hooked on him, and I did feel that I owed him at least an understanding of who I was and what he might expect to happen while I was away—personally and not just professionally.

The day before I was to leave for Virginia, we were sitting beside each other on those bus station-like chairs in the visiting room when he took my hand and surreptitiously pressed something into my palm, then closed my fingers around it. He glanced at me, eyes narrowed to let me know this was something we couldn't talk about, not here, and when I sneaked a look inside my hand, I saw a necklace with a gold lion's head with ruby eyes and a diamond nose. "It's a Leo," he whispered. "For a Leo from a Leo." Our birthdays were just two weeks apart, both in August.

He pressed a finger to his lips to remind me that no one was allowed to exchange things in the visiting room, so this was contraband. I could never ask how he came to have it, though obviously someone had smuggled it inside, and now Will was smuggling it out to me. He smiled that confident, "I'm making you happy," kind of smile. For a long moment I didn't know what to say. No one had ever given me a diamond. All my exes, including my soon to be ex, Dean, had prided themselves on their disinterest in showy gifts. My first wedding band had been a simple gold band, and while I was just fine with the idea that romance had nothing to do with the exchange of jewels, the sight of that lion and his diamond nose sent a shudder of pleasure through me.

But I couldn't accept this gift. I had just been about to tell him that I was fairly certain that while in Virginia I might have an affair. That he'd have to understand that he and I weren't officially any kind of couple, certainly not a monogamous kind. Just as I was about to say we couldn't have any kind of hold on each other, here he was giving me a gift. And beyond the necklace itself, he was taking a risk for me—if he had been discovered with the necklace in his possession, he would have landed in segregation. He would have been written up. If he wanted to cascade through the system and reach the parole board in three years, he had to toe the line and make sure not to do anything that could blemish his record. But I steeled myself and said, "Will, sometimes at these colonies I have affairs."

He dropped my hand and fell silent. I had endured a few of these heavy silences of his. They often felt volcanic, as if at any moment he might erupt with all the words he was holding inside. And this silence felt even hotter than usual. I could see I had to wait it out. And so I did for several long minutes before he finally reached for my hand again and squeezed. "If you do," he whispered, "when you come back and visit me, don't wear the lion."

"What will you do if …?" but I couldn't say the words again. I began to imagine that future visit, me waiting the five or ten or twenty or even fifty minutes before correctional officers called him down from his range. He enduring the strip search and the walk across the room towards me, wondering if he would see the necklace around my neck.

But why did I owe him anything? Defiance welled up inside me, and then, before I could say another word, he said, "I'd probably turn around and leave but I can't know until it happens, can I?"

"No," I agreed, and then we kissed.

I was sad to say goodbye, and when I did, as I drifted across the parking lot with tears in my throat, I had no idea what was going to happen.

chapter twelve

I was always happy at the Virginia Center for the Creative Arts, writing in a studio in the renovated dairy barn with a view west towards the Blue Ridge Mountains. I always felt centered there, with time to wander and write and time to spend with people I had come to love over the years, people like Charles, the groundskeeper who had moved to a nearby funky bungalow, people like the co-directors, Craig and Sheila, and Jessie, the director's daughter whom I had known nearly her entire life. It was late June now, two months into this story, and when I told Charles about this "thing" back home, he offered to let Will call me on his phone at home. The grounds had only a pay phone near the dining hall, one shared by all the residents. It could not accept collect calls, and so every evening I walked out the back gate and down the dusty road to Charles's house. There, surrounded by barking dogs and the thick humid Virginia air, Will and I talked on the phone.

I confessed that I missed him. It was easier to say this from this long distance, but he felt farther away than anyone ever had. In an emergency he couldn't come to me; if I needed to reach him, I couldn't. I missed him the way I often missed my dog and cats—creatures I couldn't talk to unless they were right beside me. The space between us felt unbreachable, and it deepened the ache of missing. I had grown accustomed to such long hours of talk—more talk than I had ever shared with someone I was coming to love—and on the phone his voice sounded thick with sadness. In the background I could hear the roar of the range, the shouting men and the blaring music.

"I love it here," I told him. "I hope you understand."

Even as I worked to understand what words would hurt him and what words would not, I wanted at least to try to be honest with him.

Sometime between our goodbye in the visiting room and my arrival in Virginia, I had made the decision that if this was truly going to be a romance, it couldn't include lies and pretense the way life with Dean had come to.

"I'm glad you're somewhere that makes you happy," he said, and I believed him.

"You deserve to be happy."

In those days he didn't seem to begrudge me any pleasure. Rather, he seemed to relish my happiness, as if it were contagious and might bleed into him. My warmth towards him seemed to have softened him, and over the phone we laughed and gossiped about my fellow artists and his fellow convicts. "Some of the other artists were shocked when they heard I was seeing a prisoner," I told him, "but there's one novelist here who's been supportive… Bruce. He acts like it's his job to protect me from people who are too uptight to deal with it."

He interrupted me as I was talking about Bruce. "Don't talk about us. They'll judge you. Everyone will. Besides, what's between us is just between us."

But I was sure he was wrong. I saw the understanding and generosity Charles and Bruce and Craig and Sheila were offering—their kindness and, yes, their curiosity. But who wouldn't be curious? This was an unusual situation, an unusual way to meet someone, an unusual person to fall for. Beyond being open with Will, I was determined to be open with everyone, determined to push people to understand, and though I had taken tentative steps back home to talk to people about this, in Virginia, in this community where I had always felt so safe and at home, I had opened up still more.

"Keep it quiet," he said, again and again. But I believed that anyone who knew me and saw how happy I looked would accept us and celebrate my happiness. I was that lost in that vaporous cloud of early romance—every early romance I've ever known or seen. I was even enraptured by the romance of our beginning—"ah, we met when I was writing a story…" Artists especially, accustomed to defending the way they spent their time, would never judge. And those who did pass judgment would risk my judgment in return. I would know them to be prejudiced and blind to complexity.

Will and I didn't talk much about Maynard. He didn't like to talk about it, and besides, I wouldn't have understood that what was happening inside could actually affect my life beyond the way it might affect Will's mood.

In Ontario summer had still felt distant—that late spring chill hung in the air—but in Virginia summer was blooming, and the lake across the road from the colony was as warm as bathtub water. That's where Jessie, the Director's daughter, and I decided to go one particularly hot afternoon.

Jessie had just turned 11, but she had always had the soul of someone older. I first met Jessie when she was only 6 or 7, but our friendship began when I told her how much I admired the cowboy boots that she wore rain or shine, with every outfit, even in searing heat. The boots were white leather with fringe, and when I told her I loved them, she told me that they represented everything good in her life. Her parents were in the midst of a rocky divorce, and those boots were sacred to her, the one stable thing in her life. So I treated them as sacred, too. On every visit to VCCA since, Jessie and I spent time together.

As we drove to the lake, she told me that some jerk had just been teasing her about the boots, and I agreed with her he was a rube who had no understanding about the important things in this world. We drove across the road, past the stables filled with the horses that belonged to the Sweet Briar College girls, past blooming magnolias and southern belles sunning themselves on those emerald green rolling lawns.

When we reached the lake, we lay our towels out on the deck, and Jessie stood her boots beside our towels. We lay down to warm ourselves before taking a dive.

After a few minutes she reached over and touched my lion necklace. "That's beautiful," she said.

"It's a gift. From a new…friend."

"Cool," she said. "A guy, right?"

I nodded. "I haven't taken it off since he gave it to me," I told her because that was true and because it was the kind of thing she'd understand.

"That's so cool," she said.

For a moment I worried about where our conversation might lead. Jessie's mother had cheated on her father, and everyone knew about the affair. Her father had cheated too—or at least most of us thought he had. Jessie was aware of more than she wanted to be, and I worried that a mention of love might make her uneasy, but if I tried to dodge the subject or fudge the truth, would be even more uncomfortable. So I said, "Jessie, there's a problem with this man. He's a prisoner," and I gave her a brief rundown about how we had met. Then before I knew I was going to say it, I said, "And I'm sort of falling in love. But I don't know what's going to happen."

She cocked her head. "No one ever knows what's going to happen."

His status and my emotion hadn't seemed to throw her at all. We closed our eyes and rested in silence, and after a few minutes we stood and dived into the lake and began to swim across. Halfway to the far side, suddenly she grabbed at me; she seemed frantic, and I reached to rescue her, but the moment she touched the lion's head resting against my chest, her body and her breathing relaxed. She cupped it in her hand and said, "I suddenly was afraid you'd lose it. You can't lose it."

We both looked down into the dark, weedy water, and I felt my heart clench, and something inside me shifted.

I had never imagined myself being sexually faithful to any man, not even to a husband. Maybe that was the result of the time in which I came of age; maybe it was my rebellion; maybe it was just because that was who I was—a woman with a roving eye and a feeling that most faithful people were only faithful out of fear. The way Jessie's parents' marriage had disintegrated was a shame, but only because it made her so sad, and I thought she would learn to accept the fact that breakups were part of what made the world go around. My parents who had never slept with anyone but each other seemed like the weirdoes, and much as I longed for the kind of connection they shared, I was sure they could not understand the real world in which people were forever cheating on their spouses, nursing broken hearts, surviving broken homes. I had long blamed them for leading me to believe that love could be everlasting.

But suddenly, while I was swimming with Jessie in that lake, faithfulness seemed like the only thing good in the world, my parents' connection ideal in every way. In that lake I decided that no matter what,

I would be faithful to Will. I would try, at least. I would give it my all. It would be hard, but the rewards I reaped might be as rich as those my parents had from their marriage—security, yes, happiness that was genuine and easygoing, comfort that did not compare to any. The gift of devotion came to me in that breathless moment when I imagined seeing the lion drowning, when I inhaled the devotion Jessie felt to sacred things. That day my desire for anything but faithfulness drifted away.

* * *

After that I began to tell Will as many stories about my life as I could. I decided he had to know that I was taking an antidepressant and had been for the last couple of years. Over the years I'd taken them on occasion to stave off the kind of depression I couldn't attribute to anything other than a chemical propensity towards depression.

He almost laughed. "Why use a crutch?" he asked. "You don't need a drug to be happy. You need to feel loved."

A few nights later I began to tell him that a therapist had once told me that my dad's denial of his sad history and my parents' over-the-top passion for each other had come at the expense of their children.

Will interrupted, and for one of the first times, he sounded angry with me. "Stop blaming things on other people," he said coldly.

Instantly I felt self-indulgent. The problems I was talking about—bouts with depression, parents who loved each other more than they loved me—were silly compared to what he encountered every day behind those walls. A stand-up person never laid blame—not on others, not on society and certainly not on one's parents. A stand-up person took responsibility for who he or she was.

"Accept who you are," Will said. "Don't be ashamed and don't blame other people for the things that you do." He convinced me to give up the antidepressants—he had never believed in them. And I gave them up, a gesture of devotion to him.

Seven years after we split up, I found the only letter I ever wrote to him that I'd kept. I wrote it on that visit to VCCA—it was nearly 10 typed pages long. Reading it made me blush but also helped me to see how much I was already in in his thrall. Every word in the letter was overdone, but reading it I saw that no matter what I was telling myself, I had dived all the way in.

Friday night, nearing 9 p.m. (from VCCA, 1992)

Two more cards from you today, and a phone call. So the day was good. …

…Damn Will, I want to do everything with you.

… This sort of celibacy is new for me. I like it, but it's new, and sometimes it makes me nervous. I sometimes sit and wonder: Who am I? What has happened? How did this happen? …How easily we could have missed each other in the world…

I just keep saying thanks to something, or someone…. I miss you, my darling.

… Every time I begin or try to begin writing to you about making love I feel as if I'm going to burst wide open if I can't have you. …

…why aren't you here? Why aren't you waiting for me upstairs in my bed? I'd close this, fold it, walk across the dark lawn looking up at the stars and grinning, and then I'd climb in bed and kiss you everywhere and hold you and…

But you're not here. But you are.

chapter thirteen

For many years afterwards I tried to tell people about events at Maynard that spring. I tried not only because those events wound up conspiring to hurt me, but because I still thought people should know how prisons worked. But ultimately, no matter how badly administrators and guards and editors and lawyers behaved, Will was in prison for murder and most people felt that whatever happened to him—and by extension to me and others who loved him—was justified. Anyone who loves someone guilty of a terrible crime and in prison learns to understand that's the way things are.

But myriad small things happened that led to our marrying, and once we did, I wanted friends and family at least to understand my decision—even if they didn't think it was right. It was hard to explain because the story was composed of so many small events that created a perfect storm that began the day I left for Virginia. That same day Warden Claussen left to attend a National Warden's Conference across country; Louise Salem remained behind as acting warden. A little after 8 p.m. at Maynard, a squirrelly young inmate named Pierson showed up in the nurses' station bleeding from his rectum, and reported to the nurse on duty that four men wearing bags over their heads had gang raped him in a weight room off the gym. He told the nurse he had just managed to get away with his life.

The nurse sent him to the city hospital and reported Pierson's story to Louise Salem who locked down the institution—confining prisoners to their cells, closing down visits and the yard. She called in the Pen Squad—cops employed outside the prison—to investigate which was protocol in cases involving serious violence inside the joint. Right away Salem announced to the whole population that a gang rape had occurred in the gym. She also contacted Claussen, who gave this news to the gathered wardens at the conference. Within hours, Maynard became known as one of Canada's most dangerous institutions, on the verge of exploding, and the next morning a young and inexperienced reporter at *The Whig* dutifully reported on the paper's front page that four men had allegedly gang raped a young inmate in the prison gym. Although Kingstonians were largely inured to tales of violent outbreaks in prisons, this was precisely the kind of story that helped fuel the belief that inmates were explosive devices waiting to detonate.

Will, meanwhile, was skeptical of the story, and he and Luke, as chairmen of the Inmate Committee, tried to calm their fellow inmates by putting out a memo stressing that this rape was allegation only. The gym was always packed with men in the early evening, and the idea that four men with bags over their heads could sneak in without anyone seeing them seemed unlikely to Will. When the Pen Squad left after interviewing only a few inmates, Will understood there were no rapists at large. If the Squad even half-believed there were, they would have questioned every inmate and guard. He also knew—inmates did—that addicts often hid their stashes inside various body cavities to avoid discovery, and sometimes when trying to retrieve those drugs, they hurt themselves. Will figured Pierson, who was young and an addict, invented the rape to avoid the humiliation of having harmed himself, and that Louise Salem's decision to call a lockdown was possibly illegal.

I knew none of this while it was happening. By the time I returned from Virginia, the lockdown had ended, and Will told me only a little about these events. I could see that he was incensed by Salem's actions in the face of a population already so on edge. "They're fucking idiots," he said. "Salem especially. She's trying to stir up the pot. That's what these people do."

I held his hand and tried to calm him down, but for the first time I didn't suggest that he consider Salem's point of view. That I said nothing surprised even me, but I felt myself changing, electing to place myself on Will's side, and for the next seven years I would side with Will in nearly every disagreement—with almost anyone, about almost anything. I didn't countenance his anger that day because, in this case, it seemed justified; he had also just told me the warden had rendered a decision about our trailer visit. He would make no exception for us; we would be allowed to have a trailer visit—in one year.

"What's wrong with these people? Don't they get anything?"

Will laughed. "What happened to open-minded Amy who always sees both sides of every story?"

But I was choking back tears. I couldn't believe Claussen had denied us, and his decision led me to believing Will had been right all along, these people cared only about punishment. Prisoners, and by extension their loved ones, were renegades and outlaws, and the coppers and cops and Straight Joes would never understand us, would never try to understand. Why couldn't Claussen see that encouraging us to be together would transform this man? I could breathe happiness and new (and productive, fulfilling, non-criminal) life into him. I deserved support in that.

I didn't see it then, but all these years later I finally see that I was suffering a kind of Stockholm Syndrome, bonding behavior considered by most to be a common survival strategy often observed in battered spouses, cult members, abused children, concentration camp survivors and prisoners of war. I had felt the same kind of passive and blind devotion to Dean for much longer than I had loved him. Only much later did I see that, and did I begin to understand that I had long been prone in that direction and that, at least in part, it was because that was what I saw in my parents—that was what love was supposed to be. A true love was meaningful and all that ultimately mattered in this world, and true love meant absolute devotion, a commitment that brooked no separation or disagreement. And there was something more. Both men had carried me into worlds new and unfamiliar, with customs and rules I didn't wholly understand—for Dean I moved from the urban commotion and buzz of America's New York City to a small farm town in Canada, and for Will, in essence, I was moving to prison. In each case these men were my only familiar ground; in each case, for a long time, many had urged me to reconsider my decision to make such dramatic changes. Added to this, my nature was, from childhood, empathetic. I had always been drawn especially to anyone who was hurt in any way, and here was hurt that seemed to have no end. And the day the warden turned us down in the wake of my colleagues turning their backs on me, on us, all those nay sayers became enemies, and Will became my only true ally. I would have to develop strategies to navigate the rocky, unfamiliar terrain of prison, and among the world of people I knew, only Will was offering me kindness.

He pulled me close. "There is a way around this…" he whispered. "A way we could have a trailer visit."

I rested my head against his chest and listened to his heartbeat. I looked up at him, silently asking how, and he said, "They can't turn us down if we're married." He touched my face and looked me in the eyes and said, "Amy, marry me."

Surely I hesitated. Surely I thought I would faithfully wait for him until he was out of prison. Surely I didn't think that waiting a year to spend private time together was an impossible feat. And marriage? I didn't want to be married. I liked the fact that he seemed to love me— passionately, even madly. But marriage wasn't what I had in mind when I thought of romance. And then he said it again. This time it wasn't a question. "I love you, and I would have asked you anyway, but now… well, if we get married, they have to approve the trailer visit."

I wish I could remember exactly what I said. I wish I could watch a film of every second of that visit, frame by frame. I wish that the way I have always wished I could watch a film of Patricia Hearst as she transformed from kidnaped heiress's daughter to gun-toting, bank robbing SLA Tanya. But I don't have a film, and I don't remember those next several minutes. All I do know is that by the end of that visit—within a few hours of learning about the warden's decision—we were talking dates. And within two months we would become husband and wife.

chapter fourteen

Although prisoners frequently married while they were still doing time, weddings were permitted only in the trailers, so we would have to wait for his next scheduled trailer visit, that is another eight weeks. He would ask his friend and hometown minister, Russell Davis, to officiate, and we would invite the kids, his mom, Bernard and Connie, and my Kate. Mom still was dodging me, and I couldn't imagine how I was going to tell my parents about this news; I hadn't managed to breathe a word about anything that was going on with Will, or Dean who would be returning in late August by which time I would be not only moved out, but married. I was probably thinking about that when Tim Thomas, twitchy and wide-eyed, interrupted Will and me in the visiting room.

Tim was a handsome young man who had been raised in the toniest neighborhood of Montreal. Boarding school educated and a heroin addict, he had been sentenced to serve 10 years for robbing a number of banks. Something about Tim made me feel maternal. It might have been that he was almost as much in thrall to Will as I was. That day as he approached us, he stammered apologies. He was clearly in despair about something. "Will, I'm sorry, I had to tell you about the meeting..." he half-bowed. "I told Salem that you're pissed off," he said. "It just slipped out."

I noticed Will swell up with that angry silence and the strain of composing himself. "Shit, Will, oh, shit, man, I'm so sorry..." Tim continued, "I told her we don't believe there was a rape..."

Will glared at him. "Repeat the words you used. Exactly."

"I said, well, you, you know, that you think there was never a rape and that her lockdown might have been illegal."

84

At the time this sounded like a meaningless melodrama to me, melodrama that couldn't possibly matter to us. I just wanted to kiss, but when Tim left and I leaned in towards Will, he didn't kiss me. Instead he looked at me and said, quietly, "Listen, if anything happens to me, call my lawyer. He'll know someone down here."

He had given me Mike Martin's phone number in Ottawa and told me I was always welcome to talk with this man who had defended him in the murder trial. It was Martin, he said, who could tell me every gritty detail, anything I wanted to know whenever I wanted to hear the whole story.

But I hadn't called Mike Martin. I didn't think that I was going to have to.

* * *

The first stranger I did talk to about Will was Ron Bergeron. He'd called me a day or two after Will and I filed our marriage request. Before Maynard, Will had been incarcerated for 6-1/2 years at Middle Harbor where Ron Bergeron was a member of the Citizen's Advisory Committee. When Ron called he told me that, and he explained that he felt that he and Will knew each other well. "Always liked the fella," he said, "and Harry Windsor tells me you're a great gal, so I was just calling to congratulate you on this news I heard that you're planning to get married."

"Thanks," I said, but Will had never mentioned this man, and from what I knew about his feelings towards Citizens' Advisory Committee members, I doubted he and Will actually knew each other much at all.

Ron invited me to meet for a coffee. "Just to talk about things," he said. And although I was reluctant, I agreed to meet him the next day for lunch at Morrison's, the greasy spoon where all the *Whig* reporters hung out.

Ron was a paunchy, jovial man in his 50s, though he looked older— as old as some of the prisoners who were in their 50s looked. Prison took its toll on everyone, even the volunteers. "I like the guys more than Harry does," Ron told me with a wink. He explained that he and his wife had many dear friends among the convicts and ex-cons. "Been around the block with lots of 'em," he laughed. He described some of the fights he'd helped guys inside wage against "the machine," and he told me how he and his wife had invited a few men to live in their home as they were making their way back to "civilian life." He was impossible not to like, at least a little—he was so blustery and friendly and eager to talk about those ex-cons who had made it on the street and those who hadn't. And then he began to talk about some of "the gals" they had loved, and his face darkened, and his tone turned somber.

"Amy, the life of a convict's wife's can be downright ugly sometimes. It's not a life for the faint-hearted...."

I wanted to stand up and leave. Here was another protector who was going to try to convince me to turn away. "Listen," I said, "It's not like Will hasn't told me about the hurdles we're going to face...it's not like we haven't already."

But he waved away my words. "I'd like you to talk to some of the wives," he said. "You need to do this for Will's sake. I brought some numbers for you and I've already asked these gals if they'll talk to you." He reached into his pocket and pulled out a piece of paper. "They're glad to help in any way they can. These're stand-up gals..."

Why would he think I wanted to talk to strangers about Will? If he was as savvy about the prisoner's life as he claimed to be I couldn't imagine how he'd think I would talk to any other prisoner's wife. Will had told me time and again, that until he had a chance to scope out and advise me on the women I might run into—in the Sally Port, in lines waiting to visit, in the yard and in the V&C— I was to keep my distance. Anyone could be lugging drugs inside. Anyone could be married to a rat and looking for dirt. "Association" with the wrong people could bring trouble, and simply talking to someone could be construed as an "association" and entered as such in the prisoner's file. If I talked to an addict's wife, Will's file might wind up including information about his "association" with that addict. I had to be careful. So how could this stranger expect me to call these strange women?

"Thanks," I said and pocketed the paper knowing that the moment we said goodbye I would throw it away.

I couldn't afford to "associate," and I had one more reason for not wanting to talk to another prisoner's wife. I had convinced myself that other couples were different. Much as I had distanced myself from those women I saw on the side of the road waiting for a bus to Kingston, inside I distanced myself from the other women—and Will from the other men. Maybe Susan Musgrave and Stephen Reid were like us, and perhaps one or two others here and there. But I saw us as savvier, more intelligent, and I firmly believed that we were more likely to succeed both in partnership and in winning and coping with freedom than were most other prison couples.

I never said that to anyone because I knew how naïve and cocky that made me seem, and I also knew everyone would argue with me. But I did truly believe that—just the way most people will believe anything for at least a while that serves their desires—and so I listened politely. Even to Ron. When he leaned forward and said, *sotto voce*, "Amy, I hope you realize you're making Will's box even smaller than it already is," I blurted out, "What are you talking about?"

"Just so's you know, and I shouldn't tell you but I'm going to. You're currently Correctional Services of Canada's biggest headache." As he told me this, he puffed up with pride the way people with any kind of insider knowledge usually do. He rested his chubby hands on the table, tapped his fingers and looked hard at me. "You're drawing attention to Will, and it's always better for the guys if they just quietly do their time, just lay low and wait it out. But with you in the picture…" he let the words hang there, a lingering accusation, and after he felt enough time had passed to let this idea land, he went on. "I like Will. I'm on his side. And I want to make sure you don't make things harder for him than you have to. Women do that sometimes."

The comment inflamed me, but I was learning from Will. I didn't say a word, just let my anger roil around inside, wondering who the hell this man thought he was. Maybe the paper had put a stop to my writing about prison for the time being, but I intended to overcome that barrier. I would become their biggest headache. I would write about the dirty laundry prison authorities didn't want aired in public—needless lockdowns (and there would be many more in years to come), doctored security files, unearned releases, threats to inmates' lives, wasted public monies on poorly run programs, guards who worked the system to earn triple time, guards who smuggled and lied and made trouble. I would write the stories Will was telling me. Like the one about Papa

Lavine who died because of improper medical attention and Pete who had been locked up in segregation on the word of a drug addict who was then transferred to lower security as reward for this lie. I would write about threats the head of security had made to Will from the day he was elected chairman of the Inmate Committee and about that same security officer's warning him to withdraw from the Committee if he really wanted to marry me. He told Will that the day we filed the papers.

I smiled politely as Ron paid the bill, and I promised him I would keep his words in mind, though I had no intention of doing so. I was naïve enough to think that if I was, in truth, CSC's biggest headache, that that was a good thing. I believed no one could actually hurt us if we were smart enough and tough enough and together in what was beginning to feel like a battle against all odds.

chapter fifteen

For a while, however, I wasn't focusing on the intrigues at Maynard because I was also moving out of the farmhouse to live for a month at Alicia's house. Alicia was my publisher's secretary and a friend who lived just outside Kingston, on the shores of Lake Ontario. She and her family were going away for the month, and because she knew I was looking for a place of my own, she offered to let me stay there. Summery Kingston is blissful, and her house was lakeside and roomy enough so that I could invite Will's kids to stay with me. Alicia didn't mind—she was one of the few who wasn't unsettled by the idea of prisoners or their families.

The three kids came by bus on a day Maynard was having another social, and this one was especially festive because the lockdown had recently lifted, the weather was finally summery, and the food was abundant. The inmates even had a pony for the kids to ride, and as I sat wrapped in Will's arms, surrounded by the kids, I felt, again, like that cheerleader dating the quarterback, princess of the prison yard. Every few minutes one of the inmates brought us a platter of fruit or some other offering, and Cass was giggly from the pony ride. In photographs of that social we all look happy, and nothing screams prison except the barbed wire fences that surrounded that large sunny yard.

When it was time to leave, Will pulled his son aside. "You'll mow the lawn for Amy," he coolly instructed him, but I protested. I didn't know why he wanted to ruin the day, and besides, I wanted to spoil his kids. Their mother was poor, and besides losing their father to prison when they were very young, their life ever since had been peripatetic— they lived in a succession of tiny houses with a mother who was always just one step ahead of bill collectors. Because Laura had had two more children with another husband, Will's kids often served as babysitters and caretakers for their half-sister and brother while their mother worked odd hours as a waitress in a sleazy bar. "Don't make him work today," I told Will.

But Will insisted. "A little work never killed anyone."

The day before I told Will about Alicia's fast-growing lawn, and in that moment I wished I hadn't. "You're the man of the house," Will told his son. "You have to take care of these girls." He tousled the boy's hair.

Willie just nodded, and I backed off the way I had already begun to. Besides, I liked Will's intention—he wanted to take care of me, help me out with the chores the only way he could. In Dean's house, and in all our years together, his children's needs always came first. And there was this. Will and Molly had both told me that the cops had recently caught Willie throwing rocks at ducks in a lake somewhere, and they were keeping an eye on him. Unlike the girls who were so vividly their father's daughters, with pale skin and hair and their quiet and composed demeanors, Willie had his mother's dark skin and her flare for drama. Maybe some discipline couldn't hurt him. And I would see to it that he felt appreciated when he did help me.

When we returned to Alicia's house, in the fading heat, I suggested before anyone did any work, we take a swim. For all our romancing, and despite the joyful day, visiting yards were thick with the stink and sweat and noise of too many people crammed into too small a space. I walked them down to the dock, and we all dived into the water, and after a few minutes I left them there to enjoy the lake while I went up to the house to fix a feast—Farmer's market pasta and pesto and vine ripe tomatoes. As I was grating cheese, I heard a wail coming up from the lake, and a second later the girls, soaking wet, were breathlessly charging up the lawn towards the house. "Willie threw Cass's shoes into the lake…" Sarah said. Cass burst into tears.

I ran down to the dock, the girls on my heels. I was a strong swimmer, and as I dived to search, I thought about a story Molly had told me about Will as a daredevil kid diving from a towering bridge over the Ottawa River. As I dived down into the darkness, I imagined us diving from bridges together, fearless, swimming free, and each time I came up gasping for breath and saw Cass in tears, I dived down again until I knew it was useless. I couldn't find the shoes. I swam to the dock. "Cass, honey, I'm sorry. I'll buy you a new pair."

That quieted her. Willie scowled. Swim time was obviously done.

As we trudged back towards the house the girls surrounded me. "I love your clothes," Sarah said for the third time. "Are you really going to buy me shoes?" Cass asked. "I love this house," Sarah said. "I love swimming," Cass said. They were brimming with happiness, but Willie lagged behind, silent, and just before we reached the house he said, "I'll mow now."

"You don't have to," I said.

"It's fine." I could see he was as stubborn as his father, so I led him to the mower that was tucked into a corner of the vast garage. I followed him as he rolled it onto the lawn. "We'll call you when supper's ready, okay?" I said, trying to sound cheerful.

The girls and I cooked the pasta and baked brownies, and as they worked I admired their beauty in the glow of the setting sun washing the room. Through the wide window I could see Willie scowling and sweating as he steadily pushed the mower across that hilly lawn. The whine and whir burst from the mower's belly like bullets or backfire, and I left the girls to finish up while I walked outside. The mown grass smelled sweet, and the dampness of the humid earth rose up around my ankles. When I reached him, I cut the motor. "Really, it's fine," I said. He was drenched with sweat.

"I have to do it. Dad said."

"It's okay, you've done enough….It's time to eat."

He gave up and the two of us walked the mower back to the garage. As we were walking, tears welled up in his eyes. "Why do I always have to be the man?"

"You don't, Willie, you don't…"

He dried away the tears and angrily said, "What do you know?" And I didn't know, so we walked back to the house in silence. Although the meal calmed him, and he was pleased to discover he would have his own room, from that moment on, Willie cleaved more tightly to his distance from me as the girls drifted ever closer. After those couple of days Willie and I never spent any real time together, and I always felt his anger about his father loving someone who wasn't his mother as a palpable presence.

The girls, though, were a different story. Early the next morning Cassandra, in her penguin pajamas with her sun-kissed skin glowing pink, appeared at my bedside before I was awake. "Know what?" she bent close, her hair curling around her pretty face. "What?" I sat up and smiled at her.

"People are always saying I look like a doll, and I just looked in the mirror, and it's true. I do. I look like a doll."

That's when I fell in love with her, and I never stopped being in love—not even during the teenage years when she did her best to break my heart—and after those few days with the kids, I felt my attachment to Will and to his family deepen. I swore to myself that it would never fall apart the way all my other loves had.

The next night, as soon as the kids were asleep, I called my mom and dad again. I was sure if I could lure her up and introduce her to the kids, Mom would love them and would eventually find a way to tell Dad and make this okay. But for the third time she dodged my invitation and quickly handed off the phone to Dad. When we hung up I was frustrated and angry and wanted to find someone in the family who might take my side, so I decided to try Mom's twin sister, Aunt Ruth. She had always been a kind of extra mom, and although she lived in Israel, she was visiting her kids in the States, so I called my cousin Jim's house. He and I chit chatted, and then I asked to talk to his mom. And I told her I had a secret to tell her, but she had to promise not to say anything yet.

"I'm in love with someone, and I need your help to find a way to tell Mom."

I imagined that my mom or Ruth could offer me some wisdom and comfort that Molly and Kate could not—they were my blood, and they both had known me from the moment I took my first breath. They knew I had always been emotional, yes, and even volatile but always empathetic. At *The Whig* people were atwitter about me—Alicia had told me the publisher was wondering aloud whether I was mentally stable. I needed my mom and Ruth to tell me I wasn't crazy now. "Ruth, the man I love is in prison," I said.

I heard her exhalation, and then silence.

"We're getting married. Next month. I want to tell Mom, but only in person, and only up here because I can't tell Dad, not yet. But every time I try to convince her to visit, she puts me off, so I thought maybe you could tell her to come visit me."

For their whole lives, until Alzheimer's descended on my mom, both she and Ruth could talk nonstop to anyone about anything—politics, family lore, books. But now Ruth was silent. I could hear her breathing. "Ruth?"

Finally she promised she would do what she could, and then we said goodbye, and my cousin's wife picked up the line. We talked for a few minutes, but suddenly Jim was on the phone again. "What the hell did you tell her? She says she can't tell me. She's never kept a secret in her life."

"She promised me," I said. When we hung up I began to think about my sisters. Maybe I could confide in Rachel who was a free spirit and seldom judgmental. I called her but before I could say a word she said, "Listen, I'm pregnant. And I'm having the baby but I'm not getting married. Karen's coming to visit me to help me tell Mom and Dad. I'm scared Dad's going to kill me, but I'm doing this, damnit."

I had to laugh because I knew her news would inspire his joy, more so after he heard mine. I couldn't tell her my news now. I hung up and thought about the nickname my father dubbed me when I was a kid. Sarah Heartburn. I did tend to live large, to wax poetic over broken friendships, to cry in movies or when teachers were upset with me. I always wove long, dramatic tales from the smallest adventures.

In the fairytales, legends and myths I was researching for my kids' column, *The Bedtime Story*, I discovered that nearly every culture has its version of *Sleeping Beauty* in which a fairy, somehow insulted by one of the parents, stands over the baby's cradle and utters a curse. "You will prick your finger on a spinning wheel on your 15th birthday and fall down dead…" "You will wander the world for three thousand years," "You will lie as if dead until wakened by the kiss of a prince…"

In a sense my father had cursed me, although it didn't always feel like a curse, and even then I was at least partly aware that the allure of this romance was its drama. But I couldn't talk to Dad. Not yet. I didn't want to hear him say it—curse or blessing—out loud.

chapter sixteen

Ottawa, where the kids lived with their mother, was a 90 minute drive north, but before I drove them home, I let Willie sleep in and I took the girls to visit my office at *The Whig*. Willie slept in. I introduced Sarah and Cass to a few of the people I liked best in the newsroom—Josie, Meghan, the crime beat reporters. Then I took them into my office to meet my assistant, Candace, who was hard at work putting together the copies of the stories I worked on with my illustrator's artwork. Candace was preparing the package for the ten other papers running the column.

Six months earlier Candace had walked into *The Whig* looking for work just as *The Bedtime Story*, only in its third month, was drawing interest from the Southam Syndicate papers around the country. A local publisher had just fired her for reasons I forgot as soon as she told me what they were. She was shy and Betty Boop cute, and I liked her. Plus, I needed help—the scope of the job getting out of hand with all those new papers. And Candace seemed the perfect solution. She had brains, editorial experience, and best of all, she was immediately available. I talked O'Connor into hiring her as my assistant to do the administrative work for the column while I focused on the creative side. And as an editorial assistant, she was required to join the union, something I had never done since I was still considered a freelancer.

I had always been a union supporter, and I could have joined, but I was waiting for the union to negotiate a new contract that offered those writers (like me) whose work was being syndicated proper compensation for syndication. I had talked to the union reps about this, and although they said they understood my stance, because only a few of us

94

had work of any interest to the other papers, negotiating this was not a priority.

For the past five months Candace had been a lifesaver, and when I introduced her to the girls, I said just that. We chatted for a few minutes before I walked the girls downstairs to Morrison's where we took a booth and ordered hot chocolates. The moment our drinks arrived Sarah said, "I like Josie and Meghan, but Candace's NG," and Cass nodded in agreement.

I shook my head—both at the incongruity of such prison slang coming from such innocent-looking faces and at the very idea. "Candace's great," I said.

"Don't trust her," Cass said as she licked whipped cream from her lips. I looked at those sun-freckled, cherubic faces and wondered at the fog of paranoia enveloping them—that was their birth-cradle curse. And then, in the same somber tone Sarah had used, I said, "Girls, don't judge people before you know them."

They rolled their eyes and looked at each other, and I decided to change the subject. I didn't want to spoil the mood of our weekend. After our hot chocolate we walked across the street to the Farmer's Market, and as the girls perused the stalls that sold jams and breads, scarves and ceramics, I sneaked to the silversmith's booth where I'd seen a ring that would be perfect for Sarah's upcoming 15th birthday. It was the figure of a woman arching backwards into the circle that was the ring. To me it seemed the image of a girl on the verge of womanhood, a girl like Sarah.

Back in the car I handed it to her. "Happy birthday, a few weeks early."

"Oh my god, it's beautiful, thank you, oh …." It fit her perfectly, and I watched her mistrust and Lolita-like guise drop away as she admired it on her finger. Then we picked up Willie and headed for their mother's house.

I don't know why I had agreed to drive them home. They often took the bus on their own. Maybe I wanted to save the bus fare. More likely I wanted to meet Laura. As we reached the village outside of Ottawa where they lived, Sarah directed me down a narrow road teeming with low-rent townhouses. I snaked my way between cars parked tightly on either side. Suddenly a skinny, barefoot girl darted into the street, and

I slammed on the brakes and watched as the child, her hair a tangle of blond curls, her cheeks smudged with dirt, called out happily, "Hi! Sarah! Cass! Willie!"

Sarah rolled down the window. "Vivi, you have to be more careful!"

So this was Laura's fifth child. Vivi and her brother, James, shuttled back and forth between their parents' homes, pawns in a never-ending custody battle that went on for the next several years. Molly had described Laura as Peter Pan—a woman often surrounded by a mob of children—her own five and many of her lovers' kids, her children's friends, her neighbors' kids, and runaways. Some of those kids became her babysitters, some became her friends, some her cleaning people. Some became her thieves. But I didn't know all that yet, and after I parked I followed the kids into a stuffy townhouse where Fred, a giant macaw, sat in his cage squawking, "Hellooo…"

In my memory, Laura's voice is a nasal squawk like Fred's, and though she has changed markedly since those days, I still picture her as she was that day—pretty and slender with a cascade of wild auburn hair and breasts spilling out of her low-cut blouse. She wore skintight cropped pants, and she sourly invited me to come in. I was right behind Sarah as she walked past her mother and reached out, grabbed Sarah's hand squawked, "What's that? Sarah? That's a guy's ring." She studied it and began to howl with laughter. "Girls don't wear naked girls!"

Sarah backed away and quietly said, "Amy gave it to me. For my birthday."

Laura squinted at me. "Well, first off, it's not her birthday, and pardon me, but I sure wouldn't wear something like that!" She nodded to a chair. "Oh well. Go on. Sit."

Not wishing to make the kids feel uncomfortable, I sat and smiled and looked around the crowded living room, searching for something to talk about besides the kids. I settled on the carved wooden masks hanging on one wall. "Nice masks."

"Will and I bought those on one of our trips to Jamaica," she said.

Maybe it was my imagination, but I could swear she puffed out her chest as she pointed out other paraphernalia on the tables and shelves and walls. "Those baskets we got in Mexico, and that's a rug we got in the Caribbean or maybe Belize…."

I glanced at the window half-hidden behind Fred's cage and saw massive purple clouds rolling in from the south. A storm was on its way, and I wanted to get the hell out of there. Laura's house was overheated and overstuffed with a sink overflowing with dirty dishes and an open peanut butter jar sitting beside a carving knife on a crumb-strewn table. The place felt on the brink of danger, and little James was peering at me from around the corner. Vivi skittered around us, talking and flirting.

I think our dislike of each other began that day. I suspect some of mine stemmed from envy—mostly that she had had the good fortune to give birth to these marvelous girls. I did also wonder if she saw them as marvels given Laura's self-involvement. She was a woman who often left her children in danger. But that day, and for a long time afterwards, I didn't know much about her. What I did know was that this clan—all the kids and their parents and grandparents— kept things more than close to the vest. Silence had been bred into them by their Scottish blood and by the criminal demimonde they inhabited. They had inherited this credo: Come hell or high water, they would never rat out anyone, and that meant they must never tell some of the truths that could ever hurt their parents.

Naturally in the town where Will grew up and where the children had been born, everyone knew about his crime. The murder and arrest and trial had been big local news, gossip for years. When the kids were small, some of the local families refused to invite the kids into their homes because of Will, and also because of Laura. Even 15 years later when I first someone from that town and mentioned the family name, the first thing out of his mouth was, "Oh, the murderer…" One of the reasons Laura had moved was so that they could live in greater anonymity, but the kids had grown up being "those people." They had learned early that the less they revealed, the more they protected themselves.

* * *

From Laura's house I headed to Molly's, to the house where Will grew up. A fast-approaching thunderstorm trailed me on the road and reached me just as I pulled up her drive. Bullet-sized pellets pounded the square brick house, an ordinary place except this was Will's house so it looked beautiful and significant. Kell, my collie, had come along and waited patiently in the car while I was at Laura's. Now, when I opened the door, she dashed from the car and raced right through the door Molly opened to us. She sailed right onto a big red and white armchair. "Kell, no..." I said, "I'm so sorry..." and I moved to shoo her off, but Molly laughed and said, "No, no, I love dogs. Leave her be. That will be her chair from now on," and I felt instantly warm and safe and loved.

Molly had a way of making those around her feel that way. She and Kell and I sat together in the sunroom Will had built for her and talked as we watched the storm through the large southern facing windows. We talked about the social, the kids' swim, Willie mowing the lawn, how much she adored Sarah and missed her now that she had moved back home. Later we watched *Jeopardy*; she was both addicted to and masterful at the game. That night and every night after, whenever I stayed in Molly's house I wished I had known Will the boy growing up in that little mill town, in that house full of women. The house was small and neat, with just one bathroom, and sometimes I closed my eyes and tried to visualize Will the teenager waiting as his three sisters locked him out to finish primping—Gina especially, the oldest, who could spend hours fussing with her makeup and hair. I imagined him the man of the house, builder of sun rooms, hockey player and paperboy. Sometimes when I walked around the neighborhood, people stopped me and offered fond memories of Will. "He changed my storm windows," "He shoveled my walkway..." "He delivered our paper..." In their voices I also heard the words they didn't say—"Ah, that boy had so much promise...if only..."

Not far from the house, the Ottawa River wound its way towards the Rideau Canal, and in the local library and town hall, I studied everything I could about the place. I wanted to know everything I could about Will, something that might offer me clues about who he was, and maybe too, where things had gone wrong. The town had thrived as a logging paradise before the Depression, but when the lumber market declined, so did the village. The forest took over, and that is why it always smelled piney and clean.

After supper that night, Molly spread a pocket binder upon the kitchen table and picked through its contents. She pushed a stack of Will's report cards towards me: He had gotten A's in everything, sometimes even A-pluses, and teachers called him *sharp* and *able* and *astute*.

He had been a star athlete, and Molly had saved every article about every hockey game he ever played. In photographs he looked like a muscular surfer, laughing on a beach or standing proudly beside his blue Corvette, always wearing that lopsided grin, the trace of a dimple in his left cheek, eyes alight.

I looked up and saw Molly's eyes were moist. "There's something else I want to show you," she said. The letter she showed me then was an offer of a full scholarship to play hockey at Dartmouth for the class of 1971.

"He turned it down," she said. "I tried to talk him into it but he was always stubborn, and he didn't listen." Grief swallowed her. I took her hands. We sat silent.

Later I would sometimes joke with friends about the Dartmouth scholarship Will had turned down. If he hadn't given up on hockey, and on school, if he hadn't started dealing drugs in a serious way, we might have met at Dartmouth. When I was an undergraduate at Barnard, one of my dearest friends was at Dartmouth, and I visited the school many times during those years Will would have been there. Certainly I would have at least seen him—on the ice, in the net fending off rivals, his cheeks red with exertion, sweat rolling down his face, eyes alight.

But I probably wouldn't have loved him. He would have been just one more Ivy League boy.

And still, sometimes I imagined him on that Dartmouth hockey team, bursting with hubris, no tattoos or criminal record, no Laura or children. I imagined him holding me. Lying in Will's childhood bed, I felt his ghost. Often when I visited and slept there, I cried myself to sleep. I suspect that in her room downstairs, Molly was crying too.

chapter seventeen

The moment I saw the bungalow on the banks of the St. Lawrence River, its lot dense with sumac and lilac, its lawn drunk with dandelions, I knew I had to live there. Kate found it. She and her husband had once many years ago rented property on this spit of land, and that is how she knew Nesta and Clare. They owned the land and the bungalow next door. They had always loved Kate, and although they were trying to sell the place, she had convinced them to rent it to me while they waited for it to sell. And so, on the last day of July, one day before I turned 40, I moved onto Willowbank Road, into a house that seemed the perfect haven for me, the girls, and eventually Will.

Dean hadn't yet returned from Europe—he would be gone another month, still. And without telling him, I moved out all my belongings—the few pieces of furniture I'd brought from New York, my clothes, my computer, not much more. I see now what a coward I was. I left a note. And knowing how afraid I was even to tell him I needed to leave, I understand how captive I actually felt. My new place was only 5 miles from the farm; I knew when he returned we would have to see each other and talk this out. But I tried not to think about that.

I loved the crooked yellow house with no foundation, sinking into spongy earth. It sat at the end of a swampy road. The road from the two-lane highway down to my house was lined with suburban-style structures with basements, storm windows, two-car garages, and paved driveways. Those houses faced a canal that separated two sides of Willowbank Road, west and east; those houses faced each other's yards, but my house and Nesta and Clare's next door faced only the river. From the living room, looking south over a deck and sloping lawn, I could watch herons, ducks, and boats chugging out of the marina around the corner, and from every window of the bungalow I could watch the wide, changing river.

Nesta was thoroughly maternal, and from almost my first day in the house she insisted I looked too exhausted, overworked, and thin, so every night she made an extra helping of supper for me and sent her husband, Clare, to bring it to me. Sometimes when he came over to give me the food, he told me that potential buyers would be stopping by to look at the house. But I convinced myself no one would take this house from me. Besides, it had been on the market for a year already.

Some days as I drove down the road towards the bungalow, I wondered about my neighbors—if their lives were as stable as their houses. Most of those houses held a husband and a wife and a couple of children, and in their backyards they all had boats tied to docks that jutted into the canal. Their yards were tidy, their lawns weeded. The river lots had an edgier feel. Nesta's garden overflowed with iris and peonies, but both our houses had chipped siding and slanting decks. Our trees were overgrown, our roofs mossy. We shared a gravel laneway that Clare frequently scattered with rocks to fill potholes when they turned to deep pools after a thunderstorm.

To the west of my house stood another bungalow where Carole and Austin lived; like me they were renters. They were just a few years older than me, and right away they were friendly. Austin was a jack of all trades, and he became a savior who helped me with myriad chores. Carol was a nature lover who taught me to recognize trees and plants and flowers and stars. Naturally there were some problems in my haven. Some nights Carole and Austin got roaring drunk and I had to close my windows to block out the noise of their fights. One day the massive maple tree on their lawn that canopied my house and spilled its bark and leaves, collapsed onto my roof. Clare could be overbearing in his paternal passions. But most of all I felt free, relieved to be in my own place and surrounded by kindness.

The house had three bedrooms. I claimed the one in front with the best view of the river, though most nights I slept on an old sofa a friend gave me. I huddled under blankets near the sliding glass door in the living room because I liked to watch the moonlight on the river while I talked on the phone to Will. By then most nights we talked until 10 when prison lights went out. And mostly in those days we talked about the future—how bright we were sure it would be.

And just a few days after I moved into the bungalow, I moved out of my office at *The Whig*. Pamela Dion, the prison reporter, had launched a grievance against me, claiming that a union member could write and edit *The Bedtime Story*. Since I wasn't a union member, she wanted me fired. I tried to discuss the need for the union to negotiate on behalf of its syndicated writers, but she refused to listen.

Lawrence O'Connor, the publisher, assured me he would fight to keep me on, but now a few months had passed since Pamela first launched the grievance, and he invited me into his office to discuss matters. He suggested it would be better if I worked from home. "If you stay here you're in everyone's face every day, and they remember the grievance. Go work from home, and tempers will cool. We'll save your job, don't worry." Summer sun was streaming in through his floor-to-ceiling windows, and his tie and shirt were wrinkled, his face prison-pale. I noticed his paunch was expanding. "You understand. I know you do, Amy." He promised to furnish me with a fax machine so Candace could send me anything I needed for work.

"That's why we hired Candace, right? To help you out. You'll see. It'll be great."

I thought it might be. If I didn't have to be at the office, I could visit Will almost every day and work in the early mornings and late at night, before and after phone calls.

* * *

That same week at Maynard, Louise Salem opened the door to the outdoor visiting area as arbitrarily as she had closed it, and one afternoon while I was visiting, Will and I walked outside to share the sun for the first time in months. It was hot and sunny, and he was wearing shorts, trying to acquire some color on his ghostly legs. "I'll get a tan today," he laughed, stretching his legs out in front of him. I lay down on the bench and rested my head in his lap. He placed a hand on my forehead and combed my hair with his fingers.

"You know, Amy," he said, "no one ever gets parole at his eligibility date except the rats." He often said this, frequently cautioning that I might have to wait four, five, even six years before he lived outside. Did I understand? Was I sure I was ready for this?

I always simply nodded when he talked about how hard our road would be, but that day I was concentrating on his touch, and warmed by sun, lulled by the creaking of the rusting swing set, I fell asleep, or at least I think I must have because at some point I half-opened my eyes, and was for the first time that day aware of the guards in the towers above us, the metal of their guns glinting in the sunlight. I turned my head slightly and the rolls of barbed wire atop the fences surrounding that dingy yard came into focus. I looked down at the angry tufts of grass and up at the walls of cold stone, and suddenly I felt—viscerally— that I had come to prison so that I could understand—no, more than understand, but actually feel—the way my ancestors in concentration camps had felt surrounded by guards who despised them. Whenever I had thought about those ghosts in my life—my father's grandparents and aunts and uncles and cousins he never knew—I had always envisioned lives thoroughly hopeless, focused on their imprisonment. That day I understood something more about them. I felt, truly felt, that despite guns and guards and bleak surrounds they had felt a thousand things—including love and lust, longing and compassion. Their entire beings had not been focused on captivity, at least not at every moment. And that day those ancestors became people instead of remote, one-dimensional caricatures.

I sat up. "Will," I said, "I know I'm supposed to be here."

He certainly must have thought I meant here with him. But again, I didn't tell him otherwise. I was always careful not to say things that might hurt him.

* * *

In that haze, obsessed with Will and irritated with almost everyone at work and with my mother and nearly everyone else, I moved my work out of the office and into the bungalow, and for a couple of weeks everything felt perfect. I woke at dawn to the thrashing carp in the river, and I fell asleep at night listening to the call of loons across the river. Candace sent me work and responded to my phone calls. She also suggested that maybe she could write some stories rather than just doing

103

grunt work, and without a second thought, I encouraged her to write some. I edited them. I printed them.

Ron Bergeron kept calling me and suggesting I call some of those wives, but I didn't follow his advice, and whenever anything unnerved me—a funny look from a guard, a word from Will about possible failure—I confided in Kate. She lived her life with a courage and gusto I admired. I didn't yet know that Kate's devil-may-care attitude had created disasters in her world. She was the perfect friend, and whatever I wanted, needed, and desired, she said, I could make happen. If I complained that I was having trouble concentrating, that I couldn't write, she pushed me to sit down at my desk. "Just write. Stop complaining and write." Dean had taught me the same lesson—never to sit around waiting for the muse, that the way things get written is by sitting down and writing. And just as I had listened to Dean, I listened to Kate. I went on writing both columns—sometimes staying up until 2 or 3 in the morning, often waking at 6. No wonder Nesta thought I looked tired. I was.

And although I hadn't known what it would be, it turned out my limit for deprivation and privacy was three months. By mid-August, a little more than two weeks before Will and I were to finally share a trailer visit, my patience faltered. All I could think about was making love with Will, and everyone and everything irritated me. I yelled at Kate, I snapped at Candace, I complained when Clare showed up at my door.

I am older, and my sexual desire has softened, yet I still cannot imagine being forbidden to embrace the man I love. I no longer know how I could bear being unable to touch Will without fear of someone shouting, "Watch those hands..." And so I wonder what my desire for Will would have felt like and looked like without all that deprivation? What would I have wanted from Will and with Will and for the two of us if we hadn't been denied any privacy, if we hadn't been swimming in longing and in fear of what might never be. I imagine our sexual desire might have burned itself out and with it our desire to commit to spend our lives together. That is possible. And without the barriers separating and the rules punishing us and people diminishing us, we would, at least, have had a chance to discover what our connection was meant to be in a humane, indeed human, way.

chapter eighteen

Will was sure they were going to find some way to stop us from marrying, but he couldn't convince me of that. When he described what was going on at Maynard—the politics of the place, I got lost in a tangle of stories. Louise Salem's behavior, security's, the drug addicts, the stories sounded melodramatic. I was, though, obsessed with one glitch. Our request to marry had not yet been approved. It had been weeks. Most people applied and heard within days, but day after day in those first weeks of August, when we asked Barbara if the papers had returned from the Attorney General's office in Ottawa where they were usually stamped quickly, she told us they had not. She said the warden was waiting for them so that he could sign his approval, and he had no problem with that, according to Barbara. Barbara had no idea what the holdup could be.

One afternoon I called the Attorney General's office. The bureaucrat I spoke with looked up our names and assured me the papers had been signed and returned to Maynard weeks earlier. That night, I passed this news to Will, and the next day he let Barbara know. Her response was to tell him to withdraw from his position on the Inmate Committee. Earlier the head of security had given him the same "warning," but I had scoffed at the idea. The implied threat struck me as ridiculous.

Part of what I loved about Will was that he was willing to stand up for the other men, to work on their behalf. I couldn't let him back down because of someone messing with our paperwork. It sounded petty to me, but when I told him that, he smiled and told me he wasn't so sure. Barbara had been working in the system for a long time, and he thought she smelled a rat, and he trusted Barbara as much as he trusted anyone. He thought he ought to take her advice and resign.

"You can't," I argued. "They can't stop you from trying to make things better."

"They can do whatever the hell they want," he said. And still I dismissed the idea. I was certain everything would work out. Barbara had, after all, arranged for us to meet with the prison chaplain, Stephen Foyle, and Will's minister, Russell Davis, had agreed to perform the ceremony and was scheduled for a visit the next week. Will had to remain a stalwart defender of justice. That was the Will I loved.

I still have the photograph of Will and me and the chaplain in the visiting room, sitting beside the soda machines. Mike looked more like a high school coach than a prison chaplain. I liked his laid-back manner, especially because he said he saw no reason not to approve our marriage. We were obviously in love. Our plan sounded fine to him. When we said goodbye that day we asked him to check on those missing papers. He promised he would.

But in the meantime, Will told me, Louise Salem and Joe Book, a snake-oil salesman type who was head of security, were still talking to reporters about that rape back in June. They still insisted that rape had happened, and although Will didn't talk much about it to me, he was continuing to try to nail Salem and Page for mishandling events by locking down the institution and alarming the population. He was convinced there had been no rape, but they now had to cover up their decisions by insisting there had been. As the weeks passed and the story became one of those rumors that circulate prisons—this rumor being that rapists were everywhere in the joint now that it was integrated with sex offenders and thus everyone was in danger all the time—Will's name began to surface amongst the inmates and staff as somehow having been one of the players in the night's event. Prisons are like small towns with their gossip mills and cliques, and as inmates grew edgier about the integration of sex offenders into their midst, administration was able more easily to institute draconian measures. Fear is the necessary ingredient for instituting laws that otherwise, to a thoughtful man, would make no sense. Those who had protested the lockdown were put in segregation. Ease of movement became more difficult for everyone, and I encouraged Will to keep fighting to maintain as many rights for the prisoners as he could.

* * *

He seldom talked about these things on the phone, and so I wasn't thoroughly aware of all these tensions. Most evenings just before Will called, I walked Kell into the empty fields beyond my house, down to the riverbank where someone had discarded a sofa. I sat there amidst the tangled vines and overgrown sumac hidden from everyone's view, staring at the river. I would try to imagine Will sitting with us, and sometimes when we talked I described the fiery sunsets and the mist rising off the river. I described "our home" as beautiful, always careful to call it "ours." But sometimes when I began to talk about some lovely moment, he grew quiet and told me it was easier not to think about what he was missing.

This intensified my internal struggle about what I could and couldn't tell him. I described the way Kell looked when she barked at the bull-frogs, and the way she sometimes stood at attention in the field tracking "road kill." I told him about her bringing home dead hedgehogs, proud, as if she'd hunted them down. He laughed. He loved dogs, which made me happy. When she was the subject I relaxed, stretching out on the sofa and staring up at the spreading stain on the ceiling—a spot that no matter how many times Austin repaired it, reappeared. I tried not to complain about such things—the bills, the repairs others had to help me to fix because he wasn't there. But then one night before I could stop myself that spot on the ceiling got the better of me. "Damnit, I wish you were here to repair this fucked up roof," I said. The minute I said the words I wished I could take them back.

A silence followed. Then came his voice, thick with misery. "You need me out there."

I instantly felt awful for saying something that aroused his helplessness. Besides, Austin had told me he would fix the roof again, and others were helping me. Charlie Donevan at the hardware store had always been a great friend. It was Charlie who had introduced me to Kate, and Charlie had promised to help me out if there was anything I needed with the new house. And Clare treated me like his fifth daughter. There was my friend Al, director of the home for young offenders who understood prison better than anyone I knew and who had offered to help out too. In fact despite people like Pamela who was making trouble at work, and my mother and father, I knew how lucky I was. Plenty of people were ready to help. Still, with Will I avoided talking about most of them. Conversation about men felt impossible. Although he hadn't expressed jealousy, I'd been careful not to tell him how much Austin had done for me or all that Charlie and Al had promised. I could tell him later, when we knew each other better, when he understood how outgoing I could be, how many people I cared about and how many cared about me.

"It's fucked up I'm not there when you need me," he went on, but I interrupted without thinking. "Will," I insisted, "I don't *need* anyone."

I heard his quick intake of breath, followed by silence, followed by the distant clicks of recording devices. When he said nothing else, I asked, "Are you still there?" We had, once or twice, been disconnected.

But I could hear him breathing. "Will, are you still there?" I asked again.

Finally he exhaled, and when he spoke again, his voice was steely. "What did you say?" he asked.

"I just said I don't need anyone..." I suppose I was going to tell him it was only a figure of speech or that I was just tired and cranky, or maybe I was going to finally tell him about how helpful so many people had been, but he didn't give me a chance. He interrupted saying, "...I thought that's what you said," he said. Then I heard the click and the buzz of an empty line.

I sat and stared at the phone. I didn't know what to do. I couldn't call him back. And there was no one I could tell, no one I could turn to for advice. Even Kate would have told me to stay away and let him stew. Kate was a romantic, but she wasn't a romantic fool like I was quickly becoming. Still, I was convinced that only I understood Will—that despite his bravado, he felt helpless. I empathized with him in his upset at my petty complaints because I felt I already owed him loyalty, and I couldn't moan to other people—to people who barely knew him— about his small tantrums. Of course he lost his temper with me. Who wouldn't lose his temper living in that cauldron he described? I couldn't turn to anyone lest they puncture the vision I had of Will, the idea that only I understood him, and my silence allowed that to remain intact.

Still, I didn't know how I was supposed to fix anything if he hung up on me. Out in the real life it would have been a fight, but one that could eventually be resolved. In prison everything took on an extra barrier, an additional hurdle to climb. I had to find a way to talk to him about this, and anyway, I rationalized, maybe I was wrong. Maybe he hadn't been angry. Maybe something had happened on the range that had nothing to do with our conversation—I had seen and heard about sudden lock-downs, outbursts of violence. Maybe he had gotten hurt, or maybe one of his friends was under threat, and he'd run to the rescue. I would have to wait to clear the air tomorrow, at the next social. In person we could easily sort out any misunderstanding, and I told myself this was exactly that, a misunderstanding. I would show up at the social, he would kiss me, and everything would be okay.

But that night I barely slept, and by noon when it was time to leave for Maynard, I was a mess, worried that he was in fact angry, worried about what would happen to us. It had only been 3-1/2 months, but 3-1/2 months of constant conversation and kissing can feel like a long, long time, and I had made myself and him a promise. If I was going to learn to be devoted, I had to be devoted through thick and thin. My mother survived months of not knowing if my dad was alive; he'd gone missing before they learned he was a prisoner of war, and she'd been rewarded for her devotion. I thought about Mom as I shuffled along in the line of visitors outside the Sally Port.

I must have sensed what was going to happen. I felt numb. I kept myself moving only by pretending everything would be just fine as I walked into the small gym where this social was taking place. It was a grim, smelly room with grubby tables lined up in rows. Outside it was raining and humid. The doors to the outdoors were cracked open, but everyone was crowded inside to stay dry.

I spotted Bernard and Connie sitting at one of the tables, but Will was not yet there. That didn't worry me too much. Whenever a visitor arrived at the prison, the guard at the Sally Port called up to the range. Sometimes, though, a guard might "forget" to call—that had happened to us a few times. Sometimes the guards couldn't find the person—that too had happened to us one day when Will was in a meeting with the warden and no one on the range knew that. Sometimes guards simply neglected to go out of their way to search, and often visitors had to wait for what seemed like forever. Some days Will was downstairs within minutes, but I had waited for as long as an hour, and once or twice his strip search had taken extra time and involved a dash of harassment. I could never predict when he would show up, and I reasoned that something was holding him up this time. Obviously this time something was holding him up, so I took a chair beside Connie.

Bernard and Connie and I began to chat—about the rain, about the news from Nova Scotia and the Westray Mine disaster. As usual our talk tended towards dark subjects, and as usual after a few minutes the conversation flattened out. Each time someone appeared in the doorway, I looked up, but it was never Will. As the minutes ticked by, fear worked its way into my body, and I leaned across the table and whispered to Bernard, "Where is he?"

Guards stood in every doorway, watching, listening, searching for culprits of any kind. By then I had come to understand that all of us— prisoners and their loved ones alike—were always under suspicion, and I could not let on that anything was wrong. If anyone thought there was a rift between us, they would find a way to take it out on him. They would question him. Throw him in segregation. Place a black mark of some kind on his file. Something bad would happen to him, I was sure. So I kept smiling.

Bernard reached across the table to hold Connie's hand, and I wished I wasn't intruding on their time together, but Bernard was the only person I could lean on. Tears were rising into the corners of my eyes. I swallowed. Bernard smiled, leaned across towards me and whispered through his teeth, "Don't cry, sweetheart."

I noticed one of the female guards glance at me and at the empty chair beside me, and I whispered to Bernard, "Can you do something? Can you go up to the range and find out what's wrong?"

Still he smiled. "Amy, he can be a stubborn dude, but nobody asks Will what's wrong. If he's not here, he has his reasons. You gotta just accept it."

"But Bernard…" with panic my voice began to rise, and like a gentle conductor, Bernard raised his hand and guided me to lower the register. "Stay calm. Smile," he said.

By then, despite my wishful thinking, it was obvious I was going to have to stand up and find a way to walk out of there without raising anyone's suspicion. "Maintain your dignity," Bernard whispered, and under the table Connie squeezed my hand and said, "Smile."

Dignity was going to require deception in this case because the truth was Will had abandoned me—he was the one who had put me in this position, although I suspected that he would argue I had put myself in the position by showing up when he had made it clear he didn't want to talk. I whispered to Bernard, "I have to leave," and he stood and walked around the table towards me. He touched my elbow and with feigned ease, we walked towards the exit. As he walked, he laughed lightly and whispered, "Laugh."

I tried, and at the exit, I looked directly into the guard's suspicious eyes. "Will isn't well," I said. "I just found out. He doesn't want to infect anyone, so he won't be coming today."

She glared.

"So I'll be leaving."

I could see she didn't believe me. I looked down at the ring of keys stuck into the front pocket of her trousers. "Follow me," she said, and with my eyes I thanked Bernard.

I don't know how I kept myself from crying as I followed her down that hallway. I don't know how I steadied myself enough to walk across that parking lot in the rain. Cameras followed us across those lots so I had to wait until I was out of there to let loose, and the minute I was on the road, I began to cry. I couldn't stop crying when I was back home, and finally I called Molly and told her what had happened. She was the only person I trusted not to turn on Will for his bad behavior.

"Please, will you talk to him," I wept to her. "I don't know what I did, but I'm sorry…You know I'd never try to hurt him."

She gently promised she would talk to him. "Don't worry," she tried to assure me. "He's just like me. We both have these quick tempers, but he'll get over it just the way I always do."

He called the next day.

The minute I heard his voice, as light as he had ever sounded, I felt my body loosen and relax. "So, Miss Independence Who Doesn't Need Anybody," he said with that joking tone of voice, "how's it going?"

I was quiet for a while. I was waiting for an explanation, an apology, something. "What happened? Why…the social …"

"You said you didn't need me," he said flatly. "I take people at their word."

"You knew what I meant," I argued.

"Did I?"

"I meant I can take care of the house. I didn't mean to hurt you…" I yammered on, and the despair that had lodged itself in my gut began to dissolve. When he laughed and asked when I was coming to visit, one more layer of the deception between us was cemented into place. I never told him he could not hang up when he was mad. Instead from that day on, I was more careful, understanding and patient whe he lost his temper. From that day on I was a prisoner, too—and not only of the system, but of the commitment I had made to Will. Of course I didn't let myself see it that way.

chapter nineteen

Another week passed when our marriage papers still hadn't surfaced, and paranoia kicked in. The book I had finished at the Virginia Center and that had just come out, *Nothing Sacred*, was critical of the Attorney General's office so I began to think the that office had lied when I asked about our papers. That seemed far-fetched, of course—that anyone in that office could have actually read the book and made that connection. But a lot of things that had once seemed a stretch suddenly weren't.

Three months earlier, as an "Official" prison visitor, I had never waited in a line at the Sally Port. Then I could walk the halls of Maynard wherever and virtually whenever I wished, carrying anything I wanted to carry. Now I was just like all those other women—the ones I had always perceived as so different from me—waiting in line, locking my purse and all my belongings but ID and change into a dented locker. Now I waited sometimes for what seemed like forever behind a mother carrying her baby and arguing with the Sally Port guard about how many diapers she would need inside. Now I waited and read the sign over and over again that informed us that everything we carried, our bodies included, was subject to search at any guard's discretion. Now, it seemed, anything was possible.

Three months earlier I'd been above suspicion. Now I was suddenly suspicious. I watched each day as I stood in line with other "prisoners' visitors" and every guard and official swept past us, past security while carrying duffle bags and suitcases and garment bags but risking no search. One day, I asked a guard why no one but us was subject to a search, and she sneered at me, said I was paranoid. I laughed and said, half-joking, "Just because everyone hates us, we don't have to be paranoid, is that what you mean?"

She didn't answer, just looked down at her pad of paper and scrawled a note that I was pretty sure would turn up in Will's file one day. (Later it did—in the form of a note about one of his visitor's resisting a search.)

Some guards, of course, behaved respectfully towards us, gently even, but they were the exceptions, not the rule. Once I watched a guard snatch an inmate's wife from her children and shepherd her into the tiny room behind the Sally Port desk for a strip search. The child began to cry, but no one said a word. We didn't talk to each other; each of our husbands and lovers and brothers and fathers had instructed us just as Will had instructed me. And being a witness to so much sorrow and frustration and hurt and anger began to stir up my rage—moved me still more firmly to the other side, the prisoners' side. Some days when I walked into the Sally Port, there were large dogs waiting to sniff our belongings and our bodies. One day a new machine appeared in the entryway, one that measured in nanograms—billionths of a gram—those meager belongings we could carry in; testing for traces of drugs. I was fairly confident no one would ever try to charge me with anything, but Will was vulnerable to everything I did, to every word I spoke. Sometimes I couldn't help but question guards' actions—questioning came naturally to me and I had been trained. When I was an official visitor, the answers I got were polite. Now those answers often were growls.

As we waited for our marriage papers, I tried to tamp down my anxieties and my wariness, but I was walking around haunted by questions: Why had falling in love with Will transformed me—an innocent—into a potential criminal? Why couldn't guards and administrators see that their behavior was doubling despair, tripling fury, quadrupling hostility between guards and guests? Or did they see and was that the point?

Waiting in those lines, I always sensed impending trouble just beneath the surface. Now when the warden locked down the joint, I was just like every other family member. A lockdown meant I couldn't visit or talk to Will. Those nights when a phone call didn't come, I sat and worried about what was happening, and now I had to rely on officials to get any information, or on the newspaper which ever since the twisted version of the rape story, I no longer trusted. I was beginning to learn more about prison life, beginning to understand the fear and longing prisoners and their loved ones felt, to see that small injustices were daily fare—the kinds of injustices no one cared enough to write about or confront or change but that affected those who were serving time. Like waiting an extra hour because a guard decided not to call the range. Or being strip searched or if our children cried or if a guard decided to write up something meaningless as being meaningful. No one cared.

So, just as I was beginning to get prison a little bit, I wasn't allowed to write about it, and this new understanding led me to disbelieve every account in every newspaper of every prison event from that time on. Even today.

* * *

The month of August moved at warp speed and in slow motion. I visited Will for two or three hours nearly every day and at night we talked on the phone for an hour or more. He told me about his family. His sister Emma was a prominent doctor in Toronto. On her first visit to see him seven years earlier, one of the guards had so insulted her, she had never returned. His eldest sister, Gina, had lived in California for the past 20 years and came home only once in a great while, so he seldom saw her. Nora was a nurse and the mother of four girls, and with little time to spare, she seldom made it to see him. She was the sister I had met because she lived just across town from Molly, and Cass and Sarah spent time with her family. Whenever I visited, I spent time with them too; I adopted two kittens their cat had had, one for each of the girls—and everyone was glad about that. I was falling in love with Will, yes, but I also fell in love with his family who treated me with warmth and kindness. They were grateful that I saw in their son and father and brother, the man they saw—not a "cold-blooded killer," but a man who was intelligent and promising, a man who had done something terrible and was being punished and still deserved to be loved.

Most nights Kate chugged up the laneway to the bungalow in her noisy Toyota with her Afghan hound and her little brown dog tucked into the backseat. Once inside, especially when the girls were visiting, Kate sent me to my room to write while she and the girls prepared supper. She taught them how to set a table, how to bake lasagna, books they must read, plays they must see, music they must hear. Despite her many years in Hollywood and New Hampshire and Ontario, Kate was an Arkansas debutante at heart, a southern belle who prized good manners and her own ability to tame any wild thing, and those wild things included not only her wild dogs but Will's daughters.

I told Will everything was great, that the girls loved visiting which they did nearly every weekend, that Kate loved them, that I loved Molly and his sisters and nieces—what could be wrong? Obviously everything would be just fine. I promised eventually I would tell my parents but for now we ought to appreciate those who were on our side. His chaplain, Russell Davis, was set to visit to plan the ceremony. I still believed those papers would appear any day. We would marry, we would keep visiting, and three years would pass; he would be paroled. Me and Will in the bungalow, with the girls and the cats and the dog, would live happily ever after. I hoped.

chapter twenty

On a Sunday morning two weeks before the wedding day, I walked into the Sally Port with the girls, but as we signed in, one of the guards stopped us. "You can't take these kids inside. They have to visit with a parent or a guardian. You're neither." Sarah stepped coolly forward and handed the guard her mother's permission letter. Will had already anticipated we might have some trouble, and the girls had convinced Laura to write a letter giving permission. It was only then that I understood that Sarah had been carrying it with her for months, just in case.

He didn't smile. "I'll have to give this to someone to look over, but no visit today."

We were accustomed to these irritations, and it was a beautiful day outside—Cass wanted to go to the beach or a park anyway. So we put up no fight. That night I explained what had happened to Will, and his voice sounded icy when he said, "Something's wrong. File a grievance. They can't keep you out."

Grievances were the only option we had whenever a guard did something questionable, but the grievance process took weeks, even months. The entire time I would visit, no matter how valid the grievance we filed, the administration never once sided against the guards. I didn't know that yet, and I had already figured that the next time the girls and I visited, a different guard would be on duty who would let us in.

"It'll be fine," I said, "It's just one guy wielding his meager power…" I tried to change the subject, tell him about something funny one of the kittens had done or something Kate had cooked, but he kept veering back to the guard's refusal. "It's not right. Something's going on…"

Early the next morning Will called again. He had talked to Security officers, and Doug Killen who was the assistant head of that department had assured him Laura's letter was on file. The girls could visit with me anytime. He wanted me to come right away, so I woke the girls and we drove over to Maynard. Again we walked to the Sally Port to sign in. A different guard *was* on duty. But he shook his head. "Correctional Directives are explicit. You need written permission if you want to bring these kids inside."

I could feel the girls watching me. I had, on a few occasions, raised my voice at guards when something frustrating happened. When I did they bristled and urgently whispered to me to keep cool. They never wanted to draw attention to themselves, certainly not from prison guards.

I remained calm. "The letter is on file," I said. "Call Mr. Killen if you don't believe me." And then I couldn't help myself. I had read the Correctional Directives. "And besides the Directive you're referring to applies only when a child is visiting an inmate who is not her parent. These girls are here to visit their father."

The guard looked right at me. "He's an inmate, he doesn't have children."

Blood rushed to my head, but I held my tongue. I mentally noted the name on his nametag: Buddy Gray. Then, still calm, I said, "Mr. Gray, call the Warden, please."

He nodded, dialed, listened a moment and hung up. "No answer," he said.

"Then call your superior," I said coldly.

Stone-faced, he dialed again. I heard him mumble something unintelligible into the phone, and a few minutes later a slender, bespectacled bureaucrat, Rich Rivers, arrived at the desk. He offered an ingratiating smile. "Miss Friedman, will you excuse Mr. Gray and me for a few minutes?" They disappeared into the strip search room behind the desk.

The girls and I stood there waiting, but as the minutes passed, 9-year-old Cass said, "They're not letting us in."

"Yes they will," I promised her, hoping, and she shook her head. "They won't," she said. Sarah nodded in agreement.

A few more minutes passed before Gray and Rivers returned. "Okay," Gray said tersely. "I'll let you in. This time."

I grinned at Cass. "See?" I eagerly thrust my ID at him, but Rivers reached for it. "Miss Friedman, you owe Mr. Gray a thank you. It's his decision to make this exception to the rule."

"Thank you, Mr. Gray," I half-snarled, but I began to think that Will might be right. And if I was starting to think that Will was right, there was something wrong.

* * *

I filed that grievance the next day and forgot about it the moment I did. I was busy fixing up the house, planning the wedding and writing my columns. And Russell Davis was arriving on Friday, four days before our scheduled wedding and trailer visit. The papers still hadn't surfaced, but I remained sure they would. I talked to Russell on the phone. He and Will would have some time alone that morning. The girls and I would come for the last half hour of morning visits, at 11:30. Friday.

That week, on Wednesday night, Will phoned and said, "Bad news. Bernard's in segregation. A so-called 'reliable witness' named Fougault put something on him."

I couldn't imagine Bernard doing anything that might jeopardize his upcoming Judicial Review. A good Review could reduce his sentence. Surely he must have done something to be thrown in seg. "What did he do?" I asked.

I could hear Will's frustration with my continuing ignorance about the way prison worked. I still wasn't completely convinced that someone who didn't do anything wrong—at least a little wrong—could be thrown into segregation. "Amy," he sighed, "Fougault's a paranoid schizophrenic drug addict. The fuckin' rat owes money for bad drug debts, so he tells Security Bernard's involved in some kind of conspiracy…."

I was lost. "What kind of conspiracy?"

"Amy," he said, "Fougault is batshit crazy. He needs a transfer outta here to save his ass from guys pissed off about his debts, so Security uses him to stick it to Bernard."

I asked him why Bernard if the guards and administrators really wanted Will. He explained that Bernard was his friend and thus a mark. "You get that by now, don't you? I'm telling you, something is coming down on me."

It wasn't that I didn't believe him. I did believe that some staff were upset about our plan to marry. In fact Rick LaFlamme, Will's unit manager, had told my boss at *The Whig* that Will was still married, but I knew he wasn't, and I felt sorry for O'Connor for believing his friend's lie. I felt sorry for him for being so afraid of prisoners that he was willing to buy into any story he heard about them.

My world had become a hall of mirrors inhabited by people like Lawrence O'Connor and Rick LaFlamme who saw themselves as "the good people" and to whom every prisoner was the polar opposite—unworthy of respect and incapable and unworthy of love. I also knew—one of the crime reporters with his access to police and their reports had told me—that O'Connor's two sons had walked away from more than one serious drunk driving incident. If they hadn't been sons of the town's publisher, they could easily have been just two more losers in prison.

I still didn't understand how Bernard's being thrown into segregation on the word of a drug addict had anything to do with Will. He had tried to explain, and when Barbara Baker left for vacation, he warned me that any day now something might go down. But when I couldn't catch on to the shorthand and codes, he decided he couldn't explain it to me, so he instead he told me he had a meeting scheduled for the next day with three people from Correctional Services national headquarters. "I'm going to tell them about all the shit that's going down in this place. Who knows, maybe they'll do something useful."

I was glad to hear that note of optimism—rare for him—but I was also paying little attention. I was focused on everything I had to take care of before I moved into the trailer for three days. Because I would be locked away from the world where no one could reach me and where I couldn't reach anyone outside. I couldn't tell everyone where I was going to be, so I had to cover myself for those days I'd be away.

Just before we hung up Will asked me if I could find a lawyer for Bernard. I knew plenty of lawyers in town, but I immediately thought of Ginny Ball. She and I were fellow members of the Board of Directors for Revelations House, a group home for teen offenders. We got along well. Ginny was a local celebrity, less renowned for her legal prowess than for her prowess in a boxing ring, but I knew she stood up for prisoners.

And Will had heard of her which was no surprise. Kingston had only six criminal lawyers, and all of them had reputations in the joints. "I hear she's tough," he said. We agreed I would contact Ginny.

I called Ginny the next day, Thursday, and she agreed to see Bernard. That evening, just twelve hours before Russell was due to arrive, the girls and Kate and I were laughing about something over supper when Will called. He, too, was now in segregation.

"Time for the lawyer for me," he said. He sounded calm. "Nothing to worry about. It's bullshit. I met with the National Headquarters people and told them everything going on. Naturally next thing I'm in seg. Same rat. Same story as Bernard."

He assured me he would be all right though he would need a lawyer. When I asked if this would affect our meeting with Russell, he told me we could have a closed visit—one behind glass. "Like I said, it's all bullshit anyway," he said. "Maybe it'll all be resolved by morning, but find a lawyer just in case."

I told Kate and the girls what was happening. Kate suggested I call the Warden. "Why waste money on a lawyer," she said. "The timing and circumstances are so suspect. Surely he can do something."

The Warden's home number turned out to be in the phone book, and the more Kate assured me, the more I became convinced that he could straighten out this tangled mess. Clearly his penitentiary was out of control. Surely he wanted to regain control.

I dialed.

I quickly apologized for bothering him at home. I hurried to explain the problem—our marriage papers had never surfaced, then the girls were refused a visit, twice, then first our friend Bernard and then Will had been locked up in segregation on a trumped up charge by a drug addict. I told him I thought there might be people working for him who were upset by Will's efforts to change some of the unsavory things going on at his prison—some things about which he might not be fully aware.

"Miss Friedman," he said coldly, "are you threatening me?"

I wanted to laugh. The question was absurd, and I felt as if we were in a bad TV movie. Threatening him? With what? And why? And how had he interpreted what I had just told him to be a threat?

122

"Sir, I think you've been in the system too long. Think about it—missing papers, being refused a visit, Will's meeting with National Headquarters and boom he's in seg. Obviously someone's messing with him...with both of us..."

"I'll look into it," he said. He hung up before I could thank him.

"Don't worry, he has to play tough," Kate reassured me. "He'll look into it."

I believed her.

Still, I left a message on an answering machine asking for an appointment to see Geoff Jarvis, a criminal lawyer whose name and reputation I knew, just in case.

* * *

When I read the letters I wrote in the weeks and months that followed, I cringe. Those letters were dense with the minutia of the next several days, bristling with accusations about the various prison officials who were out to keep us apart, to hurt Will. I saved all the letters on old computer discs, and years later as I pored over them, I understood that despite the way the system in its bureaucratic, plodding and sometimes vile way steamrolled us, I had started to sound a little mad.

The next day, a hot, dusty Friday, the girls and I walked through the front door of Maynard at 11:30 as planned. I pulled out my ID, but when I did the guard pushed it back at me and nodded towards the glassed-in room with the visitors' lockers. "Your friend's over there," he said, and I turned and saw an unfamiliar gray-haired man sitting in one of the chairs. "Minister Davis?" I asked the guard, and he nodded.

But at that same moment Russell turned and recognized the girls. He stood and walked toward us.

"He's supposed to be with Will," I told the guard who only shrugged and said, disinterestedly, "Will's busy.

"Busy?" I nearly spit the words back at him, but the guard looked over my shoulder at the woman waiting in line behind me. "Next..." he said, and before I could react, I felt Russell's warm hand in mine. "You must be the marvelous Amy..." he said, happily. "I'm Russell."

I tried to return his warmth, but then I was feeling prickly and angry, and I turned back to the guard and stepped in front of the other visitor.

"Will can't be busy, And this man you've had sitting here waiting for hours is his minister."

Russell touched my shoulder. "Amy, it's okay."

"It's not okay," I said to Russell, and to the guard angrily, I said, "Call Joe Book down. I want to see Will. Now."

Will had mentioned three people who I ought to watch out for, who I should not trust. One was Louise Salem who I already despised, two was Doug Killen, who I didn't know, and the third was Joe Book. I'd met Book, the head of security, on my first day at Maynard and we had crossed paths a couple times since. Waiting for him, I envisioned his graying moustache curved into a kind of snarl and his colorless eyes. I hoped he would see that I wasn't going to back down, that he ought to resolve this problem, and that he was creating a mess he didn't have to.

The girls had turned somber and quiet, and they pressed close to me. "Don't make a fuss, Amy," Russell pleaded. "I didn't mind the wait...." He nodded at the girls, letting me know I needed to calm down for their sakes. "I'm sure there's a plausible explanation for the wait."

I looked at the girls and knew they wanted to believe everything would be fine, but too many visits, too many changes of circumstance, too many days like this made it hard to believe. More than I, they recognized when trouble was brewing. "We'll just wait for Book," I said. "We'll straighten this out here and now."

Book appeared within a few minutes, and directing himself to Russell he said, "I'm sorry. I apologize for the inconvenience but something's come up."

"It's fine," Russell said, but I interrupted before he could finish and snapped, "We want to see Will now."

Book turned those colorless eyes on me, then looked down at his watch and smiled. "Look, morning visits will be over in just a few minutes. Why don't you four just go have a bite to eat and come back at 12:30 for the afternoon visits?"

"Sounds good," Russell's voice boomed in that small space, and he put his arms around the girls' shoulders and turned them to leave. I looked at Book again and said, "Now. We want to see him now."

Book tapped his watch. "By the time we call up to the range..." his voice trailed off, and Russell said gently, "Amy, come, we'll come back in a little while."

I saw I had no choice. We trudged under the pounding sun across the wide parking lot towards the entry road, and we continued out, walking out to Highway 15. Russell made cheerful small talk while we walked, but as we waited by the side of the road for traffic to pass before crossing to the shack-like diner, I said, flatly, "He's going to be gone when we get back."

Russell laughed. "Don't be silly," he said, and we ran across to that diner that was the kind of place I never went. It was a prisoners' family place; no one else would have any need to stop there. They served greasy grilled cheese sandwiches with slabs of half-melted orange cheese and vegetable oil slathered on white bread. The coffee tasted like dishwater, and all the other diners were people just like us—people who had to wait and do whatever we were asked, who had no choice but to do whatever guards demanded of us. There wasn't another restaurant within six miles of Maynard, and for anyone visiting from far away. It was and felt like the last-chance.

My fears that Will would be gone when we returned were founded in fact, not paranoia. That day I began to understand how thoroughly I now lived in the realm of most prisoners' families. I was no different from any of them. The Maynard that had seemed an alien spacecraft was now home, and those months of hanging out with prisoners and their families whose lives depended on the whims of their captors had changed me. The lens through which I viewed the world had narrowed, and I was like anyone who has been cast into a brand new world—like a soldier on an unfamiliar battlefield, like a terminally ill patient first hearing the news, like an astronaut on a new planet. The world looked and was entirely different to me that day.

Truthfully, it had been brewing. It had begun with small things—the call from Cal Costin telling me that Will was the one prisoner I couldn't talk to; the letter to my editor casting me out of prison. It snowballed to include the lost papers and refused visits and things that had happened outside the prison walls: my column had been cut from once weekly to once every two weeks, and it wasn't only *The Whig* that was withdrawing privileges I had once enjoyed. I had been teaching for years at a local college, and earlier that year they had invited me to apply to their Board of Directors. A decision was to be made in late summer, but in July they called to let me know they had withdrawn my application from consideration; they didn't say it was because I was visiting a prisoner, but I knew of no other reason for their decision. That summer the office of Barbara MacDougall, Conservative Minister of Parliament and a member of then-Prime Minister Mulroney's cabinet, had called to let me know she had enjoyed my latest book and hoped we could meet on her next visit to Kingston. In early August MacDougall's office called to let me know that meeting wouldn't happen.

In retrospect, I see that with each person who turned away and each moment that tried to separate me from prison, and thus from Will, I became more defiant and less reasonable—about prison generally but especially about Will and our need to be together. My nightly anthem became Bruce Cockburn's *Lover's in a Dangerous Time*—he was one of Canada's folk heroes, and his song contrasted the hopefulness of new love with the despair and foreboding of the Cold War. The Sarah Heartburn in me felt as if Will and I were in a war. At night, staring out at the river, I listened to that song over and over. I watched the moon rise. And I vowed I wouldn't stop fighting for Will.

* * *

At 12:30 Russell, the girls and I were back at the Sally Port where the guard said, "You'll have to wait. The warden wants to meet with you at 1." I glared at him. "We want to see him now," I said. But I knew nothing I said would change anything. I knew this man was just doing his job, and part of his job was to follow orders. I had begun to hate everyone who wore that prison uniform. Hatred felt like a physical thing seeping into my body as we shuffled into the dingy locker room and sat on hard metal chairs to wait.

The moment the clock struck one, I stood, and the guard at the Sally Port nodded and buzzed us inside. I ran ahead of Russell and the girls, through the maze of hallways leading into the administration building. I'd walked that route a dozen times, and I knew the way, and I was damned if I was going to wait one more minute. The girls and Russell hurried after me as I took the well-worn stairs two at a time.

Unlike the rest of the prison, the administration building was well-kept with walls of dark wood and polished floors and a hushed sound. As I reached the second floor, I looked down the long, empty hallway towards the Warden's office and saw Tim Thomas, treasurer of the Inmate Committee and one of Will's allies, pushing a mop along the polished floor. When he saw me, he pushed the map towards me, and when he was close enough he whispered, "Give me your phone number." I scribbled it on a scrap of paper and handed it to him, suddenly conscious of the fact that I had just passed my first *kite*—slang for the anonymous notes passed, letters mailed, journals stashed in mattresses, often the only secure means of correspondence with people outside. They were used for nefarious means, of course, also just to communicate information that wasn't permitted. In this case I was fairly certain administration wouldn't want any communication between me and Tim.

He pocketed the paper and moved back down the hall just as Russell and the girls caught up to me. The Warden's office door opened and the secretary smiled at us.

"Come on in," she said brightly, and she proffered a bowl of candy towards us. "Like some candy, girls?"

And even that smiling secretary offering sweets to Cass and Sarah suddenly looked suspect, not like someone doing her job but like the wicked witch from *Hansel and Gretel*, with her candy as a trap. I wanted to warn the girls but before I could speak, the door to the warden's inner office opened, and Doug Killen stepped out. I knew him by his name-tag, and when I saw that, the hair on my arms stood on end. He was holding a piece of paper, and he waved it in the air at me before past us and into the hall.

Right behind him came Warden Claussen. "Ms. Friedman, hello," he said. "And Reverend Davis? Please, come in."

I took Cassandra's hand to lead her in with us, but Claussen shook his head. "I think it's better for everyone if the girls wait out here."

"With the candy!" the secretary cooed.

"They can hear whatever it is you have to say to us," I said, but again Russell lightly touched my shoulder and softly said, "It'll be better." And turning to the girls he said, "Have a piece of candy for me, too, okay?"

They took the chairs the secretary offered them, and Russell and I walked into the warden's office. Claussen directed us to the couch and moved to safety behind his wide, cluttered desk. His face was expressionless and he said, "Good news and bad," and lifted a piece of paper from the stack on his desk. "The marriage papers have arrived! And they're signed, sealed and approved. It appears some signature was missing or some other nonsense..." his voice trailed off, and I could see he hadn't the strength to elaborate this particular lie. Besides, I was just waiting for the other shoe.

"Unfortunately," he dragged out the word, "Will is no longer with us. He's been transferred by Emergency Involuntary Transfer for the Good Order of the Institution out of Maynard."

If Russell hadn't been squeezing my hand, anchoring me to that sofa, I would have flown at him. "Transferred where?"

"He's on his way to Middle Harbor, and naturally I'll give you directions to find your way there...it's just 30 miles west, give or take, but then you know that, Amy, don't you?"

I moved to the edge of my seat. "We're supposed to get married in four days. In a trailer, here," I managed. My face flushed hot. I wanted to run—to catch the van I knew was ferrying Will away as we sat there pretending to be civil.

Claussen swallowed. "I hope you don't think your marriage plans have anything to do with this transfer...entirely unrelated..."

I couldn't listen to another lie. "Listen," I said, hoping this time that he did feel I was threatening him, "Not one of you has kept your word, ever. There's no reason for me to believe a word you say."

He didn't flinch. He knew I could do nothing to hurt him, and in a few minutes I would no longer be his problem. With a signature he had shifted me and Will and everything about us on to someone else's plate, and he already seemed relieved. I thought I even saw him suppressing a smile. "Very well, I can see you're upset. I have spoken with Chaplain Foyle and I've instructed him to speak with the chaplain at

Middle Harbor about your wedding plans. Of course, there's likely to be a bit of a delay…"

"How dare you…" I began, but now Russell moved forward and hurriedly said, "We're grateful for any help you can give us, and naturally we'd like to know the reason for this transfer, what you allege Will has done that would warrant this dramatic move."

"You do understand it is my responsibility to protect the safety of every inmate under this institution's care. We employ the Emergency Involuntary Transfer, well, in extreme measures…"

* * *

For years that moment remained a still image in which Russell and the warden talked forever and ever but said nothing. And words no longer mattered because I no longer believed that anything anyone told me was true. The anger and panic that rose up inside me that day never vanished altogether; they still lurk somewhere inside. Whenever I hear anything about what a prisoner has done to warrant punishment, I'm suspicious. I understood, if only vaguely, how someone who has been wrongly accused of a crime must feel when she first hears the accusations. I felt a roaring silence inside, and a war between the sense that nothing mattered and everything did. No words would change the circumstances, that was clear, but a deep desire welled up inside me to find a way to clear up all misunderstandings, to rewind the tape three months and somehow convince everyone—my bosses and prison authorities, friends and family, strangers —that Will and I meant no harm to anyone and that we might, together, even do some good.

I do know this. I was suddenly and thoroughly sober, no longer drunk on romance. Every single detail mattered. I became the hunter and gatherer of information. If wardens and security officers and deputy wardens and my newspaper bosses had purposefully set out to create an enemy, someone who would fight at every turn, they had nailed it. While I didn't necessarily believe that had been their purpose, circumstances had created an enemy in me, and from that moment on, I knew I would muster every resource I had—my intelligence and wiles, my friends, my contacts—and prove how wrong they had been in their treatment of us. And I would turn them inside out and upside down if I had to.

* * *

Instead of brushing away the details of the stories Will had been try- ing to tell me, I pored over every document I got from IPSO, the inter- nal police security office, in essence the prison's secret police. Those documents accused Will of conspiring with Bernard to murder another inmate. Their information about this "plot" came from an "unnamed but credible inmate." I already knew it was Fougault, the man who put Bernard in segregation, although in the IPSO papers (as in all prison documents), the name of the "source" was blacked out. IPSO reported that Will had been "involved in unsavory activities," and that an inter- nal biker war had led him to conspire to kill.

The papers also stated that Will was free to take this matter to court, should he wish to do so.

I was bred on movies of the '60s and '70s—*Klute* and *The Parallax View* and *All the President's Men, Chinatown* and *The Conversation*— and all of those movies with innocent victims and corporate corrup- tion, with officials on the take and secret surveillance and cover-up, came roaring back. I knew as well as anyone knew that information coming from a secret informant was seldom reliable. But I should have remembered something I conveniently forgot, that rumors can stick to anyone, and anyone in prison is stickier than any civilian.

But I was still living my version of a more contemporary movie, *Murder in the First.* Based on the story of Henri Young, a prisoner on Alcatraz who, in the 1930s, was charged with killing another prisoner, and in the movie Young's lawyer puts the prison on trial. Revelations from that trial ultimately helped to shut down the morally bankrupt Alcatraz, and in my secret, inner vision and version of our story, the same would befall those who were lying to us. Their injustices would be their ruin.

The fact was, though, no one was interested in IPSO's secret files laced with blacked-out names. I learned that over time. Most prisoner stories unfold with people either not listening or simply not believing the word of anyone who has been convicted of a crime. Still, I believed,

130

again, that our story would be different. Our story would shine a light on this.

But in the warden's office that day, I looked the warden in the eye and said, coldly, "What do I have to do?" And he told me that all emergency involuntary transfers were investigated by Regional Headquarters. He lied and said there was no telling what they would decide—and it was a lie because in nearly every case Regional Headquarters backed up the decisions made by Institutional heads. That's how things worked.

As I asked what would happen if Regional Headquarters supported Maynard's decision, Russell put a hand on my hand and whispered, "Everything will be just fine."

"Then you can grieve to National Headquarters," Claussen told me. I would take this grievance up the ladder, eventually, as I would the grievance about the girls' visit being denied and at least twenty more grievances over the years. And every time, higher-ups concurred and supported the decision that had been made at lower levels. I suspected that then, but I believed if I fought hard enough, I could change that as well.

The Warden explained that Chaplain Foyle would give me directions to Middle Harbor and would make sure that Middle Harbor took care of all the details necessary for our wedding to proceed. He stood, indicating the meeting was over, but as I stood I looked at him and said, "Sir, you do realize you shouldn't trust Joe Book and Louise Salem, don't you?"

He looked me in the eye, and he nodded, and he said, "I'm not sure exactly who to trust," and for another second we looked at each other. Russell took my hand and said to the warden, "Thank you for your time," and he led me out the door.

The girls were chewing big wads of gum, and when we appeared in the door they stood, and I put an arm around each of them. "Let's get out of this place," I whispered. "Your dad's not here anymore."

Cass looked at Sarah and said, "Told you so."

chapter twenty-one

Will had told me that he never cried, but that night when we talked on the phone, I was sure I could hear him choking back tears. I also heard fury in his voice and decided I had to instill some serenity. I said firmly, clearly, calmly that I wasn't going to let anyone stop us from marrying. They would stop us somehow, he assured me just as he had assured me that everything was going to go wrong, and now it had. But I tucked all my misery inside. I had called the lawyers, Geoff Jarvis and Ginny Ball. I would be the defender, the promoter, the cheerleader. I could take on everyone and everything. I would take care of Will and his kids, and I would help out Bernard and Connie, too. And anyone else who needed help.

Besides adoration, I had adopted other qualities my dad possessed, traits he taught all his kids to cherish. When he was needed, he was the man who always stepped up to the plate, and he taught us to do the same. He told us regularly that he had raised his kids to be just fine—meaning strong and brave and independent, able to take care of ourselves and others, too—even if we were dropped onto another planet. One of the stories we were nurtured on was about the day of his liberation. He hadn't told us many stories about being a prisoner of war—not the day-to-day misery, the loss of friends. But the day in June 1945 when the Allied tanks rolled into Stalag 9b in Ziegenhain, Germany where Dad and other members of the American Army's 106th Division had been prisoners since January—that day he talked about. The tanks couldn't stop—they were still chasing the Germans—so the soldiers tossed some boxes of crackers to the starving soldier prisoners to tide them through until they could be evacuated. That food—just crackers—wouldn't be enough, so the only three men who were strong enough— Dad who at 6 feet tall was down to 120 pounds, and two others in similarly weakened shape--drove 100 miles to the nearest Army depot to get food and supplies. The implication was that that's what you did—when it was important to help others, you did. When it was vital to save others, you did what you had to do—you found the strength.

The warden had given me Chaplain Foyle's home phone number and told me to call, but it was Friday afternoon, and when I got to a phone and called, the woman who answered told me Foyle had just left for the weekend. My heart sank at the news, but I gave her my phone number and explained that this was an emergency. I needed to speak to him right away, I said, and she said she would see what she could do. Then I studied the map to find the best route from my bungalow to Middle Harbor, Will's new home, the high security penitentiary, west of Kingston, in the middle of nowhere, 30 miles away along the winding lakefront road and tucked just north of the lake in a corner of the county I had never noticed. I phoned Molly and Willie and, for their sakes, sounded as cheery as I could. I assured them everything would be just fine. I fed the girls supper and put them to bed. Then, when everyone and everything was quiet, I began to write.

And I wrote screeds. To friends. To family members. To everyone I could think of who might listen to a cry for help. In each letter I begged for understanding, pleading with everyone to see things the way I had learned to see them over the last few months. The prison system, I wrote, was thoroughly corrupt, and nearly every guard and administrator I had met was in collusion to harm me and Will. I described Will as heroic. I insisted everyone understand that though he was a convicted criminal, he also was a human being, and one who was being unfairly punished—and so was I for trying to be part of his life. I decried the editors and publishers and railed against the censorship both the newspaper and the prison had imposed on me. And using the fax machine supplied by *The Whig*, I sent out these missives far and wide. To colleagues at newspapers in Kingston and Toronto and Vancouver and Montreal and New York and Ottawa. To family and friends in New York and Ohio and California.

And I saved every one of those long, operatic letters. And when I read them again a decade later, beneath the stream of words that I hoped sounded convincing—even inspiring—I could hear my cries of frustration.

Reading them all those years later sent waves of embarrassment coursing through my body. But there was something else—this tight little ball of sadness lodged in my belly that grew whenever I recalled the way I felt that night, the way I felt so often back then. The way I felt for so many years. That night I felt certain that everyone who knew me would come to our aid. My dad and brother and the lawyer cousins, the relatives with clout and money and powerful friends. If I could just explain fully who Will was and how I had fallen in love and what was happening to us, I knew that with a little help I could bat down the lies being told about us. I was equally certain that Chaplain Foyle would ride in on a white horse and fight for our right to marry as we had planned—in just four days. I was dead certain that my colleagues at the paper would help, would stand up for my right to write what I wanted and needed to write. And I was confident that friends from the board of directors, from the College and from Chez Piggy's would rally all the forces at their disposal and help me to counter this injustice.

But that isn't what happened.

Chaplain Foyle never did return my phone call. Many friends and family members shuddered at the woman I'd become. Many tried to talk to me about how impossible I had become to talk to, how unreasonable I was sounding, how I ought to calm down, reassess, rethink this decision, let some time pass before leaping with both feet into marriage with a man I had only just met. A man in prison. A man in prison for murder.

But here's the thing about those kinds of conversations. It's like trying to convince a drunk that she is drunk and must lie down. Once obsession is in play, it isn't possible to talk someone out of that obsession, and starting that night and every other night for years all I thought about and could talk about were the injustices towards prisoners that I had known and seen and experienced firsthand. And there was another problem with my obsession. There were a dozen or more kernels of truth in what I was trying to explain to everyone. It was true that Will and Bernard had been unfairly targeted and transferred. It was true that those transfers would affect everything about their lives from that day on—making release for Bernard nearly impossible and sending Will's parole date farther forward by as long as it took for him to cascade back to a medium security prison. It was true that my boss at the newspaper had no interest in hearing my point of view on how prison worked and who prisoners were. It was true that a number of events had conspired to separate me from Will, and it was true that a few people at the paper wanted me fired. True, too, I was offering them opportunities for labeling me and cornering me and belittling me, but it was also true that before I became obsessed and angry and planted myself firmly in Will's camp, and only his, some people had turned their backs on me. Most people didn't want to hear a prisoner's side of any story unless that prisoner was someone who had been wrongfully convicted. But a guilty man, especially one who had killed someone? A guilty man was guilty through-and-through. That's the way I saw it then. It's the way I still see it now.

Will, too, wrote over-heated letters. He wrote to my parents to tell them that he loved me. "I would lay down my life for her," he added, and even then the line embarrassed me; it was the kind of thing a lot of prisoners wrote, melodramatic and corny. He wrote that letter on lined notebook paper—the only kind he had because his belongings had not been transferred with him. (And it would be weeks before he had his clothes, his radio, his books and papers and pens, and when he did finally receive those, a great many things were missing, another one of those "that's the way it happens in prison" things.) He wrote the letter in pencil (he had no pens), in his blocky handwriting. But I didn't complain about the paper or the pencil, and I didn't tell him I was embarrassed. My complaints seemed pitifully unimportant in the face of what he was going through—the double bunk, the higher security, being suddenly sent back to what felt like the beginning of his sentence. Middle Harbor was where he had begun.

A few people wrote me back. One lovely poet friend I barely knew sent me money and a kind letter offering his support and concern. But one letter that came back broke my heart, and that was from my brother Peter, seven years younger than me and someone I admired and adored. Peter was a lawyer, and like my youngest sister, his wife had just gotten pregnant. "It looks like the stream of insanity in the family runs deep," he wrote to me. When I read that line I wept.

I thought I knew what he was referring to. It was my grandmother Pearl, my father's mother. Grandma Pearl, the original family drama queen, the first Sarah Heartburn, though she had her reasons to be. At 16, she met my grandfather as he was traveling through Poland on his way towards home from Siberia where he had been a World War I prisoner of war. She left with him for the States, for Pennsylvania where his family had emigrated in search of a better life. But she left her entire family behind, and they ultimately perished at the hands of the Nazis. Then, when her youngest son was captured in the Ardennes and went "Missing" (it would be weeks before they learned he was a prisoner of war in the heart of Germany), she must have felt pushed over the edge. By the time I was born, she was in the parlance of the family, "mad." Today she might have been diagnosed bi-polar.

From earliest childhood I had felt a special bond with Grandma Pearl. The bond came from my heart, but it also arose out of those stories we were raised on. Everyone said I looked just like Grandma Pearl. She was a large-boned blonde, the opposite of my petite, dark-haired mother, and the opposite of all my dark-haired siblings. And despite her sadness and her madness, she had a kind of *joie de vivre* about her, an energy I viscerally connected with, even if it was one that had been quashed by too many traumas. Mom and Dad were forever talking about how lucky I was—lucky unlike Grandma Pearl. If she had been born in the 1950s, raised in the '60s like I was, she would have had opportunities— to study, to work, to travel. But she had been raised in poverty at a time and in a place where women had few options. So it was up to me—at least that's what I felt—to take those gifts I had inherited from her and to use them well. And there was that other thing: If I messed up, I could wind up "mad."

It was also Grandma Pearl who unwittingly inspired me to be the writer I had become. By the time I was 12, Grandma had stopped talking. I suppose her illness had silenced her, the deepest kind of depression. One night I was in my bedroom that was over the den where the grownups hung out in the evening. They didn't know about the heating vent I sometimes pressed my ear against to listen to their conversations.

That night as I was listening, I heard my father and my grandfather berating my grandmother. I've no recollection of their words or why they were angry—the memory is purely instinctive. But I do know that I was so upset by the conversation and by her silence that I went to my desk and sat down and wrote the first short story I'd ever written—it was the story I thought my grandmother would tell if only she could talk. I no longer have the story, though it is the first story I ever sent to a magazine—to a contest *at Seventeen*. It was never published, but it was that night that I decided I would write, and I never changed my mind.

So when my brother wrote that line, I was so hurt, I decided I couldn't talk to him, or to anyone in the family. And I didn't for the next two years. I turned my attention away from my family and focused everything I had on Will and his.

chapter twenty-two

Over the next few weeks when I wasn't writing letters, I studied the Correctional Service Directives to learn everything I could about emergency involuntary transfers and the grievance system. I sat at home poring over every paper I could find on the subject. Like most legal documents, Correctional Directives were designed in large measure to cover asses, and to give readers a headache, and I had a perpetual stress headache. Still I did not stop reading. Although I had never enjoyed reading legalese, the writing wasn't pure Greek to me either. Like the diligent graduate student I had once been, I circled and starred and underlined passages, and afterwards filled the letters I continued to write with references and relevant Criminal Code numbers. My brother wasn't completely off in his assessment of me at the time. Anyone who did read those letters would have recognized a kind of madness in them. Like Russell Crowe playing the lost genius John Nash in *A Beautiful Mind*, I whirled around my house, filling walls with post-it notes, with reminders and arguments and counter arguments and numbers until my letters were as indecipherable as a treasure map to legendary Atlantis, or John Nash's code.

Will had begun his sentence at Middle Harbor seven years earlier. In his six years there, he had no trouble at all—no fights, no run-ins, not a single black mark on his record. Now, on the heels of the transfer, he was warding off anger, and though he never acknowledged it, he was suffering depression. Still, he was confident that Middle Harbor's Warden White, an old hand in the system, would see the transfer as bogus. White or one of his designated staff members was required to meet within 48 hours with the transferred offender to discuss the reasons for the transfer. Correctional Directives advised that the receiving warden

138

could withdraw support of the move. So Will had two days to respond to the reasons offered for the transfer. Transfer papers alleged that an unnamed source had fingered Will and Bernard as gang members who were conspiring to kill a rival gang member. The allegation was pure invention, a story concocted to sound as plausible as most prison concoctions are. We both put our minds to the task of writing a coherent, meaningful response, and we counted on Warden White's overturning the decision on Monday morning. We sat together in Middle Harbor's cramped, smoky visiting room writing long, detailed explanations of everything that had happened over the past three months.

That day I also begged the V&C guards to call Middle Harbor's Chaplain Kennedy down to talk to us. Stephen Foyle was supposed to call, I told them, but he had dropped the ball. We had been planning to marry in just four days. Right away I learned that Middle Harbor was different from Maynard in a thousand ways, and one was the temperament of its staff. From the warden down, this staff was less hardened, more wise to the system, aware of all the ways injustices towards prisoners and their families (and towards staff) was the stuff of daily life. Fewer of the guards—particularly the two V&C guards who had been there forever—seemed interested in making things any harder than they needed to be. So they called in Lloyd Kennedy.

Chaplain Kennedy was a small, reedy man with darting eyes and thinning gray hair. The minute he came into the room in his khakis and pressed blue shirt, he reminded me of Woody Allen, and I felt immediately grateful towards him for responding to the call. Lloyd was soft-spoken and gentle, one of those people who actually seemed to care about prisoners, to recognize them as human beings, and as I told him what we wanted from him—to keep our wedding date for next Tuesday—he looked sorry to have to explain that that seemed unlikely. Rules were, after all, rules, and prison rules stipulated that all weddings were to take place in trailers. Our next Catch 22 was this: Because Will had just arrived at Middle Harbor, he would have to wait his turn. There was a long waiting list of men signed on for trailer visits. Will wouldn't be eligible for several weeks, perhaps months.

"Big surprise," Will muttered. He wouldn't smile at Kennedy, wouldn't shake his hand, barely looked at him. To Will this whole thing had proven that every prison was the same, that every rule was designed to make the prisoners and their loved ones unhappy, that this was just one more piece of evidence to prove his point. Still, I refused to accept Kennedy rendition of the way things were. I was insistent. I told him Molly and the children had planned on this, that everything was set. "They're coming to town," I said. "Everything's arranged—the kids with school, my job, my life, everything..." and I just kept talking until he finally agreed he would look for some way to resolve this problem we had. He promised to get back to me. And even though Will said "He won't," I held out a sliver of hope.

The next day passed without a word from anyone, and on Monday morning we received Warden White's decision: He and his staff at Middle Harbor had accepted the terms of the transfer. That meant Will would have to stay at Middle Harbor, though of course he could file his grievance to the next level—to Regional Headquarters. And so, the day before we were supposed to marry, we sat in the visiting room and wrote out more papers. These we sent to Andrew McCabe, the Regional Director, and I prayed that he would eventually see through this contrived story and make things right, would send Will back to Medium Security where he belonged—and where he could get on with his work to cascade his way to parole.

Monday would have been a rotten day except Chaplain Kennedy came to the visiting room. He was grinning ear to ear, and I pressed my hand against Will's and whispered, "Look, look who's here," and even he looked happily surprised. It was the first time he'd smiled since the day of the transfer three days earlier. Kennedy told us he had worked things out, and we would be permitted to marry in the prison chapel, the only couple ever granted this privilege. He looked down and apologetically explained that of course we wouldn't have a trailer visit for a few weeks. It couldn't happen the next day as planned, but everything was set for the following day, Wednesday.

I was so grateful I nearly threw my arms around the man, the first person who was working to make something possible for us. And I focused on the idea of being the only couple ever permitted to marry in the prison chapel. With that line my overheated romantic sense we were somehow special deepened, the sense that come hell or high water, we were meant to be together.

And that is how it happened that just five days after the Emergency Involuntary Transfer, on a hot August Wednesday morning, just a few weeks after I had turned 40, the girls and Willie, Molly and Kate and I drove out to that looming, barbed-wire monstrosity that was Middle Harbor to celebrate a wedding.

The perimeter of the place was surrounded by a 30-foot razor wire double fence, with observation towers at the corners. Armed patrol vehicles with Cold Canada C7 rifles and parabolic microphones were on guard 24/7, and motion sensors had been placed in the outlying property, with multiple camera units throughout the grounds and buildings. Every visitor once on the property here, was subject to search, and listening devices were installed in each table in the visiting room. Middle Harbor had seen its share of violence over the years, and J unit (where Will was now living) was considered one of the most dangerous places in Canada's entire prison system, built on native burial ground which meant, inmates said, that it would forever be a cursed place of darkness. When years later Middle Harbor built a new division to house foreign citizens being held on security certificates, it was dubbed Guantanamo North, and whenever I was there I felt afraid, unhealthy, heavy with all kinds of sorrows. I sensed everyone did.

Chaplain Kennedy had warned these were the downsides of our decision to go ahead: Will wasn't permitted to wear anything but his "greens," that hideous uniform they wore; he wasn't allowed to keep the wedding ring I'd bought the week before, rings Sarah had helped me select; we would have no private visit after the ceremony. But neither of us cared. I made light of them, and to show how much I didn't care, I even wore a green dress to match his greens. I assured Will that I didn't care what they tried to take away from us; we would defy everything and everyone. We would be as bold and strong as Etta Place and The Sundance Kid, as Barbara and Clyde. All the hardships had, for me, only upped the air of romance.

Middle Harbor's halls were darker than Maynard's halls, and as our wedding troop followed Kennedy along the halls towards the central chamber, I could hear our footsteps echoing back at us. In the center of the prison, eight arms of the edifice shot out to the sides like an octopus, and as we walked I felt as if I could almost hear the screams encased in the cement surrounding us. I could only half-see the bodies in those hallways, but I could feel the muscles and tattoos, and I heard whistles and catcalls and the thud of my heart. I held the girls' hands and watched sullen Willie shuffling ahead of us, his hand in his grandmother's while Kate sashayed at the head of our line right behind Kennedy. Nothing could wilt Kate.

When we reached the chapel I first noticed a woman I didn't recognize leaning against the doorway. I did recognize Ron Bergeron who stood beside her. When I saw that he had come to show his solidarity with us, I felt myself softening towards him—he hadn't had to do this. And as we walked past, he squeezed my hand and smiled. He nodded at the woman and said, "Amy, this is Erin Dolan, she'll be Will's new C.O. Erin, Amy's a great gal…." We exchanged half-smiles. Unlike savvy Barbara who knew the system inside out and who, I still believed, might have been able to stop the transfer if she hadn't been on vacation, Erin was very young—in her late 20s—and she seemed almost afraid.

Inside the chapel I saw Will looking just as shell-shocked as he had for the last five days. His face was markedly pale, and he was expressionless, but when I reached him, he took my hand and squeezed it, hard. He leaned in and kissed me, and then he turned and ruffled his son's hair, hugged Sarah, then Cass, then his mother. He shook Kate's hand. He looked at Russell and asked, "You all set?"

"I'm ready when you are," Russell said. He lined us up in a row before him, with me and Will in the middle, the others fanned out to our sides. Will clutched my hand as Russell began to read the ceremony. I noticed sweat was pouring down Will's forehead, and out of the corner of my eye I saw his mother handing him Kleenex after Kleenex, saw Will wiping sweat away, over and over again. If I hadn't lost my sense of humor over the last few weeks, I have laughed sweetly at this. But obsession tends to blunt one's humor. And so I remember little beyond Will's sweat and my promise to be faithful. I remember meaning it and being relieved that I did, feeling as if now, at last, I deserved to be loved the way my mother was loved.

Before I knew what was happening, I was wearing a wedding band and there was a ring on Will's finger, too (officials somehow changed their minds about making him give it up), and our parade was on its way to the visiting room—Will escorted from one direction, rest of us from another. In that tiny room, crowded among strangers, we hugged and kissed. Then the hour was up and it was time to kiss goodbye. Again.

chapter twenty-three

Three weeks later we took our "honeymoon," our first trailer visit. The administration even tacked on an extra night and day—84 hours insteads of the usual 72. But Will's throat was coated with cold sores, and he had a high fever and a throbbing headache. His illness which began a few days before the trailer went untreated until days it was over, and then only after I threw a temper tantrum with Erin Dolan, his inexperienced Correctional Officer. She finally sent him to see the prison doctor. I didn't remember that he was ill until years later, after I re-read the letters I wrote to Erin.

And I do not remember the first time we made love, odd considering the longing leading up to it. But perhaps it is perhaps not so odd because of the one moment of that visit I have never forgotten. We had probably just made love, and we were lying in bed beside each other in the dark cave of a room. The lumpy mattress was covered with the new sheets I had brought along (and would bring to every visit ever after), and Will's arms were wrapped around me. He pulled me so close I could feel every muscle in his body as they moved. He kept pulling me closer and closer, and then, although I hadn't asked him, he whispered, "We were drunk. We'd been drinking all day, me and Danny." His warm skin turned instantly clammy, and his grip on me tightened, and I understood he was talking about the day of the murder.

He was whispering in my ear. "We must have downed a case." I felt his body reel as if he were drunk again. Then in one long breath, like a confession, the story rolled out of him. I didn't breathe or say a word. I just listened.

He and his buddy Danny had been talking about driving over to the house where another dealer lived. Joe, the dealer, had been pushing Will to take his business out of Joe's territory. Danny and Will were drinking and smoking dope, and when they decided to go, Will tucked a gun into the waistband of his jeans and pulled out his shirt to hide it from sight.

I know next to nothing about guns. I've no recollection of what kind it was or how many he owned or why he owned any except that he was a drug dealer, and drug dealers owned guns. I imagined they often tucked those guns into their waistbands and hid them under their shirts. In my entire life I have fired a gun just twice, a single-shot rifle—once in the back fields of the farm where Dean taught me how to shoot because it might be necessary on the farm, and a second time when a rabid coyote wandered into the farm's summer kitchen while I was home alone. I had always felt squeamish about those rifles tucked up on the top shelf of an upstairs closet, the bullets downstairs on a shelf hidden behind books. But when that coyote appeared, I ran upstairs, grabbed the rifle and shot the creature, and then without taking a look, I called Animal Protection to come get it. Guns have always seemed like symbols of misery waiting to happen, pieces of metal that launched despair for countless people I came to know in prison, and for so their victims. Guns and alcohol were involved in the vast majority of stories I heard.

But in bed that evening—or it might have been day with the shades drawn tight—asked no questions—about guns or anything else. I stayed as quiet as I could so I wouldn't startle him out of this story that was clearly tucked so deep inside. I rubbed his arm. I touched him so that he would remember that he wasn't back there and drunk and carrying a gun, ready to kill or be killed. But on he talked, describing the drive into the countryside. "He threatened my family's life," he whispered. "I couldn't let him hurt my family." He may have described the weather, I don't remember. I no longer even remember what season it happened in except when I think about the story, and when I calculate back from the date when he went to prison, I envision a day in late winter or early spring, and I see remnants of snow on muddy earth, and bare trees, though perhaps that's only because his body felt so cold and tight. I don't know what he drove. I'm not even sure if it was he or Danny who drove. I do know he had once driven a Harley—guys in his crowd did. But I also knew he owned a Corvette. I am absolutely certain that whatever he drove it was something he could have bragged about. He was raking in money from construction and dealing, and he always liked nice things, was proud of his status as evidenced by what he owned, the way he had been proud of being Chairman of the Inmate Committee, the only outward evidence of status a prisoner could possess.

The year was 1985, a few months before I moved to Ontario. On the day of the murder, I barely knew where Ontario was on a map much less that tiny little town where the murder took place. In the foggy memory I have of the story he told me, the victim's house was in the faraway bush of the Ottawa Valley, surrounded by towering pines. In my imagination, perhaps my memory, the house was open to the elements, though it may have been a snazzy, modern place—and that is more likely since so many drug dealers and bank robbers and shady stock and gun traders I met had once lived so well.

Will and Danny drove fast. They knew the back roads. Will had lived his whole life in that part of the world. Before he knew it they were there, in this place far from neighbors. But Joe wasn't home when they arrived, only his wife was—an innocent, although she was well aware of the business her husband was in. She welcomed Will and Danny but seemed to have no idea anything was wrong. If she did, she wasn't letting on. She told them her husband would be home soon. She asked if they wanted a beer, and they said yes, despite the fact that they were drunk. Will watched her open those beer bottles as if she were moving in slow motion. I half remember his description of the blessed taste of that cold beer. His mouth must have been cottony with anxiety.

Did Joe return home on a Harley? In my memory, or perhaps it's only my imagination, I hear a Harley roaring up a leafy path. I don't know what Joe thought when he saw Will or if he first spotted the car. I don't know if either Joe or Will knew someone was going to die that night. I don't think so. I don't think Will ever imagined killing someone although he had been in "the business" for a decade—and he had used his fists plenty of times. Was Joe as drunk as Will was? Did Danny think they ought to leave? Did Will? Did Joe's wife notice a change in mood when her husband returned? I don't know the answer to any of those questions. I don't remember if I had those questions then. They come to me all these years later.

Somehow in the next part of the story, in my memory and in my imagination, the four of them were inside the house—though I recall their drinking those first beers outside. Now the wife was across the room, busying herself with something. Maybe she was cooking supper. Maybe she was opening another bottle of beer. I don't remember if Will told me or if he knew. The next thing he and Joe were talking, their voices hot with threats. They were standing beside Joe's gun rack, and then again as if in slow motion, Will saw Joe reach for a gun. He reached into his waistband. He fired first. Joe fell.

Will and Danny were already running, nearly out the door, Danny ahead of Will when something—the wife's scream perhaps—prompted Will to turn back towards the house. Then, without thinking or looking or aiming he fired his gun—in her direction—and without knowing whether or not he had hit her, he raced to the car, and they were speeding towards home. They must have headed to Danny's because Will and Laura were separated, and Will was staying in his mother's house, trying to get things together, an emotional wreck about the way his personal life was unraveling.

The next morning he was still half-drunk when the cops showed up at the place where he was staying—not his mom's—and arrested him and charged him with second degree murder. "I didn't kill her," he told me, referring to that shot at the wife, "but I shot at her. If I hadn't, they would have charged me with manslaughter."

In that trailer, in the darkness, I could barely see him, but I could feel his body shaking as he went on talking about the woman he had shot. He shook harder as he told me everything he knew. "She needed surgery. That's all I know. I didn't want to kill her. I didn't want to hurt her...I was crazy. I was drunk. I don't know why..."

I closed my eyes. I could feel his tears, or maybe it was my tears I felt. He stopped talking, and right away, in that moment for no rational reason except that the image was too painful, I tucked that woman's fear, and those screams I could almost hear, and her wounds into some corner of my mind, a place where I wouldn't have to think about them. I tucked them away so I could pretend Will had acted only in self-defense, subconsciously consoling myself (and his mother and his children), rationalizing my devotion with the idea that although this man I loved had killed someone, if he hadn't, he would have been dead.

He laid his head onto my chest and cried. After that night, we never again talked about the murder. He said he couldn't. And neither could I.

chapter twenty-four

The night after our trailer visit ended Will told me over the phone that Erin had asked him about our argument. That's how I first found out that guards had listened in on our "private family visit." Someone had reported us as having had a violent argument, although it had been far from that. It had been heated, yes. And I had cried. But there was an explanation, and the moment Will told me the guards had listened in, I felt a knot in my stomach, a knot that stayed there for a long, long time. Back then I tried—and often failed—not to imagine what else those guards had heard. Later, whenever I tried to explain to anyone what being under surveillance felt like, I couldn't find the words. "What do you care if you're not doing anything wrong," they often asked. Or "They have to listen—it's prison. People do bad things in there." That always silenced me, but I secretly wanted to scream because I was picturing those guards huddled around and listening to us making love.

In 2006, years after I had stopped visiting prison, I went to see the German film *The Lives of Others*, a film that had received worldwide acclaim. The film was about the Stasi, the German Democratic Republic's secret police. As I sat in the theater watching Stasi officers placing bugs in a (Communist-leaning) theater director's apartment, I felt that familiar stomach clench. The officers were bugging the director's flat because they had been ordered to dig up dirt their boss could use in order to seduce the director's lover. I watched the director and his girlfriend talking to each other in what they thought was privacy, and I was launched right back into that trailer, into those visiting rooms, inside the sickly fear that lived inside my body all those years I visited prison.

Later I learned that the movie's director, Henckel von Donnersmarck, had been prompted to make the film because his parents had lived in East Germany before the Berlin Wall fell. Whenever he visited that country he could feel the fear every East German felt as spied-upon subjects of the State. The opening scene of *The Lives of Others* was set in Hohenschonhausen Prison, the site of a memorial dedicated to victims of Stasi oppression. The quiet hero of the film turns out to be the Stasi agent whose conscience overcomes his need to fulfill his duty. Reportedly Hubertus Knabe, head of the memorial, had tried to convince Dommersmarck to change the film. He felt strongly that no Stasi agent should be portrayed as a hero. And I loved the film, but I agree.

Once I realized that Will and I were dependent on the whims of those who were listening to us to interpret our lives, my uneasiness blossomed. So did my paranoia. But I still wonder: Is it paranoia when those who are actually listening have already proven they do not care what happens to you? Fear blossoms, and fear can be paralyzing, but borne of something real, fear is hard to suppress.

Once again, on the heels of this news, I sat down and began to write. This time I wrote Erin a long, detailed letter about everything that had happened since our wedding—noting the fact that when Will and I had finally had a chance to spend some private time together, at last I had had an opportunity to learn about his crime. I requested—no, I demanded—that she put every letter I wrote into Will's file. I decided I would document every last thing in an effort to override lies and misinterpretations tucked into the file. My mission rose one more notch. Determined to ensure he would be transferred back to medium security status and then smoothly cascade through the steps to his eventual parole, I convinced myself if I could articulate everything that had happened and how it had, Regional Headquarters would see through the sham of Maynard's transfer. They would overturn it. I told myself I could survive three years and that in the summer of 1995 when Will became eligible to apply for day parole, all this would be behind us.

To Erin I wrote: "...you clearly did not understand the extenuating circumstances involved in this case..." followed by two single-spaced pages reiterating the precise events of the previous months. I offered her what I always offered in those overwrought letters—a description of us as innocent victims of a conspiracy designed to keep Will's side of the story (and every prisoner's side) out of the papers. I wrote, and believed and believe still, that it was at least in part designed to discredit me so that if I did manage to publish any part of the story, whatever I wrote would carry no weight.

"In general I think Will and I have handled ourselves with astonishing grace in the face of these abuses," I wrote. I described my discovery about the truth of private family visits. Our argument, I told her, ought to be easy to understand. First, he was ill; second, I was exhausted; third, we had just endured weeks of stress. In my view, our argument had only proved that Will cared for me.

It had happened on Monday morning, the last day of our visit. I was scheduled to leave at 1, but early that morning I woke suddenly remembering that I hadn't rescheduled my doctor's appointment. I'd made the appointment when I thought our visit would be just three days. I had rescheduled everything else in order to free up 72 hours during which time no one could reach me. When Middle Harbor officials extended our visit, I forgot to reschedule my appointment with Sam Shortt, my long-time physician, someone I considered a friend. I was to meet with him so he could write a letter to my publisher attesting to the fact that I was not mentally ill.

The publisher never told me he thought I was crazy. He did tell his secretary, Alicia, and she told me (and who knew who else he had told). I believed Alicia because it explained a lot of the behavior I'd encountered in the newsroom—whispers, eyes turning away by people who had once been friendly and warm. I think now he must have used his belief in my mental instability to justify the decision insisting that the newsroom editor and editorial page editor oversee each column I wrote to make sure I didn't overstep any lines.

When I thought about people conspiring behind my back "for my own protection" I was enraged. Even now the memory of it raises my hackles because the truth was that the protection they sought was for themselves. O'Connor couldn't risk my writing anything that didn't cleave to Southam's corporate standards. Others were worried about their jobs since the Syndicate was making changes—small at first—but clearly everyone's job was on the line. Already Jack Morley who had been the soul of the paper for years was leaving. A new editor, a meeker type named Daniel Scheinman, was taking his place.

When Alicia had told me about O'Connor questioning my sanity, I called Sam. He offered to examine me and to discuss the whole situation. He would write a letter assuring my bosses that I was mentally fit—depressed a little, and by nature a dramatist, but not unfit to do my job. And so when I woke and remembered the appointment for 10 a.m., I naturally told Will. I assured him I would call Sam that afternoon, as soon as I was home, to reschedule. I knew Sam would understand.

Will couldn't believe I would even consider missing such a vital appointment. "But Will," I argued, "we waited for months for this... I tried to explain to him that he didn't know Sam, didn't know what an easygoing, kind and generous soul he was, and how well he knew and liked me. Will didn't know that whenever I did something remotely over the top—visiting underground newspapers in South Africa or intervening on behalf of kids in trouble with the law or staying in a barn all night to birth a lamb—Sam always said, "There's the sensitive artist in you."

But Will and I argued. He insisted I leave, and when I said I wouldn't, he began to talk about how much better I would be better off without him altogether. Just look at the trouble he had already caused in my life, he said. Look at my having to prove to my boss that I wasn't crazy. Look what a loser he was, locked up in maximum security. I argued back. He wasn't a loser unless he gave up on himself, and on us; we would get him back to Maynard, we just had to stay with this; we had to stay strong—what else was there to do but become a loser? I insisted I didn't care what anyone at the paper thought of me.

Not for the last time, Will won that argument. He did agree we could stay together, but at 9 a.m. he sent for the guards and insisted I leave the trailer early. Then Dolan learned from the guards that we had argued—violently—though there had been nothing violent about it.

I wrote to her:

"... He wanted me to be better loved... to be married to someone who was "free..."

In other words, Will loved me the way I had always wished to be loved—enough to give up time together that he had wanted for something that was better for me.

* * *

A few weeks later, while I was still silently fuming at the publishers, the wardens and guards, after Sam had written the letter, one night I sat down to write a column. A memory floated back to me of a day when I was in 10th grade. Mr. Randall was my English teacher. My mother taught at the same school I attended, and she knew Randall. She agreed with me that he thought rather too highly of himself. He considered himself above the other teachers, and he certainly thought himself far above most of us lowly kids.

From the first day of class I disliked him, but he was the only Advanced Placement English teacher, and I was on the AP Track. The summer before I had been reading Faulkner and was hooked on him when school began and Randall assigned us Tolkien's *Lord of the Rings* trilogy. I tried to read the books, but compared to all that lush Faulknerian prose, Tolkien felt flat, so I skimmed the books. When exam time came, I looked down at the 300 multiple choice questions on *Lord of the Rings* and knew I was doomed to fail. And fail that exam I did, but instead of simply giving me an "F," Randall called me into his office. He sat, bloated with fat and pride, and began to quietly berate me for my ignorance. He let me know I wasn't up to the rigors of AP English, wasn't made of the right stuff for him or for the study of literature. He kept talking, and my lip began to tremble as I swallowed back my tears. Then he roared at me. I clearly wasn't up to the task of being a "real student." Not only wasn't I good enough for his AP, I wasn't good enough for Level Four. He demoted me to Level Three.

Now, more than 20 years after that experience, I sat in my bungalow on the St. Lawrence River and the memory felt as fresh as the day it had happened. I closed my eyes and remembered too that Mrs. P. in Level Three promptly promoted me to her Level Four. She and my mother had comforted me by agreeing the man was a bully. And that's what I wrote about—the story of Mr. R, and the harm bullies leave in their wake. I wrote about my sensitivity ever since that day to people who casually throw their weight around. I did not mention prison.

The column ran on Saturday. Two days later I walked into the office to pick up my paycheck, and as I was walking up the stairs the editorial page editor was walking down. When he saw me he whispered, "Need to talk to you," and he led me into his office. There he warned me to watch it. He said the column I had written about Mr. Randall had treaded a little too "close to the line," and if I wasn't careful, my column would be cut altogether.

This editor had always liked me. We had been friendly colleagues, and he and his wife had visited me on the farm to show their young daughter the lambs doing their springtime leaps into the air. I knew he didn't want me ousted, and that's why he warned me they were watching me. One more surveillance.

chapter twenty-five

Throughout the late summer and early fall I often enjoyed the 30 mile drive to Middle Harbor, past mansions and their spacious lawns that swooped down to the lakefront. The two-lane usually was empty, and I enjoyed the scent of sweet autumn air and the changing leaves. I had always loved to drive, and it gave me time to think. But those trips several times a week also took their toll on my car and the gas on my pocketbook, and I was counting the days until my commute was once again a mere four miles—the distance from my bungalow to Maynard.

Besides, Middle Harbor itself inspired uneasiness and the kind of violence I'd never imagined I could feel. I wanted to kick in someone's face—and the faces I envisioned were Louise Salem's, Joe Book's, Stephen Foyle's, Lawrence O'Connor's. But physical violence wasn't what I truly craved. I wanted vengeance. I wanted those people to know what it felt like to be forbidden to make love in private, to lose credibility, to feel threatened. I wanted them to know what it felt like when people who had once admired them wondered about their sanity. I wanted them to know all this and still have to work for a living, pay the bills, keep up a house, care for a spouse and children.

At Middle Harbor visitors had to walk past one gate, wait between it and another, until the guard buzzed us through. Then we walked a long path before entering the main building. There I almost always ran into an inmate, always the same man. Pancho had been at Middle Harbor for decades, and he was harmless. Everyone knew it. Indeed, staff and administration had tried for years to transfer him out and onto lower security, but everytime they filled out the papers, he did something to foil their plan to evict him. Everyone—guards and inmates and administrators and we visitors—understood that to Pancho this looming, monstrous place was and always would be home. He was the joint cleaner, fussy about his floors. Whenever anyone walked in with mud or snow caked on our shoes, he stopped us, wagged a finger and waited for us to kick off that mud or snow outside. He didn't distinguish between "official" and prison visitors. His concern was for those floors. The sight of him upset me for Pancho seemed the symbol of what happened to men stuck in there too long, the symbol of an institutionalized con.

But I quelled vindictive, depressing thoughts with the belief Will would be out of there, fast. Every staffer I met at Middle Harbor—from the warden to the secretaries to the guards—knew the transfer was nonsense. No one seemed to hold a grudge against either Bernard or Will. They understood they were no threat either to the system or to society. They said that, out loud. Some even said they hoped they cascaded out fast. But these people were cogs in a clunky bureaucratic wheel, and their first commitment was to the job. They could not be seen siding with an inmate against the Service; if they were, they stood to lose the backing of their comrades if and when they ever needed it.

The visiting room at Middle Harbor was ghastly—10 by 15 feet, with no access to the outdoors. Instead of a grubby bus station, it felt like the visiting rooms I had seen on TV, with tiny chairs and tables bolted to the floor and walls filthy with remnants of cigarette smoke. The tables were grimy with sweat. Still, the guards, overweight good old boy types with moustaches, were just doing their time. They were better than the power-hungry men and women at Maynard. They probably were pulling a scam or two for double time pay, waiting for retirement, but they had nothing against us visitors, and little animosity towards the cons. One of the two actually liked Will. He told me he liked him because he wasn't a loud mouth, and he was smart, and he made people laugh, and he wasn't high strung or nervous like the drug addicts or drunks who couldn't be counted on to behave in any predictable way. Will was polite, and so were his visitors. Whenever I complained to the V&C guards about the transfer, they shrugged. "Shit happens. Don't worry, they'll be back in Maynard any day. We've seen a lot. We know." I felt a surge of affection for their helping me to believe our troubles would soon be behind us. And they weren't voyeurs. They had to watch us from behind the glass of their little room, but if we got lost in a kiss, they didn't call over their loudspeaker to make us feel smutty. Some days Middle Harbor's visiting room felt almost like an old, familiar pub down the block where everyone knows everyone and bar fights seldom break out because strangers don't just drop in to stir up trouble.

* * *

As time passed, my world grew smaller. Since I no longer worked at the office and went in just once a week, I saw no one in the city, and I seldom any longer went to Chez Piggy's. I visited Middle Harbor three times a week (the maximum permitted), six hours at a time, and spent nights talking to Will on the phone. On weekends the girls usually came for a visit, or all three of us went to see Will's mother, Molly. When I did run into old friends, I noticed some were ducking me. Looking back, I don't blame them. I was a woman obsessed, and not everyone wanted to hear endlessly about prison. But it was almost the only thing I could think or talk about. And back then I did blame them. I felt dropped, though I also dropped those people who couldn't understand what I was going through.

And then, as if my world hadn't grown uneasy enough, Ottawa-based *Frank Magazine* ran a story about *The Whig*. *Frank* was styled on Britain's *Private Eye* and prided itself on mining details from existing stories—often the most scandalous details. Some dismissed it as a scandal sheet—stories had no bylines and the magazine relied on protected sources. But secretly many of us loved to read it. *Frank* been credited with keeping some stories in the news long enough to break cases the mainstream media had dropped. The story about *The Whig* revolved primarily around the changes in our newsroom. I had never much liked Daniel Scheinman, and he didn't seem to like me. In *Frank's* wry, sarcastic way, their story detailed "Daniel's headaches" in the newsroom, citing several. To my dismay, one of those headaches was me.

The article described me as one of the columnists who was making Daniel's life difficult and went on to say I had just rashly married a man in prison for murder, a man who on the eve of our wedding had been conspiring to murder a fellow inmate. When I read the piece, I fell to pieces. I knew who *Frank's* sources were in our newsroom. I'd considered them friends. Bill had even given me a wedding gift, and Mike was a longtime pal. Earlier that year we had spent weeks together covering a long trial. As a favor to him, I had just selected one of his friend's adaptations to run as one of *The Bedtime Stories*. I had confided and cried to both these men. Now Bill's wedding gift felt like a bribe to inspire me to feed him information he could then feed to the press to support the image of a woman gone crazy.

Thankfully some people who had always been kind remained that way. Another of my favorite spots in town was the Brew Pub. The owner, Van, a large bear of a man, greeted everyone who walked into his pub with its cherry wood walls and comfortable red leather booths, with an embrace or, at least, a friendly smile. The scent of home-brewed beer spiced the air. Music from Kingston's own Tragically Hip and from Bruce Cockburn and Marianne Faithfull blared from the speakers. Waitresses delivered huge platters of fries and burgers and the crispiest fish and chips. The Brew Pub was welcoming and nourishing, the opposite of prison. And so that's where I took the girls after we visited prison.

Van had, of course, heard I had married a prisoner. He'd also heard about the transfer. But the first time the girls and I walked in, Van rushed to greet us and shepherded us to a booth where he ordered us a round of free drinks—hot chocolate for the girls, anything I wanted. He looked at the girls with his eyes twinkling and said, "You kids are almost as beautiful as my girl. Your dad's a lucky guy. Dads and their girls have a special bond, don't ya think?" The Brew Pub became one of our havens, another place I couldn't wait to take Will when he was free.

* * *

Not long after the transfer Tim Thomas had called me at home to tell me he had a petition signed by all 500 prisoners. The petition demanded that Bernard and Will be sent back to Maynard. He also had an affidavit from the alleged victim asserting that there were no problems between himself and Will. And he had other affidavits from prisoners who knew the informant—they named him. These stated the informant needed to find a way out of Maynard to avoid those to whom he owed large drug debts. This, clearly, was his inspiration for providing any story Security asked him to provide.

Geoff Jarvis was supposed to be the toughest criminal lawyer in town, and the first time I visited his office to give him the retainer, I told him to pick up the papers at Maynard. It was important, I reminded him, to collect all the pieces of the puzzle. It wasn't just a transfer back to Maynard, Will needed. He needed the accusation that he had been "conspiring to seriously harm another inmate" banished from his file. The implication of potential violence would stick like flypaper, and at every parole would become a reason to deny parole. Thus we had to prove that Joe Book, Doug Killen, Louise Salem, and a few of the other peripheral characters had plotted to dirty his file. The prisoners' petition and affidavits were part of that proof.

First days, then weeks passed, without Geoff's making his way to Maynard. When I called the office, his secretary put me off. When the bills came, they included charges for my calls to his office. I was so frustrated that the day Connie called to say Ginny Ball who was representing Bernard wanted to meet with us, I quickly made the arrangements. We met at a booth in a dive of a diner on the wrong side of town where Ginny promised we wouldn't run into any prison suits. There she promised us she would work with Geoff to get both guys back to Maynard.

I grew up in a household that thrummed with legal arguments and rebuttals, a house steeped in conversations about justice. I'd learned elements required in order to seek an outcome so that that knowledge felt like part of my DNA. Fighting for a just result required thought and reason, compromise, intelligence, diligent hard work, attention to detail. My dad had always pointed out that no matter what, people were going to fight. If they didn't resolve their disagreements in courtrooms or around mediation tables, they would resolve them like gladiators. Dad believed in mediation, argument and compromise, not in fist or gunfights. And because he loved the law and lawyering, I grew up with a deep streak of hopeful faith in the law.

But as time passed, neither Ginny nor Geoff did anything we asked them to do, and as time passed I began to think the criminal lawyers in town cared more about their reputations than they did about their clients. And as time passed and our fight turned into mere mountains of paperwork that sat on Geoff and Ginny's desk, and then, later, on an Ottawa lawyer's desk, I lost all that faith. I wanted to see things the way my dad and brother saw them—both were usually reasonable men. In the fairness with which he approached the world, my dad was almost saint-like. I wanted to be like that.

Throughout my life I watched my parents fight for the underdog. I had long felt confident that in the end sane, intelligent, passionate conversation could sort out complications. In my secret heart I usually sided with lawyers. I heartily and thoroughly despised the way Will had chosen to settle his problem. I abhorred the decision he had made that had harmed so many lives. He had chosen to deal drugs; he had chosen to carry a gun and associate with criminals. He had chosen to be a gladiator in a ring. But in those months as I tried to wage a legal battle, I felt I was fighting phantoms. I came to see that legal recourse wasn't available to those who had ever crossed the line—no matter whether or not that person was paying the price in prison.

And as my faith in legal maneuvers dissolved, and as my connection to my brother and father faded, I started to set aside some truths in order to comfort myself with where I stood. I didn't talk to Will about my disapproval of his past criminal behavior or about my secret wish that he had never chosen to settle fights with force. I didn't complain about the miseries prison caused me. At least he and I could talk to each other. At least he didn't think I was crazy. At least he didn't want to take anything away from me. I didn't complain about my struggles because they seemed so much easier than his. At least I could leave that dreary place. At least if I wasn't in the mood to be in prison, I didn't have to be. At least I could walk in the woods with Kell, under the moonlight. I could eat in restaurants and listen to music and walk on the beach. I thought if he could survive the endless days and nights inside that place, the least I could do was manage without whining about this life outside.

But at *The Whig* life was becoming increasingly unmanageable. Candace had shadowed me for months on *The Bedtime Story*, and now she told my boss, she ought to be promoted to take my position since she was a union member. She let down all pretense of being my sweet right-hand partner. Just as Sarah and Cass had predicted, she was someone not to be trusted. And I sensed that losing at least one of my columns was imminent, so I began to look for other jobs.

And then, just as Van had cheered me up and helped me to forget those who snubbed me, Dan Dalton turned my mood around. Dan was a salesman from the Kansas City-based Universal Press Syndicate. He had come to *The Whig* for one of his regular meetings with our city editor with whom he had become good friends. Both men were outgoing and smart and tough, with a great sense of humor. Usually when Dan came in it was to give a sales pitch about a new column his Syndicate was selling—another *Cathy* or *Doonesbury* or *Garfield*, another *Dear Abby*. But this time Dan was interested in knowing about *The Bedtime Story*, this column that had been making a buzz in Canada. Universal Press was considering picking it up for its worldwide syndication.

To my everlasting gratitude, our city editor's response was to tell Dan that if he was interested, he ought to talk to me, not the publisher. He told Dan the column was my creation, that I had nurtured it from its birth less than a year earlier, that both Jillian Gilliland, the illustrator, and I had been working our tails off to develop it and that we both were wholly dedicated to giving our energy and time and attention to detail in order to make the column sing. So when Dan approached me, I talked to Jillian, and she and I hired a lawyer to protect our interests—just in case *The Whig* decided to try to make a deal for the column without us attached as the creators.

Meanwhile at home Clare came to my door one evening looking forlorn. He told me someone had offered their asking price on the bungalow and confessed they would take less than the asking price from me. They had come to think of me as almost a daughter. They hated to see me lose the place. In a panic, feeling I could not turn to my father for his advice this time (as I had so often in the past on business and legal matters), I made a few rash decisions. In just a few days I had purchased a house—my first—and to fix it up for the impending winter, I called upon my friend Charlie Donevan at the hardware store to help me install a woodstove. After that, during the afternoons after I visited Will and before I sat down to write, I often chopped wood. Sometimes at night when I couldn't sleep because my mind was spinning—with the details of the transfer, the Whig fiasco, and negotiations with Universal—I walked outside and chopped wood until I was exhausted enough to sleep. As I did, I envisioned Will beside me, and whenever I felt sorry

161

for myself, I thought of Molly, of all the work she'd done to raise her kids all alone. And I thought of Kate who never tired and never complained.

But that become one more truth I avoided telling Will. I never told him that I wished on stars about him or that sometimes I couldn't sleep because my mind whirled with everything that might go wrong. I didn't talk to him about how I was managing money. I didn't let him know that his paychecks—which he'd signed over to me—weren't helping much. Inside he earned $100.00 a month. Most months that didn't cover our phone bills and the gas to visit and the girls' bus trips. I was earning a living, and the mortgage I negotiated was reasonable, and his mother had signed over his savings account to me with a couple of thousand dollars I used to pay the fees on the bungalow purchase. But I was afraid to think too far ahead. Blind hope became part of the wishing—that I would cut a deal with Universal Press that would bring in enough money to support us all without worrying whether or not I lost the column or got another job. I convinced myself finding enough extra work—freelance editing, teaching, even modeling for painting classes at the university as I'd done from time to time—wouldn't be a problem, would be enough to cover those lawyers' fees that made increasingly little sense but that I couldn't afford to stop paying.

* * *

In late September there was suddenly a gale, and the sky began to fill with geese flying south for the winter. I could feel winter approaching—the seasons in Ontario are short and sharp. It began to look as if the transfer back to Maynard might not happen before bad weather came, and I felt increasingly uneasy about the idea of fighting not only prison officials but the elements—the long, icy roads and sudden snowstorms.

One day Pat, Dean's new girlfriend, called me. She wasn't precisely a new girlfriend. In fact Dean and Pat had lived together for years before he met me. He had left her for me, and I had heard they reunited when he came back from overseas and found me gone. He had been back only a few weeks, and I hadn't contacted him—and felt guilty for that. But I wasn't surprised to hear he was with Pat. Over the years I had met her a couple of times. I'd felt awkward around her—after all, I had stolen her lover from her, though I learned that only a few months after I had moved in with him. But she was a kind, elegant woman with a mane of beautiful hair and a chiseled, lovely face, and she had always been polite.

Now I pictured that face. "Dean is so depressed over losing you, he can't move," she said. I was quiet, trying to imagine how she had managed to place this phone call. She told me she wanted me to go talk to him, and all I could think about was how selfless she was being. She begged me, and I agreed because she sounded so brokenhearted, and worried. That worried me too.

I drove to the farm and found Dean in his bedroom, curled on the bed in a fetal position. The sight stunned me. Dean was Swedish, born and bred, slightly depressed by nature, but he had never been one for outward expressions of emotion. For all the years I'd known him, he'd seemed in control of everything within his reach. Now there he was, unable to move. Because of me? Pat had told me I was the reason he was so depressed. "I'm so sorry..." I said.

I sat down beside him. I touched his shoulder. "I'm so sorry, Dean. We weren't making sense...we didn't love each other." I hated having hurt him. I hated myself for the cowardly way I had left. I wished I had had the strength or the kindness to break up face-to-face, and sitting there I suddenly saw how cowardly I had been. I felt sick to my stomach and mean. I couldn't explain why except that I had felt trapped. But when I saw him there so unhappy and helpless, I couldn't remember how I could have felt that way.

He turned his face on the pillow and looked at me. He looked at my hand—the one rubbing his arm. He waited a moment. Then he brushed my hand away, sat up, and the tears were gone. "It's okay," he said. That quickly he appeared recovered, wholly himself. "I'm fine. Glad you came over, but I'm fine." He studied me. I'm sure he was noticing how pale I was, how dark the circles under my eyes. "How about you? You okay?" he asked.

It was my turn to cry, and the moment I began, we were in familiar territory—Amy falling apart, Dean able to tell me what to do, how to do it and why. He began to talk about the plans he had had for us. He agreed, our life together had been unhappy, and he had hoped I would move into my own place. But he had wanted me close. He had thought we might remain a couple. He'd even had a notion we might have a child together. He'd envisioned a nanny coming along as he and I continued to travel the world.

I stared at him. "That wasn't what I wanted."

"I see that now. You wanted something more conventional."

I burst out laughing. "Conventional?"

"You know what I mean. He knew about my marriage to Will. He asked for details. How we had met. When. Everything. I told him the story, and when I got to the transfer, he immediately understood. He knew war zones. He knew how enemy territory worked, how conflicts went awry. Once again he would become my mentor, a father figure and savior. He could use his position to help, he said, as he asked question after question, ferreting out the names, dates, places, times—all the elements of the story no one else ever wanted to hear.

When I got to the part about Regional Headquarters conducting their investigation, he told me to follow him into his study. He sat at his desk, scribbled a few notes and told me his plan. He was going to write a letter to Andrew McCabe, the Regional Commissioner, the man at the top of the chain in Ontario, the man who now had Will's fate in his hands. He needed the files, he told me. He would study everything about the case. He was confident he knew just the kind of letter that was needed. That's the letter he would write.

"I'm sorry we couldn't work things out between us, but since you love this guy, I'll help," he said, and just a few days after I delivered the material to him, he called and asked me to meet him again, this time in his office at the university. There he gave me the letter to Andrew McCabe he had composed. It was short and brilliant. His life's work had been devoted to studying the twists and turns of conflicting versions of stories, he told McCabe. In his research for more than 20 books, many of them award winners, he had learned how to read documents to find the truth in them. Even a quick read of the papers involved in this case made it clear that a severe injustice had been done to Will.

He handed me the letter, kissed my forehead and told me to take care, to stay in touch. I couldn't wait to show it to Will that letter. And when I did he shook his head. "Your ex wrote this?" His face registered shock. "What a guy. He must have really loved you." But he wasn't envious. He was grateful, and, I think, a little proud for having won me away.

When I later heard that Dean and Pat were enjoying life together, I was glad. Later still, I heard from girlfriends he had had in several ports around the world during all those years he and I lived together, and I understood we had never been the kind of partnership I wanted. And I stopped feeling guilty and felt, only, gratitude for his friendship.

chapter twenty-six

Whenever I drove down Willowbank Road, I wondered at all my neighbors who seemed to live such ordinary lives. I half-envied them. Only years later did I learn how little appearances ever mean—that the retired police officer and his wife had a son serving time for murder; that numerous marriages in the neighborhood were dissolving; that people were dying. But back then I was obsessed by my own troubles, and everyone around looked as sturdy as their houses and their cedar docks.

I had elements of peace and pure pleasure, of course. One of those was Kell. Someone had told me that the dogs we're meant to live with come to us to teach us what we need to learn, and Kell came to teach me devotion. She usually rode with me to Middle Harbor, and while I visited, she waited in the car. No matter how long the wait, no matter the weather, after visits I found her curled up asleep on the backseat, the wind blowing through her hair, or standing eagerly at the window, panting happily as I jogged towards her. She was never nervous or upset or angry with me. Rather, she nuzzled me.

At home I never tied her up, and I learned that she sometimes strolled down the road when I began to meet the neighbors who told me how much they liked Kell's visits to their houses. Our first friend on the block was Nesta and Clare's daughter, Diane. She and her daughters, Erin and Kate, didn't live there, but they often came around. Freckled redheads with wonderful laughs, they called themselves the Flames. Erin was one year younger than Sarah, Kate one year younger than Cass. The four got along beautifully. One of Diane's sisters was married to a prison guard. Diane was certain he was the type who beat up prisoners in their cells, lied to investigators, and set up inmates. Her sympathies leaned towards prisoners, and when eight-year-old Katie asked if Will was ever lonely, Diane decided to add their names to the visiting list and come meet him.

Will was game to meet my friends, particularly those his daughters liked as much as they liked the Flames. The first time they visited, Cass and Sarah sat on either side of Will, sidling close as if they needed to protect him. They need not have worried. The Flames and Will quickly got along, and throughout our marriage, they were our greatest supporters. One day fifteen years after that first visit, I wrote to Katie to ask her what she remembered of visiting prison. By then she was finishing college and still the bold, outgoing young woman I loved back then. She wrote back immediately, apologizing in advance because she thought I probably wanted to hear a sad story. But the story she remembered wasn't sad. Rather, she recalled talking with Will when he began to tap his knuckles on the table. When Katie had asked what he was doing, he put a finger his lips and whispered, "That's where they put the mics. I'm driving them crazy."

"Will always made me laugh," Katie wrote. "And because of that visiting prison felt fun. That's what I remember."

After their visit to Middle Harbor, I loved him more—for being kind to my friends, for enduring the trek through raucous ranges and the strip searches to sit and talk to my friends. I felt grateful to him for helping them to feel good about my having married him. When other friends met him, they stopped worrying for my safety and my mental health and started cheering us on. A few weeks after he had charmed the Flames, he also charmed Harriet, my new editor at Universal Press Syndicate who wanted to meet him. He charmed my friend Anndale who loved the girls and wanted to know their father. And Kate and he had liked each other from the start. The only ones left to charm were my parents, except even when they learned we had married, they were not ready to consider a visit.

* * *

Months were passing with no word from Regional Headquarters. One of the only things keeping me from exploding with frustration was anticipation of our second trailer visit. For this one we had invited the kids. Willie decided to stay home and keep his mother company now that the girls were abandoning her, as he put it. But the girls couldn't wait. The Flames agreed to look after Kell and the house and the cats and to check my answering machine and mail in case anything vital came in from *The Whig* or from Universal. And so this time, with Diane's support the visit felt less freighted with the strangeness and anxiety of the first.

The girls and I arrived on cool October morning and laid out our suitcases for inspection. We stood silent as guards rifled through our toiletries and underwear. Although the girls seemed accustomed to this intrusion, when one of the male guards lifted my underwear into the air, I flushed with anger. But I was learning to keep quiet because the quieter I was, the more quickly these searches ended. After they cleared us one of the guards led us into the trailer that reeked of Lysol.

Less nervous this time, I closely watched all the procedures. Per protocol our escort opened a kitchen drawer, removed all the knives and counted them, a ritual I never understood except as a way of trying to make us feel like fools for letting ourselves be locked behind doors with a prisoner. After the knives, the guard pointed to the panic button on the wall. "In case there's any trouble," he said. Once we were settled inside, another guard escorted Will from the range. Even now if I close my eyes I can see him walking into the trailer wearing a rare smile that made him look so beautiful my whole body trembled. His smile changed everything about him—his eyes grew light, his body relaxed. Even his muscles seemed to soften, and he laughed more heartily. Life outside of the range turned him into the man I imagined he would become when he was free.

And as we unpacked groceries the guards had delivered before our arrival—groceries paid for by Will's money—I inhaled the smell of apples and leeks. We spared little expense for these visits—they were our luxury. Will had invented a pasta sauce he made with tuna fish and mountains of fresh tomatoes and a secret ingredient he refused to reveal. I no longer remember if his sauce tasted great or if its deliciousness was simply from the pleasure of our being together. I do remember how happy he looked as he prepared it. In the trailers I felt as if I had been holding my breath for months and here I could breathe.

Almost immediately after unpacking, while I made the beds with sheets from home, he cleared the counters, shooed us from the kitchen and went diligently to work making his sauce. We always bought chocolate because the girls and Will were chocoholics. On that first visit together, someone sneaked half of a giant chocolate bar when no one was looking. Whoever had done it never confessed. For years "who stole the chocolate bar?" was a favorite family game, and who we selected depended upon who we wanted to tease that day. There were other stories we told again and again, like the one about the trailer visit in July for which we ordered a dozen ears of corn. In summertime, outside, in the real world, corn was so abundant farmers couldn't give it away. But the prison had charged us $15.00 for a dozen ears. Determined to address every outrage, I actually filed a grievance about the corn, but as always prison officials themselves overruled our complaint. As always I took it up a notch, to Regional Headquarters, and as we could have predicted, Regional concurred with the Institution's decision. So I grieved the cost of those twelve ears of corn all the way to National Headquarters. The final verdict wasn't returned until November, and someone at NHQ concluded that it was reasonable for twelve ears of corn to cost $15.00 in late fall. All these years later I can laugh about it, but back then I did not. Back then their ludicrous response was only more proof that the System was out to get us any way it could.

The second day of the visit with the girls we woke to a knock on the door and the girls bursting into the room, pillow marks still carved into their tender faces. "Breakfast in bed!" they giggled. They presented a tray of steaming food with eggs undercooked, bacon burned, toast soggy. But everything tasted perfect. I wanted only these people in my life, and I wanted them in it forever.

That afternoon as we were playing Hearts, I turned on the radio and on CBC, there was, by sheer luck, an interview with Claire Culhane. Claire was a renowned prisoners' rights activist, a woman who had fought for others' rights her whole life. I'd read about her. I'd heard stories. I knew that she was born in Montreal in 1918, the daughter of Russian immigrants. When she originally tried to train as a nurse, she was denied because she was Jewish, but she fought that obstruction and became a nurse. During the Spanish Civil War Claire worked for the anti-fascist movement, and throughout the 1940s and '50s, she worked on labor issues. In the '60s she fought for abortion rights and against nuclear testing. She spent six months in Vietnam as a nurse in a tuberculosis hospital which led to her leading the Canadian protest against the War in Vietnam.

As I listened to her on the radio, I fell in love. "If you believe in something," Claire told the interviewer, "you live that lifestyle." Claire's prison work began in 1974 when she volunteered to teach women's studies classes in a Correctional Center for women. On June 9, 1975 three prisoners at BC PEN who were about to be returned to solitary confinement took 15 hostages. A standoff with prison officials lasted for 41 hours. In the end the Emergency Response Team stormed the hostage takers. In the process they shot and killed Mary Steinhauser, a correctional officer who had gained prisoners' respect by implementing courses for prisoners in Solitary Confinement. Claire joined in the demonstrations outside in support of the prisoners who were staging sit-ins and work strikes over conditions inside. Then, along with a group of Vancouver area activists, she set up the Prisoners' Rights Group (PRG) whose aim was to help prisoners help themselves—especially in finding competent lawyers, filing grievances, qualifying for hearings, access to health care, educating the public. And involuntary transfers.

I left the card game to listen to Claire talk about the abuse of power wielded in involuntary transfers. I had to meet her. She had been through it all. During that BC riot she spent 80 hours locked in with the inmate committee, fearing that if volunteers left the prison, military and police stationed outside would move in and take it by force. They finally did. Her book *Barred from Prison: A Personal Account*, told the story of those efforts and of her having been barred from all but two federal prisons in BC and all prisons in the provincial system allegedly "for the best interests of the Institution." This had only strengthened her conviction that prisons were built not only to keep prisoners inside but to keep the public out.

Claire was an ally of the most valuable kind—she not only campaigned for individual prisoners' rights, but she understood the system. As she said that day on the radio, to challenge the prison system was to challenge all of society. The PRG letterhead read: "We can't change prisons without changing society, we know that this is a long and dangerous struggle. But the more who are involved in it, the less dangerous, and the more possible it will be." In *No Longer Barred from Prison* she wrote, "We can only proceed, individually and collectively, to make whatever improvements are possible in our respective areas of concern, sustained by the hope that others are doing the same."

There it was. Claire was my hope that someone else saw things inside prison the way I was beginning to see them.

The trouble was, Claire lived in Vancouver. She was touring the country, going from prison to prison to meet with individuals as she so often did. She had fought for and won the right to visit any prisoner in any prison in Canada, to hear individuals' stories and see for herself what was going on in every corner of every joint everywhere—whereas everyone else visiting a prisoner was not permitted to visit any other prisoner unless he or she was a blood relative. Claire wanted prisoners to know they weren't forgotten. She was leaving Kingston the next day for Montreal, and I so longed to meet and talk with her, for the first time I felt like an actual prisoner because I couldn't go out to meet her unless I was willing to end our visit short. I couldn't do that.

I listened as she told the story of how she had, at age 60, hitchhiked from Vancouver to Dorchester Penitentiary in New Brunswick to a riot in progress. Her courage and passion captivated me. I closed my eyes, thrilled at the idea that there was someone out there who understood this system the way she did, someone did not sit around twiddling her thumbs and wondering how she might help but who actually walked inside and asked questions and demanded answers. Hearing her voice quelled my anxiety and some of the loneliness I hadn't even been aware I felt. Kate and Diane were champions, but Claire was a champion who knew prisons inside and out.

Will and I had talked about Solicitor General Doug Lewis's quote in The *Vancouver Sun* about the public's "being fed up about offenders who can't be rehabilitated." There a move afoot to consider using the Mental Health Act as a means of keeping prisoners behind bars after their sentences ended. Claire was right on top of this, explaining that the public had to realize that such measures are historically first practiced against prisoners and then against non-prisoners. Both Stalin and Hitler secretly dispatched dissidents to psychiatric wards in lieu of offering open trials. Only an immediate public outcry against such covert methods could protect ordinary citizens.

But whenever I talked about the horrors of these ideas, I knew I verged on sounding hysterical, so I listened closely to Claire who sounded firm and calm. She never raised her voice. She never cursed. She never lost her dignity. She talked about the fact that lawyers frequently were not helpful to prisoners. She sought not wins in court but semi-reasonable deals she could strike with "the devil" as she dubbed government and Service officials. Her goal was to avoid harassment of prisoners while enabling bureaucrats to save face. Day after day, night after night, Claire wrote letters on behalf of prisoners, imploring officials to take a second look at this story, another scan of that one, to give one more thought for one more option. She sat at her Olympia typewriter pounding out letters on behalf of thousands of men and women all over the world.

When the interview ended, I sat down and wrote Claire a letter about Will's transfer. The moment we left the trailer, I mailed it to the PRG address in Vancouver. Within days Claire wrote to say she would be glad to help. She instructed me on a few things to do and via faxed letters and finally phone calls we worked together to find a way to approach Regional Headquarters.

And I began to learn. One of Claire's mantras was, "They can take everything away from you but don't let them take away your dignity." I began to keep temper tantrums at bay. I stopped crying. I began to understand that no matter how frustrated and unhappy and angry I felt, when I visited prison, when I talked to officials, when I was in public, I had to hold my head high. I had to look as if I could handle anything. If I didn't, they would take me down.

Eventually Claire and I wrote to each other almost daily—not only about Will's case but about the cases of so many others. Most nights I woke in the middle of the night to see a trail of paper spread across my study floor. Her faxes inspired me to pull myself out of bed even when I was most depleted. Even years later whenever I tried to tell the story, it was the memory of Claire that pushed me to stay with it. It was Claire who taught me that the smallest truth can dismantle a thousand lies.

From the first time we talked, whenever anyone told me I was mad, I heard Claire's voice. "Who the hell cares what anyone thinks?"

chapter twenty-seven

When I first set out to find a job in case *The Whig* let me go, I tried the local college where I had worked for years. They weren't interested in hiring me back—whether because of my marriage or not, I never knew, though by then of course I suspected. By chance I learned that someone was starting an independent adult school and looking to expand her course offerings, so I sent her my résumé, interviewed, and was hired to teach a memoir writing class to begin in late October.

A week before class was to start, the director called to ask if I would meet a prospective student. Professor Colin Miles wanted to know how I was going to run the class and wanted to talk, and I could not afford to say no. So the next afternoon I drove into the outskirts of Kingston to a hastily constructed boxy structure where the school director led me into an office where Dr. Miles awaited me. In his early 60s, he wore corduroys a little too long, eyeglasses a tad foggy, and had shaggy hair that needed a trim. He smelled like good cigars and whiskey. The minute he began to talk, I liked him. He'd been raised in Northern England, grandson of a shepherd. For few minutes we happily talked sheep. He had received an Oxford education and a Ph.D. in psychology from Cambridge, and now he was semi-retired and wanted to write about his childhood.

I'd always gotten along well with psychologists. Like writers, most are curious about human nature, and they were a breed I knew well. I had lived through college and for years after in Manhattan where nearly everyone I knew either worked as a therapist or saw one. Also, Miles was British, and for the past few years I'd been surrounded by Dean's Irish and British friends whom I also liked tremendously for their intellectual, bemused view of the world, characteristics Miles shared. "You're probably in the habit of using passive voice since you're an academic," I said. He laughed easily and said, "Impossible habit to break."

"Not impossible."

He smiled. "I think your class might be just what the doctor ordered."

I asked if he had been in private practice. He laughed and said, "No, no, in fact for 30-odd years I worked for Correctional Services Canada. In the prisons."

I can't remember how or what I told him then. I may simply have accused him outright of being a plant. Whatever I said to him, I was certain I had been set up, that Correctional Services had sent him here to catch me at something, or to psychoanalyze me. I thought maybe he was here to infiltrate my class so he could find out more about me—and Will. I wondered if he had been sent to ruin other peoples' lives before ours, if the Service paid him well for prying into innocents' lives.

I do remember saying goodbye and walking away, across the parking lot. The air was cold, and my heart was thudding so hard I could hear blood in my ears. I climbed into my car, and Colin "call-me-Bill" Miles came to my door and leaned into my window. He looked at me with earnest brown eyes and said, in a voice thick with compassion, "Andrew McCabe is a good friend. If you like I could speak to him about this transfer. Perhaps that will help. I promise, Amy, I shall try."

I nodded and sped out of the lot. I didn't trust "Bill" Miles for one second. The coincidence was too coincidental. Andrew McCabe could change the course of this story with one signature, but I didn't believe Miles would talk to him on our behalf. I was sure if he said anything it would harm us. I knew I couldn't avoid him altogether. He was going to be taking the class—we had settled that. So I silently vowed to keep my dignity, and to be careful of what I said.

* * *

When Sarah and Cass were older, they both told me, separately, that when they thought about their childhood they thought of waking in my house at dawn to the sound of machine-gun like typing. The walls were thin, and I sat in my room writing columns and letters to Claire and letters and petitions and affidavits. I wrote at least half a dozen letters to reporters at the *Toronto Globe and Mail* who were writing columns on the prisons. I wrote several letters to the reporter at the *Toronto Star* who often wrote about justice issues. I wrote to Charlie Greenwell of CJOH Television in Ottawa and to investigative reporter Victor Mallorek of Toronto's *Fifth Estate* and to Dale Goldhawk of CTV because each of them had done stories about prison. None of those reporters ever wrote back or acknowledged my letters.

I was losing hope of Will's evergetting out of Middle Harbor. The longer he remained a "high security risk," the less likely he would be paroled in three years. In November when I read an article in the *London Observer* called *Lifers: When They Throw Away the Key* (November 19, 1992 by David Rose), I culled as many facts from the story as I could and sent off one more missive to all those journalists, hoping they would consider writing about these issues I could no longer write about.

"May I draw your attention to a few key points about emergency involuntary transfers," I began. I enclosed paragraphs from Rose's piece about the aspect of the justice system that runs without courts or tribunals or lawyers, where decisions made are made in secret. By that time everything that might give prisoners a voice was melting away. Kingston had planned to host a Lifer's Conference early the next year, but one night Arsenio Hall opened his late-night network talk show using the conference as a punch line in his monologue, and the next day the conference made headlines in *The Toronto Star*: *Killers Conference in Kingston*. It was promptly canceled.

"You have to learn to expect this nonsense," Claire said when I complained. But I couldn't accept it, so I wrote more letters to more journalists about that. It had been four months since Will and I had begun going through the motions the system required for and I was still spending thousands of dollars—all of Will's savings, some of his mother's money, much of mine—on lawyers, still compiling hundreds of pages of documentation. By December I knew I was only spinning my wheels.

At Christmas I traveled to Molly's to celebrate with the rest of the family, and as I sat amidst the decorations and tree and gifts, I felt lonelier than ever. I sat in a corner brooding about being forbidden to give Will a gift, about visits not being allowed on Christmas Day. When I looked across the living room at Emma sitting in her boyfriend,

Keith's, lap, I was envious, an emotion I'd often felt when I was younger. Back then I'd felt it towards my own parents. Whenever I tried to speak to my mother about it, she scolded me for feeling such an emotion. "You have everything in the world to be grateful for. Don't envy people. It's a terrible thing," she'd say. And here I was feeling what I wasn't supposed to feel towards Emma and her new big-hearted boyfriend. I envied their being together; I envied them the trip they had just taken to visit Will's oldest sister, Gina, in Los Angeles. I felt triply bad—not only was I alone; not only was I envious; I was a bad person for feeling envy.

But envy is a hamster wheel. The moment I was on it, I couldn't stop. The harder I tried to climb off, the faster the wheel spun. By Christmas afternoon all I could think about was how much I envied these sisters who could travel and exchange gifts and sleep with their men, who could buy expensive baubles like the '60s-era Mercedes Keith and Emma had just bought in LA.

Ever the pragmatist, Molly shook her head. "Why buy something you won't drive?" she asked them when they explained it was parked in their drive under a tarp.

"Mom, it's a good investment," Emma said. Keith squeezed her and turned to me. "So Amy, how's Will doing."

The room became quiet. Everyone turned to face me. I stopped running on the hamster wheel long enough to recognize Keith's kindness. Nora began to shoo her little girls out of the room—they were considered too young to know precisely why their Uncle Will was never at these family gatherings. I never was sure what their parents told them to account for his absence since Mandy was 10 and Melissa was 8, and Mandy at least remembered her uncle. They both understood I was his wife. Only Alice was too young ever to have met him.

"He's okay," I said. "I'm sure he'd love to meet you, Keith." Maybe it was envy that prompted me to throw that invitation out like a gauntlet.

"We should go," Keith said. "To hell with how they treat us. He's family..."

"Maybe..." Emma pursed her lips. I could tell by her nervous giggle that the idea made her uneasy. She was a strong-minded and well-respected doctor, and she didn't like to admit how hard it was for her to endure a visit to prison. But Emma had champagne taste—not unlike her brother's. Her home was as immaculate and beautiful as prison was unkempt and ugly.

"I'm going this week," Gina said. "It's not right not to visit him."

When I invited Gina to stay with me in the bungalow, Molly beamed. She wanted her family together. And with her happiness, some of my misery began to ease. When Nora's husband, Sean returned from ice skating at the local rink with their oldest daughter, Jennifer, I felt better still. Jennifer was one year older than Sarah and adored her Uncle Will. For that especially I loved her. And I enjoyed the younger girls who were always bursting with energy. I liked being in Nora and Sean's house that reminded me of my own childhood home, an explosion of skis and skates, sketchbooks and puzzles and books. After our feast, the girls led me two blocks down to the sledding hill, and for hours we sledded in the bright Christmas Day snow, and for just a little while I forgot about how sad I was. Instead of envy, I felt the way my parents had taught me I ought to feel—lucky.

* * *

The day after Boxing Day Gina drove with me to our home. The next morning before our visit with her brother, she spent an hour in the bathroom preening. When she stepped out she looked glamorous—too glamorous for prison. Her bleached blond hair was tousled and sprayed into an extravagant "do," and her face was perfectly made up. She wore high heels, a low-cut sweater, form fitting slacks. I thought telling her this wasn't the way to dress for prison, but I didn't know her well enough to criticize. And when Will walked into the visiting room and saw her, he grinned and said, "Wow, what a babe," and I saw he was not only unembarrassed, he was impressed. He was proud. I felt a shiver of worry about us creep under my skin for the first time. But as always at the first sign of any kind of trouble between us, I batted my concerns away.

Throughout the visit, the feeling nagged at me. I was dressed nicely as I always was at visits—I usually wore a skirt or slacks, a nice blouse, good shoes. But at heart I had always been a jeans, tee-shirt and tennis shoe kind of girl. I wore my hair short enough to towel and finger dry—I had no time for hair dryers or sprays. I wore no makeup beyond the occasional lipstick. I thought of myself as beautiful the way athletes are, but never glamorous like Gina was. I was battling a few extra pounds— a not unfamiliar struggle—and although muscular and fit, I wasn't long and slender like Gina, and my nails weren't manicured like hers. Until that winter I had never colored my hair, though it was turning gray, as if overnight. Just a month before I colored it for the first time to keep it blond—like it had always been, like Will thought his own hair still was.

But I wasn't interested in talking about looks. I wanted to tell Will about my latest efforts on his behalf. I had concocted a plan to visit Tim MacDowall at Clarendon, the minimum security prison where he had moved and where the alleged rape victim from Maynard turned up. I'd employed Claire's help to compose a strong argument to Regional Headquarters asking for permission to visit Tim. He had no family, and he was a friend who needed help. Naturally I omitted the real purpose of my desire to visit. The truth was I wanted to talk to the man who Will and I both saw as the turning point in the story of his transfer out of Maynard. He had already confessed to Tim that there had never been a rape. I planned to tape a confession from him that our lawyers could use as further evidence that Louise Salem and Joe Book of Security had had reason to discredit Will—and me.

I felt brave about my plan. I believed this was the kind of thing women like Gina, no matter how glamorous, would never do. I hoped the lengths I was willing to go to help my husband reach parole would impress him, and that he would find me still more lovable. I told him what I could about the plan, using the prison slang I was picking up so that we wouldn't risk being understood. And then we chatted about nothing much. When Gina and I stood up to leave, they hugged tightly. When he smiled over his shoulder at me, I saw that his eyes looked bright, and that niggling insecurity returned as I wondered if his happiness was a result of Gina's visit or my plan. I would never know because I wouldn't ask.

Gina and I walked back through the gates and mazes, across the cold, windy lot to the waiting car with its frosted windshield. Two days later, after she had left for L.A., I received my approval to visit Tim at Clarendon. It felt like a major victory—only Claire received such permissions. I invited Cass to join me because from the start she had amazed me—this girl with the angelic face and deep concentration had an extraordinary ability to maneuver worlds that frightened so many. And like me, Cass loved the intrigue of adventure. She readily agreed to come along.

At Clarendon inmates were permitted to come and go—not exactly as they pleased but since minimum security was the first road leading to release, the first chance for inmates to prove themselves, restrictions on both inmates and their visitors were far fewer. Cass and I parked across the road—far from the cameras that hovered above the lot. And there Cass helped me strap the tiny recorder to my arm, covered by a sweater sleeve.

"Okay, let's go," she said. We drove across the street and into the lot and walked inside. There were no security checkpoints to cross, so we simply walked into a big, sunny visiting room with clean tables and comfortable chairs. We smiled at each other. "It'll be good when Dad's here," Cass said. I couldn't have agreed more. This room was the Ritz compared to Middle Harbor's visiting room.

We chose a table for four. Cass sat across from me. When Tim arrived, he took a chair beside me. The fourth chair, still empty, was where Pierson would sit. "He'll be here," Tim whispered. "I told him he better get here."

If I had been paying closer attention, I would have noticed Tim's heavy-lidded eyes. I'd have realized he was still using heroin, turning his mind and body leaden. But I wasn't paying attention to Tim—I was distracted by our mission. Cass looked up and tapped my arm, and I turned and saw a minor commotion—one inmate pushing another towards the stairs. She raised her eyebrows and whispered, "Bet that's him." Her knowledge of prison was like ancient knowledge.

Tim nodded, yes. And then Pierson was there, sitting across the table from me. I sneaked a hand under my sweater and pressed the recorder to "on."

"This is Dryden's wife," Tim said, sounding tough. "And she has a few questions for you." Pierson looked younger than I had imagined him, scrawny and pimply, like a terrified kid in the principal's office. For a moment I felt sympathetic, but I steeled myself. It was, after all, partially his fault that Will was in Middle Harbor. I needed him to tell me everything.

He shook his head and whispered, "It didn't happen."

"Louder," Tim said gruffly. "Talk so she can hear," he leaned towards Pierson and cast him an angry look.

"Nothing happened," he repeated. "I wasn't raped. I made it up. When I got to the hospital, there were prison officials and RCMP officers. They told me I had to stick to my story. That's all. I had to keep saying it happened or they were going to move me back to Maynard. But I couldn't be there. … They'd kill me there…" He shifted as if about to stand, but before he could move, two inmates I hadn't noticed appeared at his side. Putting hands to shoulder, they pressed him back in place.

He looked to his right, his left, eyes skittering everywhere.

"So Will was right that you were never raped?" I asked.

He nodded. Tim snarled, "Talk."

"He was right," Pierson muttered. "I made the whole thing up because—well…" he looked at Cass and squirmed. "Because I hurt myself."

Tim shifted forward. He was nose to nose with Pierson. "This is his daughter. You think she likes going to Middle Harbor to visit her dad? You think they like seeing the man they love locked up for some shit like you?"

Pierson looked at the table. "No. I shouldn't have lied."

"Okay," I said. I could hear the whir of the recorder. I couldn't believe Pierson couldn't. "It's okay," I said. I stood. I couldn't bear another minute of this.

Back home Cass and I listened to the tape. She beamed. We had caught every word. "You have proof that Dad was right," she said. "Now you can give it to the lawyers and maybe they'll do something."

"And if they won't, I can give it to the press," I said.

The next morning, first thing, Tim called from Clarendon. "Pierson's gone. No one knows where he went."

I understood at once. Someone had seen me talking to him. Of course they had. The lack of security at the entryway didn't mean we weren't being watched. And without Pierson to testify or talk to a reporter, I had nothing but a lousy little tape recording of someone saying, "I wasn't raped." For the next seven years that tape sat useless in my drawer, amidst the mountains of paper.

part two

chapter twenty-eight

Five months after Will's transfer, on January 24, 1993, Claire sent me a letter that I read and re-read the way I did all her letters. But I'd forgotten it, and only years later did I re-read it and realize that although I believed I was listening to the wisdom of others, she was offering me lessons not only in political maneuvering but in how to love a man in prison, lessons I wasn't taking in.

She wrote:

…No one understands the Yiddishe Mama syndrome better than I do. But believe me, the best way you can help Will, before and especially after he comes out, is to let him stand on his own feet and find a way of supporting you and the kids, not how hard you can work to support him (and others). Shell out all the TLC you can, but know where to draw the line so he doesn't feel "smothered"—the going word when guys rear up and bolt after years and years of faithful V&Cing. Please forgive if I'm over-stepping…

But Claire wasn't over-stepping. I should have been drawing the line. Instead I was putting everything I had into this fight for Will.

It wasn't just Claire I didn't listen to. The more I got to know Bill Miles, the more I liked him. After a few weeks of working with him in class, I understood he hadn't been a plant of any kind. There was still such a thing as sheer coincidence. It was coincidence that he had signed up to take a class from me at the same time I was whirling in the paranoia prison creates. Among the many things Bill taught me in what turned into a deep friendship, was that Correctional Services was frequently in the wrong, but much of the wrongdoing didn't originate with malice. Problems often arose because of staff incompetence or laziness, stupidity and carelessness. C.O.s who didn't complete paperwork weren't necessarily plotting to destroy a life; wardens who abided by foolish rules weren't always power mad. Bill cautioned me that my believing that people in the Service could set up something as elegant as a trap that relied on a retired psychologist taking a memoir class bordered on a kind of madness. According to Bill they weren't capable of such complexity. He wanted to help me—I came to see that he did. And he also wanted me to help myself.

"Focus on your work, Amy. You're a terrific writer and teacher. Don't forget that." But in my zeal to get Will out of Middle Harbor, heading towards this dream of the love of a lifetime, I lost sight of other ideals and dreams—like my dream to write good books and to teach and to try to make some kind of difference in a world larger than my world at home. Nothing Bill or Claire or Kate said shook me out of the thrall I was in. And things happened that thrust me right back into the whirl of my belief that I needed every ounce of energy to protect us.

One day the Board of Directors of Revelations House sent me a fax to let me know they had held a meeting they hadn't bothered to inform me they were going to have. At that meeting they had taken a vote. They had made a decision that I no longer was fit to serve on their Board. The Director of the home, Alan Park, was the only one who objected. He argued that my growing knowledge about prison was precisely the kind of knowledge the Board required. But Ginny Ball and the three other members called my marriage to Will a conflict of interest. They thanked me for my years of Service but let me know in no uncertain terms I was no longer a member of their Board.

Just a few days after that ouster, I was again called into the office at *The Whig*. This time the publisher let me know that he was canceling my column, Hard Lines. Negotiations for *The Bedtime Story* were continuing. For now that column would remain, he said. But as for *Hard Lines*, the column that I had been writing for more than eight years, the column that had run my stories on everything from lambing to the IRA, the column that had inspired my first visit to prison—that one was finished. He wanted me to finish up—two columns in January, two in February, two more in March, and that was it. "Nothing personal," he said without looking me in the eye. "It's a cost-saving measure. We've had to make some hard decisions. You won't be alone."

I don't remember how I took the news. By then I was half-inured to rejection. I didn't argue. There wasn't room. He was simply delivering the news, and then it was time for me to leave the room. Ultimately I wasn't alone. Over the next several months, the weekend magazine where my column appeared was sliced in half. Other writers and editors and auxiliary staff on the paper lost their jobs—though I was among the first to go.

I became wary of almost everyone, though I did also carefully seek out allies. One day on the radio I heard an interview with Graham Stewart, Director of Kingston's John Howard Society. I was so impressed by his sanity and calm and his knowledge of prison, I read up on the organization and learned that in 1929 a citizens' group led by Toronto's Chief of Police, General Draper, reactivated a group that had been dedicated to supporting prisoners' spiritual growth. They called themselves "The Citizens' Service Association." But it wasn't just spiritual support this group offered. Draper understood that prisoners on release faced terrible pressures. Those pressures undermined police work. His organization of volunteers set itself the task of providing ex-prisoners with practical help in finding housing, clothing and employment and became a model for the John Howard Society.

The stated mission of the JHS was to provide "safe, effective and humane responses to the causes and consequences of crime." I drove to their offices in Kingston and asked for Graham Stewart who welcomed me into his office. I saw at once that this tall, even-tempered, soft-voiced Scot was just as angry and passionate about the insane responses to criminals as Claire was, though he had a cooler manner.

As soon as I told him our story, he smiled and asked, "What sort of hoops are they putting you through? And what can I do?"

I hadn't realized how close to tears I was, but I started to cry and couldn't stop. Outside his office I could hear the buzz of activity—ex-inmates answering phones, typing, Xeroxing, meeting with others who had come to them in need. Through the floorboards, from downstairs where they ran a carpentry shop, I could smell the scent of pine and oak and hear the sound of saws. I tried to stop my tears by imagining that inmate-run shop as a place Will might one day work.

Graham didn't flinch. "It's that bad," he said. It wasn't a question.

I went on crying, but Graham placed his hand over mine and said, "I know, I know." I knew that he did. And I felt less alone.

Just a week or two after that, nudged by the combination of Bill Miles' personal inquiries and Claire's relentless letters and Graham Stewart's phone calls and Dean's letter, Andrew McCabe, the Deputy Commissioner of Regional Headquarters agreed to meet with me.

Graham and Bill and Claire agreed this was an excellent sign that things were moving in the right direction, but on the frigid February day I went to see Will to tell him about McCabe's secretary's phone call, he didn't smile or express any pleasure. He only nodded half-heartedly. "Yeah, yeah," he said.

I tried to explain to him that this was a big deal. McCabe didn't meet with prisoners or their wives. This had to mean he was going to overturn the transfer. But no matter how cheerful I tried to sound, Will refused to believe there was any hope. Over the past couple of months, with no movement in the case, the tenor of our visits had drifted from plea-sure and excitement to disappointment and frustration. I was becoming less the beloved wife and more the possibly deluded cheerleader. But I couldn't let myself see that. Instead I told myself again and again and again that once Middle Harbor was in our rearview mirror, everything would be as it had been. Our visits would be lovely and loving. And our future on the outside would be better still.

* * *

Walking down the polished hallway towards Andrew McCabe's office, I felt my old confidence returning. I felt like the old me—invited to important, high class places, dressed up and prepared to convince, argue, persuade. I was surprised to find McCabe's office as enormous as it was, spanning 50 yards—half a football field—with floor to ceiling windows overlooking Lake Ontario with its layer of ice. At the other end sat a circle of plush sofas and chairs beside windows that looked out on a sweeping lawn. The wood floors were scattered with beautiful rugs, and his desk gleamed with polish.

Andrew McCabe looked to be in his mid-40s, and he looked like he belonged in this place—reddish hair beautifully coiffed, expensive suit, his slender frame trainer-fit. "Come in, please," he said. "Over here." He guided me towards the hard-backed chairs.

I noticed on the window shelf a tape recorder, its wheels grinding. I was surprised to see that he wasn't trying to hide it. That fact buoyed me. The head honcho of this huge province and all its prisons, this man who dwelled by day in this posh office and by night in a near-castle outside of town, was nervous. I saw it in his eyes. He couldn't look at me.

I already knew that most everyone who worked in this system was paranoid. I understood they had to be because in some ways nearly everyone was out to get someone. I was out to have Will moved back to Maynard, yes. And I believed I only wanted justice—Will returned to Maynard, his security lowered, all traces of the lies in his record expunged. But the truth was, the truth I didn't let myself acknowledge for years, was that I also wanted revenge. I wanted Rick LaFlamme punished for his lies to to my boss. I wanted Louise Salem and Joe Book and Doug Killen demoted. I wanted Will returned to Maynard in a limo, with streamers proclaiming his innocence.

Most of all I wanted my parents and my friends and the Board of Directors and my newspaper colleagues and the editors of *Frank Magazine* and my brother and sisters to understand that Will's transfer had been based on one whopping lie designed to cover up another lie. I wanted everyone to know every detail of the last six months of our lives—that the kids had been refused a visit, that the wardens and security officers and the deputy wardens had lied to us, that no one at the paper ever asked one real question about Will, that I wasn't the only paranoid.

Naturally McCabe offered no limos or apologies or punishments. Instead he had assigned an investigator to "our situation." He had selected a man named Paul Shell to interview every individual involved, everything I had outlined in my letters and that Claire had outlined in hers. He promised he would get to the bottom of the story. When the investigation was completed, he said—offering no date—he would make a decision.

He coolly outlined the next steps in what felt like a never-ending and meaningless charade. I wanted to scream but I could hear Claire's voice in my head: "Let him save face."

I nodded. "When will the investigation begin?"

"Soon," he said. He looked at his watch and absentmindedly tapped the dial. "Anything else?"

"I just want to know when exactly," I persisted. "It's been months…"

He stood. "Mr. Shell will contact you directly."

As we walked towards the door, I offered my thanks to him for agreeing to see me. He opened the door and looked down at his wingtips. "I want you to know that both my wife and I are fans of your column," he said.

"Thanks," I said. "Unfortunately I just learned that it's being canceled."

"I'm sorry to hear that," he said. "It's the paper's loss."

chapter twenty-nine

I wanted to see Russell Davis to thank him for everything he had done for us. Along with Graham and Claire and Bill, he had continued to be a champion on our behalf. And so on a Sunday morning when I was visiting Molly I asked her if I she knew when Services began. I wanted to find him at church before Services.

 She looked startled. She nervously stirred her coffee. "It's been a long time since I went to church, but I think it's 11."

I asked if she wanted to join me, but I knew she wouldn't go. She didn't say so, but I knew—in part because I sensed it, in part because I talked with her best friend about it—that ever since Will had been convicted, she had liked to lay low. She spent time with her best friend and with family, but she shunned other invitations and seldom even walked around town. She gave me directions and I drove into town and parked a block from the beautiful limestone Unitarian church.

I pushed open the heavy doors and discovered the service had already begun. The pews were packed. I quietly closed the doors behind me and began to tiptoe towards a seat in back, but as I did I heard Russell's voice booming from the pulpit. "Excuse me, ladies and gentlemen. Someone special has just walked in…" And he said my name.

Heat flooded my body as I tried to slip into a seat, but he was talking about the privilege he had just had of marrying me to one of the community's beloved sons. When he said Will's name, dozens of heads turned to look at me. Russell kept talking. He talked about how moving the wedding had been. "And it was held in a maximum security prison chapel," he said. Everyone in the town knew Will, or at least knew his name. And they'd known his victim too. A shiver was crawling up my spine. When Russell said, "After services I hope everyone will join me in welcoming Amy for tea in the vestry," he waved at me. I waved back and slid low in my seat.

I couldn't simply run, though I wanted to. When the service ended, I had to be polite. I followed the crowds. As I was turning to walk downstairs, a couple stopped in front of me, looked at me, spit on the floor, then turned and tore outside before I could get a good look at them. I was going to follow them, disappear before that happened again, but someone put a hand on my shoulder and whispered, "Ignore them," and he helped me make my way downstairs. There, in the low-ceilinged vestry, amidst the clink of teacups and the smell of pastries, people began to introduce themselves, asking me to please give their love to Will, sharing stories—about hockey games, baseball, their sons and Will, their daughters who had had crushes on him, the day he shoveled a drive, changed a storm window, invited a shy girl to a dance. I couldn't wait to tell Molly. Although she despised what he had done, she loved him thoroughly, and I thought these words would soothe her. As soon as I could politely leave, I hurried back, curled up on the sofa in the sunroom and began excitedly to tell her what everyone had said.

She looked away. She loved me, but my gregariousness made her uneasy. She had no interest in drama. Whenever she talked about Laura, she shook her head at her dramatics. I began to see that this story felt like drama to her, too, but I couldn't stop talking—the experience had fueled my optimism, my vision of Will's one day returning to this town and being greeted by waitresses and gas station attendants, nurses and doctors. I pictured the whole family feeling embraced again. I imagined the two of us out on the hill sledding with the nieces, and everyone on the hill welcoming him home. I couldn't wait to share the warmth people had offered me with him, the warmth I believed they would offer us all when he came home.

Molly began to cry. "Amy, sometimes I worry I won't live to see him out here…"

"Impossible," I said. I believed it was impossible. She was 74, healthy as a horse. "I promise you'll see him in this very room. And if you promise me you'll stop thinking such macabre thoughts, I promise I'll stop talking to everyone."

She smiled and said, "A deal."

It was a deal I had every intention of keeping.

Just a few days later, at Middle Harbor in the visiting room, I told the same story to Will. He was even more skeptical. His skepticism was dampening my good mood when I suddenly looked up at the guards' booth and noticed a group of people staring in through the glass window at us.

"Who the hell are they?" I whispered.

"Settle down," Will put a hand on my forearm. "Who cares who they are?" But the fact that people were staring at us as if we were animals in a zoo infuriated me. I felt that same taste of disgust in my throat I always felt when we were seen as "less than." It had happened just a few weeks earlier when visits were canceled for "Family Day," the day the guards' families visited prison to see where their loved ones worked, the day they walked the ranges and stared into cells at our husbands and brothers and fathers. I looked across the room where Connie and Bernard were visiting. I said, "Con," and nodded toward the window. She looked up, saw the people staring in and shrugged.

By then my anger was almost always near the surface. A single word or gaze could ignite my temper, so I brushed away Will's hand and marched to the window. I knocked, nodding to the guards to indicate that I wanted to be buzzed out of the visiting room. I heard the click of the lock, pushed the door open, stepped into the narrow hallway and stuck my head into the guards' now- cramped quarters. I stared at the huddled crowd. There were eight kids in their 20s, fresh-faced, with nice teeth and good haircuts and clear skin. No one in the visiting room looked as good as these kids. The men seldom saw sun or breathed fresh air—in maximum security they were permitted just one hour a day in the yard. And we visitors didn't look much better, our clothes coated with the stale air, our faces were strained with the sadness and exhaustion of visits.

I am sure I envied them their youth and beauty. Perhaps I even saw myself in them—the Amy of six or eight or ten months earlier—the curious, cocky, prettier me, the woman who was stupid enough to think she understood how prison worked and now was trapped on the wrong side of the glass.

"Who are you guys?" I asked.

One of the girls smiled. "We're from Queen's. We're sociology students. We're studying prisons."

I frowned. "If you're so curious, why don't you come on into the room and talk to the prisoners. Talk to us. I promise we don't bite. We could tell you a few things."

I truly did want these people to walk into our world. If any of them had, I would have sat them down and probably overwhelmed them with details of the trumped up Emergency Involuntary Transfer, with stories about how a child feels when her mom is strip searched, of how a mom responds when her son is moved to a place farther from home. I wanted to tell them that there was nothing to stop officials from doing anything they wanted to do to prisoners, and to their families. I wanted to explain that if they asked any of us prisoners how we had wound up sitting in this lousy little room, they would learn more than they possibly could learn by listening to professors' lectures or by taking tours and staring at people through windows. Those words stuck in my throat, snaking their way up and out of my mouth, but before I could say any of them, one of the guards tapped my arm, winked and said, "Amy, you're being political."

I wasn't allowed to be political if I wanted Will back in Maynard.

I nodded. I smiled. I said, curtly, "Hope you learn a lot," and the guard tapped the buzzer again and I ducked back into the visiting room. I squeezed Will's hand. "Got smart?" he asked. I nodded. "Stay smart," he said, locking his gaze onto mine.

And even as I wished I could have said something, some part of me knew I could teach those students nothing. Some part of me was aware that I would have spewed stories with no beginning or end, with no sensible context. I might even have cried the way I so often did in those days—though usually only when alone. I couldn't let guards see my tears, and I couldn't let Will because whenever I did get even slightly upset, he would say, "Listen, Amy, if you can't take this, we have to end it."

So as the months passed, I grew a harder shell, a brittle one that cracked only when I was alone or with a few trusted friends. Many nights I lay on my sofa and looked outside at the willow tree on the riverbank and cried. Many nights I phoned another prisoner's wife, Arlene, a woman I had met a few months earlier. Her husband was serving Life though he had never killed anyone. I didn't tell Will about Arlene. I didn't know her husband, and Will would have worried that Arlene might be untrustworthy. So my new friend became just one more secret between me and Will.

* * *

Claire had three rules she told every prisoner, and every prisoner's wife. The first was "Do not bullshit me because I don't want to be left with egg on my face." The second: "Don't expect anything. I'm not the system. All I can do is get on their backs and stay there." And the third: "Don't contact me if you can't take the extra heat."

Those she fought for did take extra heat, but she understood better than anyone that prison was a business, and a business needs merchandise, and that's what prisoners were.

Victims' rights advocates pilloried Claire, but in interview after interview she faced their questions. They always asked some variation of this: "What if it was your daughter who was killed?" Claire's answer was always the same. If it were up to her to decide her daughter's murderer's fate, she would recognize that she had two choices: She could put him in prison, throw away the key and let him rot. Or she could recognize that anyone who could commit such a crime had to be sick and she would figure out how to make him not sick during the years he was in prison.

"Because if I don't," she said, "and he finds out I'm the one who made sure he had such a hard time, he's going to come out and go for my other daughter."

Her answer was the best one I ever found. Like Claire, I knew even the men convicted of the meanest crimes had a story. (It wasn't that either of us thought psychopaths could necessarily be cured, but in truth, I met hundreds of men and women who had killed, and I never met a psychopath).

Will had a story. His included his having grown up without a dad. It included hockey coaches who had trained and applauded his efforts to become stronger and tougher. It included drinking too much and taking too many drugs. It included greed. And I thought I could change his story. I thought he could become the man Russell believed he was. The man Molly loved and had raised him to be. I thought I could help him to become a man who would salve his children's wounds and make amends for all he hadn't been able to give them for so many years. I thought I could help heal his sorrow and his fury. I thought I could help make Molly happy. I thought I could teach him to express himself in words instead of with fists. He wanted to learn how to write books— that that was a dream he'd long ago lost, and I was working with him. The belief that by my loving him he could be healed of everything that was wounded fueled me.

That's what I told Paul Shell when he interviewed me. That and every other detail about the transfer. I told him about all the people who worked so hard to keep us apart.

Shell interviewed me for hours, and I supplemented that interview with letters and documents. Like all my other letters, these were pages long, and over-the-top. I had learned still more details about events at Maynard from Tim Thomas, about the other men Joe Book had tried to recruit to act as informants about the so-called conspiracy Bernard and Will were engaged in. Richie Gerard was one of those Book approached. When he refused to lie, he was locked up in segregation with no charges. He was left there for nine weeks, and then transferred to British Columbia where Claire interviewed him and documented Tim's version of the story.

* * *

One day in March, while Shell was still investigating, Tim Thomas called to ask if I would attend his parole hearing and speak on his behalf. Some prisoners' stories had more appeal than did others. Tim's had much appeal in part because he was so well educated. His grammar and diction were perfect, and he'd read all the books I'd read, and his French wasn't Ontario biker tough French. In other words, he was a familiar type, another upper middle class guy who somehow had slipped off the tracks. His story included a younger sister who had committed suicide, a Mont Royal banker dad with a cold heart, a French Canadian mom too busy at spas to attend to her children. Tim and I had agreed he had probably begun to rob banks because he suffered from deep depressions. Bill Miles had told me that interviews with hundreds of federal inmates serving time for bank robbery suggested that the act of committing bank robbery seldom had a relationship to a desire for personal profit. Rather, robbery usually served as a defense against other overwhelming drives. Often it was an attempt to be killed or an acting out of displaced rage. Bank robbers were usually impulsive. They had difficulty controlling those impulses.

I felt affection for Tim, and I felt sorry for him. Besides, he had been one of the heartiest allies, had helped me to gather information. He often seemed as devoted to the cause as I was. He helped me keep all the pieces of the puzzle straight. He agreed to meet and talk with Shell and to hand over all the paperwork he had gathered. And because he was so "stand-up," in prison lingo, I felt indebted. I agreed not only to attend the hearing but to offer him a place to stay when he was released. That had been Will's idea. He wanted me to have someone at home to help me with the house. Tim's devotion to him was so evident, he presented no threat.

Besides, attending Tim's parole hearing would offer me practice, a lesson in how to talk to those stone-faced board members. And besides my chance to learn, if I spoke the parole board would learn about me. Kingston wasn't a big city. The entire country's population was so small word tended to spread quickly in its various circles, and prison was a tight-knit circle. I thought if the parole board members saw that I was sane and smart and articulate and well-behaved, that would eventually help them to believe in the possibility of Will's success outside.

Tim was granted parole in early April. He moved into the bungalow, and right away devoted himself to fixing everything he could fix—and to building a gigantic loft bed for Sarah who wanted to move in with me, too.

* * *

And then, one day in May, after thousands of dollars spent and hundreds of thousands of words spewed, Mr. Shell completed his report, and Andrew McCabe released his order. Will and Bernard were to be sent immediately back to medium security prisons. There was just one glitch. Maynard, upon receipt of the order, sent word to

Regional Headquarters that Will was not welcome there. So McCabe issued a second order: Will would be moved to the other medium security institution in Kingston, Cataraqui Bay. Bernard would return to Maynard.

From the outside Cataraqui, a massive red brick edifice, looked like a Disneyland castle. It had towering walls and massive gates that could easily seem to a child to house princesses and kings. In truth, of course, it was the opposite of a castle, and it was farther from the bungalow than Maynard was. But it cut my drive in half, and the transfer lowered Will's security rating back to medium. And so, despite Will's fury in learning that he was going to be living in a wildly noisy range, in a double-bunked cell, I knew Claire would be proud of me when I wrote a letter of gratitude to Andrew McCabe.

Andrew McCabe
Deputy Commissioner of Penitentiaries
Kingston Ontario
Saturday, May 15th, 1993

Dear Mr. McCabe,
I wish to thank you for the support you have shown my husband.
I understand one of the most difficult tasks of your position must be sorting out truth from myth when making difficult decisions.
My distress over this past year stemmed from knowing that decisions made regarding my husband were decisions made without knowing the man. I consider myself fortunate you have taken the time to look at the individual and was relieved and comforted upon hearing that you wish to meet him.
As I believe you realize, my husband shall live up to the confidence you have shown. Rest assured that my support and that of our children and friends shall continue to be unwavering.
The path I have chosen would not be possible were hope and light not so visible, as they are when my husband and I are given the opportunity to continue spending time and working together. Will's next transfer to minimum security shall further enable us to pursue our goals.

I believed every word. I felt relieved, reprieved. The nine months had knocked a lot of bravado out of me. But I thought we were finally on the road towards Will's freedom.

chapter thirty

I must have been too busy teaching and taking on freelance editing jobs and finishing up negotiations with *The Whig* and Universal Press, and adjusting to the news that Lawrence had offered Candace my job as *The Whig's Bedtime Story* editor, and helping Will to adjust to Cataraqui Bay to pay attention to the way Tim's eyes tended to droop closed, and to his slurred speech and to the many things he broke—the clothesline, Sarah's bicycle, a bathroom tile. When Diane told me Tim had awkwardly propositioned her, I assured her he was just a boy who needed more time outside to learn how to behave well.

"He's a fuck up," Sarah said. "You should remember what we said about Candace. We're always right." She winked at Cass who nodded emphatically. "He's a fuck up," she said. So that night I asked him outright if he was doing heroin again. He stared at me, opening his eyes as wide as he could, and that's when I saw that he could barely keep them open, could barely lift his head. "Me? What?" he mumbled.

"You have to leave, Tim," I said. And he just nodded and that very night he packed his things and was gone by morning. I was sad for him, but more than that I was relieved for myself. Sarah had asked if she could move in with me now that she was nearly 16 and by law could decide where she wanted to live. Will and I agreed the move was not only a good idea—it was vital since just a few weeks earlier she and a friend of hers had been caught shoplifting at a mall in Ottawa. Now she was facing charges. And when the authorities learned she was moving in with me in Gananoque, a social worker called and asked us to come in to talk with him. Richard Pine thought he might be able to help her avoid a conviction.

He was a big bear of a man, with soft brown eyes he trained on Sarah. "Sarah," he said, "it's good you've decided to live with your stepmom." I looked over at her with her arms crossed over her chest and her pretty blue eyes cloudy with mistrust, and I felt a quiver of worry I sometimes felt around Sarah. She could be a lovely, loving, and affectionate girl—funny and sweet and as open as a flower, but she could snap closed like a flower, too, could turn in a heartbeat into a cool, wary and silent young woman.

"I'm going to ask you some questions," Richard said quietly. She nodded and looked at the floor.

"Have you ever shoplifted before—for anyone?" he asked.

She shook her head.

"Any problems at home you want to talk about? Anything with your mother?"

"No," she said so quietly I could barely hear. She coiled herself more tightly inward as he leaned towards her. "Does anyone in your house drink alcohol, Sarah?"

I stared at her, willing her to speak. She had told me her mother drank too much, and I'd heard the evidence in slurred, angry phone calls to me and to Molly whenever the girls were with either of us. I'd heard the angry voice from far across a room. I also knew Sarah had been taught from childhood that the worst thing she could be was a rat, and now she was being asked to tell on her mother. I thought it possible that her mother had encouraged the shoplifting; Richard seemed to suspect the same. I knew she wouldn't admit that, and not only did she shake her head "no," she added, "No one drinks."

"Why do you want to live with your stepmom, Sarah?" he asked.

She glanced at me. "I want to live near my dad," she said. "And Amy's nice."

"I see," he scribbled something on the pad. "Any other reasons?"

"Just that," she said.

"No problems with Mom?" he prodded.

"No," she said.

He sighed. He looked to me for help, but there was nothing I could do. "Sarah, I'd like to give you just probation but you have to help me here…" he begged.

She shrugged and crossed one slender leg over the other. "Nothing. I guess I just got greedy," she said.

Richard Pine's hands were tied. He had to report precisely what Sarah had told him, and the court found Sarah guilty and ordered as her punishment that she serve 100 hours of community service. I asked Charlie Donevan, the local hardware store owner and my friend, to take her on, and Charlie put her to work at a campground he owned, Landon Bay. So from late summer all the way until the first snows fell, there was pretty pouting Sarah pounding nails and carrying cement blocks and digging drainage ditches and muttering under her breath about how dumb all this was.

Just as I believed that I could heal Will of his wounds, I believed that now that Sarah lived with me and near the father she so clearly loved, everything would soon be fine. She would become a cheerful, happy girl, a willing student with ambition to use her ready wit and her fine intelligence, her charms and beauty to become first a high school graduate, then a college student, and eventually a woman with a flourishing career.

* * *

Not only was Cataraqui Bay not a castle, it felt like a medieval dungeon. I hated everything about the place—its visiting room guards were bitter and hated prisoners and their families; the waits were sometimes interminable; the ranges were overcrowded; the warden was a longtime bureaucrat with no imagination and no fire. Still, I remained staunch in my belief that we could overcome it all, and Molly agreed. When Will began to write, she decided he deserved a computer, and Cataraqui Bay permitted inmates to have these (maximums did not). No one inside was permitted access to the internet, but at least he could type, and once he had his new machine, he set to work, collaborating with me on a book idea he had.

Will's new C.O. was a humorless woman. Paula Greene reminded me of women usually cast in After School specials as unhappy librarians, and from the start, Paula refused to believe that Will's transfer to Middle Harbor hadn't been deserved. Because none of the paperwork in the original transfer had been changed—there was still that "alleged conspiracy to commit murder"— no matter what he and I tried to explain to her about the circumstances that had led to the transfer, Paula was convinced Will had to be watched closely, tightly harnessed. When we told her of our plan to write together, she was skeptical. "You're no writer," she told him and explained that she ought to know since she was a bit of a writer herself, had once even thought about taking a class I taught at the College. "But Will won't ever be a writer," she said. "He's not the type."

She might as well have waved a red flag in front of both of us. Though he and I were different from each other in dozens of ways, we both responded to a challenge with stubborn fury, and so I determined we would write the book we had already begun. In my secret heart, I didn't like the story; and in my secret heart, I didn't believe either of us could write this book. It wasn't that I didn't believe Will could learn to write—and write well. That was just one more challenge, and it was the kind I loved. I had always liked teaching, and I had helped many students become better at the craft. But Will had conceived a potboiler murder mystery, and my interests leaned in far different directions. I had no idea how to write this genre, and whenever he and I talked about the story, both plot and characters he was creating sounded clichéd. But I didn't criticize his ideas. I didn't press him the way I pressed my students to work harder, to think more deeply. I coddled and praised him and stayed with the project long after I wanted to. And Paula's refusal to offer encouragement only propelled me further into Will's corner. We would show her. We would show all the doubters.

And there was the fact that if there was anything Will knew about it was cops and crime. I convinced myself the story would eventually become more nuanced and enthralling than it sounded in these early pages. We worked out a system. I shelved my own half-finished novel and poured my ardor and education and intelligence into his. For the next seven years the novels I had written and meant to return to stayed in my desk drawers, and when I look back all these years later—as I pull them out to see what I had imagined and dreamed and created and abandoned—I see how like my mother I had become. When my youngest sister started school, Mom wanted to go to law school, and although Dad agreed she ought to work, he insisted two lawyers in one household wasn't a good idea. Instead she got a teaching certificate and became a high school teacher. And she was a fine teacher—smart and generous and popular. She loved her job, adored her students; that was always vividly clear. But when I was younger I lambasted and chided her for bowing to my father's needs, for letting his desires supplant hers. Yet here I was, unconsciously doing the same. Mom said she never regretted becoming a teacher, but I once believed she only pretended she felt no regrets. Now I know that pretending can go a long way toward convincing, and although some days I look at those manuscripts and wonder what they might look like all grown up, I don't feel regret, only some embarrassment because I was supposed to be a woman who stood up for herself, took care of herself, exceeded expectations. That, after all, was my generation's siren's call; we were women meant to outshine all our predecessors. But in those years I spent most of my time and energy standing up for Will and the girls. A lot of the prisoners' wives I came to know did that, and prison sucked out so much of our fire and force, most of us were paddling frantically just to stay above water and gasping for air.

For instance: Will wrote pages and when I visited, he brought those pages for me to read. I took them home, edited and revised and added new pages and returned these in an envelope I placed into the mailbox outside the visiting room. Guards checked every item we brought in—including our mail—looking for drugs or weapons or anything else they might deem contraband. Most of the time after they assessed our packages, they passed them along to the addressee later that day. Will received my revisions and added his revisions to those. And the process pleased him. His mood began to lift. And I didn't think about the fact that writing this book and all those letters and taking care of Sarah was keeping me from writing my own books. Instead I tried to hold in balance the sense of despair that sometimes came over me and the sense of the necessity to work hard; I often felt the possibility of failure and determination not to fail at the very same time.

But one day not long into our stay at Cataraqui Bay, I walked into the outer room, and as I was about to slip my envelope of pages into the mailbox, Kevin, one of the V&C guards, tapped my shoulder. "Don't bother putting the pages in," he said. "The warden has withdrawn your privilege of writing together. The material has been deemed unsuitable." Kevin had the look of a boy who had wanted to be military or police but had been turned down, gangly, awkward in his movements, and a young but tired face, pinched by a permanent sneer. He liked to ask visitors long, complicated questions about why we were there, and we had crossed swords one day when I badgered him about his harassment of an inmate's mother visiting from Italy; she barely spoke English, and he was insisting she try. Now I bit my tongue to keep from swearing or spitting at him. "Unsuitable? What do you mean?"

"You're writing material that's unsuitable," he repeated.

I knew Correctional Services Directives inside out in those days, and I knew Federal law as it applied to prisons. I had spent over a year studying these. It was illegal for guards to read our private papers, and although we all knew they did anyway, they couldn't admit it without making themselves liable to a lawsuit. Now Kevin had done precisely that, but instead of holding that card close to my vest, I said, "Kevin, it's against the law for you to read our private mail."

He shrugged. "We deemed it unsuitable. I saw the word *murder* on your pages."

"Idiot," I said under my breath. But that night, instead of writing a story or working on Will's book or marking my students' papers, or doing the freelance editing I'd taken on to make up for losing the income from my column, I wrote out a long, complex grievance citing every law and Correctional Directive that applied. The next day I submitted the grievance, as required, to the Institution.

Three weeks passed during which we were forbidden to exchange any pages. In visits Will would recite in great detail the way he envisioned the next part of the story unfolding, and I spent evenings trying to remember what he'd told me and committing those words to paper. At the end of three weeks, for the first time, a grievance I had filed (and I had filed probably 30 or 40 by then), the warden overturned his people's decision and restored our "privilege." After that, once in a while a guard would lose our papers, or misplace them for weeks, or simply forget to deliver them to Will, and each time that happened, my attitude towards the Service hardened and my willingness to forgive Will any misbehavior and any unkind word only grew.

Other things were hardening my attitude towards the people I had come to see as Will's captors. Besides stolen and misplaced mail, there were my slashed tires. One day I walked outside after a visit to find two of my tires had been slashed. As I walked around the car, distraught, I caught sight of a couple of guards in a corner, laughing to themselves, and when I looked at them, they turned away, and I always suspected it was they who slashed my tires, though I had no proof. Also, in the eight months since Will had moved to Cataraqui Bay, the warden had locked down the institution 17 times, and those lockdowns meant not only deprivation of visits, but they meant prisoners were locked in their cells 24/7, with the resulting dark moods and flares of suicides and violent brawls that kind of incarceration incurs. The Cat became my nemesis. I felt particular animosity towards Paula Greene, Will's C.O., but that feeling extended towards Warden Whelan, a bespectacled man whose solution to every unsettling problem in the prison under his command was to lock the place down.

Besides our own story that increasingly frustrated me, I was more and more haunted by the sad stories that surrounded us. I had never believed prisoners were angels, but now I was hearing too many stories of men who one day were perfectly fine and the next day were dead—stabbed by other inmates, neglected while mortally ill, overdosed, misdiagnosed, ignored for weeks at a time in segregation cells. It was Claire who told me about Mack, the photographer at Maynard, refused parole for the umpteenth time because he wouldn't express remorse for a crime he hadn't committed. Mack had been diagnosed with cancer, and now he was down to 90 pounds, chained to a hospital bed. As he moved closer and closer to death, Claire worked to obtain a compassionate release so he could go home to the Maritimes to die among his family. Months passed with no decision until at last he was flown back to them less than a week before he died.

In October 1993, during a lockdown at Kingston Penitentiary, the maximum just down the road from Cataraqui Bay, a prisoner named Robert "Tex" Gentles was ordered by guards to turn down his radio. When he demanded to know why the prisoners hadn't been fed for 21 hours, a six guard "extraction" team entered his cell, and when they left, Robert Gentles was dead. An investigation discovered he had been maced with four times the amount of mace authorized by CSC to subdue prisoners, and he had been beaten and pinned face down on his bed—there was a boot print on his head—suffocated to death. Robert Gentles, I learned, had been one of five founding members of the Prison Violence Project, a prisoner-based human rights group started six months earlier; the founders believed that the high rate of physical and psychological violence in prison contributed to violent crimes committed by prisoners upon release. Their goal was to change that cycle. But six months after PVP was founded, two of the founding members were dead, and one year later, the other three founders were transferred to three different institutions across the country. By 1995 the PVP was officially banned by CSC.

In February 1994 I wrote to Claire:

I hate Cataraqui Bay. I hate every single correctional services Canada staff member, especially [Warden] Whelan. I do. Today I do not feel anything but hatred towards all those people who believe they are the GOOD PEOPLE. Much as I know it never did anyone any good to brim with hatred, I hate every single one of them.

I knew no prisoners who were angels, and Will was not, but whenever he was in a bad mood, I reasoned that the prejudice and intransigence of the system he faced was bound to push anyone to bad days. I was under pressure, too, yes, but at least I could go home at night. I could choose not to go to prison. I could sleep in silence and wake to mist rising off the river. I could listen to the music I wanted to listen without hundreds of other men's voices and music and cries ringing in my ears. I could call anyone I wanted to call whenever I wanted to— except Will, of course. I could leave town. I could leave the country. I could go to a library, a restaurant, a museum, a friend's house, a concert or a movie or a play. I could ride a bicycle, swim in rivers and lakes and pools. I could dance or sail or ski. I could order a pizza, shop in the

Farmers' Market, buy éclairs in bakeries. I could go camping or visit Molly, or go to Kate's house and sleep on her red velvet sofa and weep. I could pet the animals, bake a loaf of bread, cook a pot of stew, drink in a bar or in a café.

And I may have been like my mom in many ways, but I was also like my dad, the man who ever since his release from the POW camp praised to the skies thin Mawbees hamburgers as if they were filet mignon, who whooped and sang when he skated on public ice rinks, who raised a toast to his morning orange juice. Like Dad I was celebrating in my way what freedom meant—it had become so vividly clear. Dad came with wonder and delight to every film he saw, every book he read; every sight was the most bounteous sight imaginable. All my life his bliss had irritated me, and just as I had not believed my mother's joy in teaching, I had never wholly believed Dad's bliss was genuine bliss. Now I was beginning to understand how truly grateful he felt for freedom.

My empathy towards Will expanded still more because Will wasn't free. Will was trapped in a double-bunked cell in J-block where the noise of 600 men was so loud he couldn't hear himself think, in a place where the stink of 600 men filled every corner, in a joint where he had to eat whatever slop was served in the presence of 600 bitter, posing, drugged out men—Native Canadians and Chinese and Filipinos, Black and White, bank robbers and murderers, slash and grabbers and rapists, heroin and Valium addicts, drunks, loudmouths, terrified, furious men, quiet and loud, all of them trapped in this world that was thick with dirt and echoes and misery and danger.

And so whenever Will expressed any affection or joy or warmth, I praised him, and whenever he was testy or temperamental, I forgave him. If anyone spoke ill of him (and most people speak ill of all prisoners), I defended him.

Dear Claire, I wrote,
Will is phenomenal. We had a silly argument today. ...I said "Will, sometimes I feel like you're too critical of everyone...."
After a long silence he said he had to think about that. Then quietly he said, "Maybe my bitterness is getting to me.

Claire, I'm very lucky. I want to free Will. I hate it that they can do anything to them. That's what makes me hate them so. AND I'm tired of thinking about them so I'll end with that. Okay? You, however, I love.

* * *

In early 1994, several months after he arrived at The Cat, Paula Greene completed Will's "Treatment Plan," and it included, along with anger management classes, therapy sessions with one of The Cat's therapists, Dilshad Marshall. That threw a wrench into our plans. We were counting on his being transferred to a minimum security prison within a year. But therapy at least once a week for a very long time meant that his time at The Cat might go on without end. Paula wouldn't offer specifics as to how many weeks or months of these sessions would be required, and Will immediately railed against the idea. He was certain that the joint therapists had no interest or expertise in helping inmates; rather he saw them as one more impediment, one more way to slow the possible release of anyone authorities disliked. Also, he believed therapy was a sham, a waste of time, designed for people who were self-involved and couldn't get over their pasts the way he firmly believed he had. He had changed his ways, given up drink and drugs, chosen a new career path towards which he was working hard. What could a therapist teach him that he hadn't already taught himself? He and I talked for hours about it. I offered my ideas of therapy—citing myself as an example of someone who had learned a good deal from therapists I'd seen, but once again he dismissed them. Hadn't I been taking anti-depressants? That, he believed, was one more example of therapists not doing their jobs; I had stopped taking anti-depressants. Wasn't I doing just fine?

I supposed I was—I couldn't be sure since life was always in such a whirl—but I tried pointing out that he was reacting not unlike the Scientologists whose belief system he found absurd. And I didn't say it, but I thought how much like my dad he sounded. My dad believed people had to tough their way out of depression, push through it, refuse to wallow in sadness, forebear becoming stuck in the past where sad memories lay. Both Dad and Will—so different in so many ways—believed that looking back could not lead one to a healthy present, but that's precisely what Paula Greene and Dilshad Marshall wanted my husband to do. Look back. Unravel. Find the key to where he had gone wrong. Dilshad truly believed she could help him. He was smart, she said. He had always had so much potential to do something positive with all those smarts.

That is what she told me when I called her to discuss the treatment plan, but by then Will had convinced me he didn't need an in-house therapist to help him work through his problems. A little insight would be useful, I conceded to Dilshad, but for the hundredth time in that phone call I ran down the specifics of the transfer, the path that had led Will from Maynard to Middle Harbor and back to Cataraqui Bay. I explained away the black marks in Will's record—those untrue statements by untrustworthy, anonymous sources. I offered her all my rationalizations for his anger and his bitterness. It was a miracle, I told her, that he wasn't crazy. Who wouldn't be crazy in the face of what they'd put him through this last year. I told her I had gone half-mad and I wasn't locked in a cell beside a Jamaican heroin addict who played his recorder until all hours of the morning.

Dilshad's accent was British/Indian, and her voice was soothing and deep. She was articulate, and she listened with what felt through the call line like thoughtfulness. "Well, Amy," she said without a trace of condescension—unusual in my experience with employees of the Service towards us wives—"he did kill someone. That's rather more to the point than all the ins and outs of this transfer, don't you think?"

Of course it was to the point. If I had been less angry with every official, less dug-in to our rebellion and our fight, I like to think I would have encouraged her to help him. I might even have helped to nudge him towards a deeper understanding of who he was and who he wished to be and how he might fulfill those wishes. But I was thinking only of how to lower his security rating, how to reach Camp with time enough to prove to the Parole Board that he was ready to be considered, first, for escorted passes, then for unescorted and finally day parole. That was a minimum of three hearings he had to face, and much time would necessarily pass between those hearings. When I looked at all the hoops ahead of him, I felt panicked. I needed this to end. I'd imagined three years inside, never four or five or more, and therapy sounded only like one more moat to cross, one made of molasses to slow any progress towards release to a standstill.

I was certain then, and I am as certain now—as certain as I could be of almost anyone—that Will posed no risk to another person. Most of the "murderers" I met in prison I know are unlikely ever to kill again. If anyone knew the terrors and demons that followed in the wake of such a heinous act, it was they, and if anyone understood the repercussions of such grave acts, it was those serving time for their commission. They also knew that without almost any doubt, a second murder, or any crime, likely spelled the end of their life too.

But it was only many years later that I saw that as much as Will understood he had to live far differently from the way he had lived before prison, he had little understanding of the source of his anger and sorrow. He had few tools for fighting depression, almost none for how to face a lifetime on parole. Had he and I allowed Dilshad to know him better, she might have helped him. But I didn't tell him that because I was too blinded by impatience and desire to see it myself.

After he had talked a few times with Dilshad, though he didn't admit it, I saw that he liked her. Whenever he came from a session with her to a visit he was calmer and softer. Still, even seeing that change in him, I withheld stories from her. I did not tell her about the day in a trailer visit when Will decided it was time that I give up cigarettes, and just as I settled in for three days inside, he took all the packs I had brought with me and flushed them down the toilet. When I discovered what he had done, in that moment I hated him. I felt his power over me, and I despised him, and as he sat beside me and held me while I shook and wept, even as he spoke softly of how he would help me through the withdrawal, I knew I was seeing only his intransigence. "All you have to do is stop. That's how you kick it," he said, and I felt his coldness, the way he demanded too much of others. He was demanding too much of me. And I went through nicotine withdrawal in that trailer, and I left the trailer, bought a pack, kept on smoking, and hid it from him. And I didn't tell Dilshad about that. I feared if I did she would only insist he needed still more therapy. She would only slow the cascade to release more than it had already slowed. And besides, I believed he was right; smoking cigarettes was suicide, and I was a weak person for being unable simply to kick them cold turkey.

I was trying to believe what he believed much the way I had always tried to believe my father. I was trying to stay calm, be sane, be intoxicant free and faithful and loving and loved. I was supposed to be a shining example for the girls, for my students, for Will. Dad had taught me that to succeed in everything all I had to do was keep my eyes open, stay on track, pull myself up by my own bootstraps. That was how he had survived the POW camp; that was how he was surviving the strain of tending to my mother as she descended more deeply into Alzheimer's (though I still didn't know the the depth of her struggles). That was how people survived plane crashes and cancer and the loss of a child. Some survived and came out the other end feeling oceans of compassion; some came out feeling empathy but covered up that empathy with a tough exterior; and some lost their empathy altogether. I didn't lose my empathy in the prison years; if anything all the sadness and longing I saw and felt only deepened it. But Will had buried his empathy beneath his desire to be seen as important and strong and brave—a desire that only grew in prison as he was stripped of that sense of himself. Too late I understood that if Dilshad had had her way, she and I might have been allies in helping him to heal. She might have helped him to learn how to connect more closely to his better self.

There was this, too. At Cataraqui Bay the warden had called so many lockdowns, everyone was squirrelly, angry. Everyone's mood was on edge. One day at the end of a long lockdown I came into a visit and began to complain about the lack of visits, about the cold outside, about the cruel guards. "I hate this place," I said.

"*You* hate this place?" he said accusingly. "Try to imagine being double-bunked 24/7. Know what it's like having to strip in front of all those bitches just to come down to a visit to hear you complain? *You* hate The Cat, are you kidding?"

As I so often did, I left that visit and wrote to Claire, complaining, seeking her wisdom. What should I say to Will? What should I think or do?

… So long as you don't let the hatred destroy you," she wrote, *instead of energizing you…for want of a better word. Must keep going. Take care, and spend more time loving than worrying about Will…might be a better idea.*

I thought I was following Claire's advice, but truthfully I did spend more time worrying than I did loving him. I forgave him for bad behavior because I worried that he would feel too hurt. I stood up for him, but I never stood up to him. I see all these years later that I could have loved him better if I had stood up to him when he behaved badly, if I had insisted he understand that it wasn't only he who suffered. After all, I could have and should have pointed out to him, he had put himself in this position because of his own desires and fears but Molly and the girls and his sisters and friends and I were in prison because we chose to stand by him. I should have told him he ought to learn to cherish and honor that gift. But I had learned what love was from a couple who presented to the world a solid and united front, and I was afraid if I did not stand firmly in his corner, Will might send me away, and I would once again have failed at love.

chapter thirty-one

As we waited in line to enter the visiting room at Cataraqui Bay most of the wives and mothers and fathers looked down at the floor. Few asked questions about the lockdowns or protested strip searches or a guard's bad behavior. There was one other woman who was, like me, often geared up for a confrontation. Mary Lee was a muscular, strident, bleached blonde, an ex-con. Someone told me she had done time for manslaughter, but I wasn't sure. That wasn't the kind of thing anyone asked someone in line outside a visiting room. I did know—through Will—that she and her husband had met when they were both prisoners, taking college courses back in the '80s when prisons still offered inmates an education; the practice had stopped thanks to political pressure—people protesting that such "luxuries" not be wasted on prisoners.

Mary Lee had been out for a few years, but her husband was a Lifer, so she was another almost daily visitor at Cataraqui. One snowy February day, she and I were standing outside waiting in line when we learned the 17th lockdown had just been called. Visits were promptly canceled. Mary Lee and I turned to each other—both of us vehemently angry. We decided we were going to join forces to fight the warden of the Cat as we called the joint. We would rally wives and parents and children and friends to write letters and petitions protesting the administration's propensity for calling all these lockdowns. That night I wrote to Claire. I assumed she would be proud of my activist spirit. She wrote only a short note in response. "Be careful of Mary Lee."

But along with my devotion to Will, I was developing a sense of devotion towards all those people standing in line waiting to visit. Although I didn't like everyone, and some were almost scary, I felt a kind of kinship, and some sympathy. I wanted to help us all, and some, like Cameron, felt like a kind of sister.

Cameron was in her 30s, tall and slim with a cropped mop of white blond hair. She wore short, stylish skirts, and she and her oh-so-handsome husband, Jack, with his chiseled cheekbones and deep-set eyes, had a pretty five-year-old named Zee. Like me and Mary Lee, Cameron and Zee visited almost every day. When I saw them across the visiting room—more like a large automat than like the Maynard "bus station"—they seemed a perfect couple. Everyone in the visiting room loved Zee. She had an irresistible smile and often she danced around the room saying hello to everyone. When Jack walked into the room, she lit up and rushed into his arms. He would raise her high in the air and twirl her around. Sarah and Cass had grown too old for such displays of emotion, but they hugged their father and kissed him, and Zee's utter pleasure and enthusiasm for her father buoyed everyone's spirits. We all saw that whenever Jack was with Zee, he became the best man he could be.

But Jack had a drug problem, and whenever he fell off the wagon and guards caught him using, the first line of punishment was withdrawal of his family visits. Every infraction on the part of a prisoner brought some kind of punishment—solitary confinement, transfers, almost always the loss of a trailer visit and frequently daily visits. This punishment had always struck me as the most short-sighted imaginable, it seemed to me that it was put in place to assure these men never heal. I had begun to talk with Graham Stewart and Claire and with Arlene and Mary Lee and Cameron about rallying the families to address these rules that seemed so wrong. They were not only working against prisoners' interests but they worked against society's.

When Jack first went to prison, his drug of choice was marijuana. But marijuana could be detected in the system for weeks after use, and because there was such frequent drug testing, Jack shifted to heroin use; its use made detection less likely. A lot of men took heroin for this same reason, and Cameron's deepest desire was to help Jack to beat his habit. She was forever fighting authorities for more drug treatment programs. I frequently overheard her arguing with guards, insisting that their taking away Jack's visits with Zee would only feed his addiction.

Marge especially, the head V&C guard, a squat, militaristic, angry woman, always snapped, "That's policy. Swallow it."

Marge hated visitors, and in return we despised her.

One day I was waiting in line when a woman I liked a lot, Aurelia, Alberto's wife who always came with her three beaming daughters, turned to me and whispered, "Did you hear?" Her eyes darted around the room, pretending she wasn't talking to me, that we didn't know each other well and thus had no "association" problem.

"Hear what?" I asked.

"Jack. He died. Overdose."

Jack was the sixth overdose that year. He died alone in his segregation cell. That happened a lot. One day we were in line with all the regulars like Cameron and Zee, and the next day they were gone. I never saw Cameron or Zee again, but losing her spurred me on in an endeavor I had recently begun.

With Graham Stewart and Arlene, I was writing a brief on behalf of Prisoners' Families. I hoped to present it to the Justice Committee of Canada's Parliament. The central idea of our brief was that prisoners' family members ought to be part of the decision-making process in prisons. I realized if there was any hope of any kind of rehabilitation, the System needed to officially integrate families into that decision-making process. I believed this then, and I believe it still, perhaps even more deeply now that I know my belief does not arise from self-interest.

* * *

I consoled myself that Cameron's fate would never be mine because Will was stubborn enough to stick to the promise he had made himself the day he was arrested never to use drugs or alcohol again. He had become a health nut. He frequently lectured everyone—especially the girls and me—on diet and exercise. If we missed a day working out or if we gained a pound, he would lean in and poke our belly and insist we work off the excess. He told us what to eat, how many sit ups and pushups and presses we ought to be doing. He was the expert, he said, in this as in so much else.

The only corner in which he ceded expertise to me was in the mechanics of writing. But his dreams were off kilter. He planned to write two books before he saw the parole board. He was sure these would sell and he would make lots of money. I didn't offer my thoughts, not wanting to disabuse him of the dream. Besides, most writers I taught possessed some variation of that dream. I thought as time passed and as he became more skilled, he would recognize how much hard work writing took—and he either would continue or find another passion.

Dearest Claire,

Yesterday Will said that if he ends up going to the parole board next year from Cataraqui Bay he'll try to explain to them that he chose to stay at The Cat because he had a single cell where he could write (and by then he'll have finished two books at least), and where he could have access to his family.

But therapy sessions and Paula's insistence that Will would not be ready to see the parole board until a full psychological assessment was complete—and no one offered a date when that might be possible—was another reason I railed against the slowness of the system. Still, I knew that Dilshad saw I was Will's best friend and doing my best to take care of him. He had talked with her about that. He told me so. And he told me he knew I was on his side. He was sorry he sometimes forgot that. And as time passed I saw that whenever anyone let him down, even in the slightest way, he dived into himself.

Later I came to understand that the first year we clung to each other to keep at bay all those forces battling to keep us apart, and now that they were letting up we were pulling apart. But in the meantime, I was growing closer to the girls and to Molly, and I vowed to keep my promise to her: She would see her son outside one day. That meant I had to keep him moving towards parole.

chapter thirty-two

Eddie and his family lived six houses down the road, in the center of Willowbank. It was one of Kell's favorite stop-offs on our walks. Eddie's dad, Jim, was a teacher, and Fran, his mom, was a social worker, and they were wry and hip. The minute I met them I liked them. Eddie had just turned six, and his brother, Jake, was 8, and the two boys rode the school bus with Sarah to the school six kilometers away. At 3:30 each day the school bus dropped the kids at the end of the road, but neither Fran nor Jim got home until 4:30. They didn't like to leave the boys alone. "They have terrible fights," Fran said. "I was hoping maybe Sarah would consider being our regular babysitter."

The job was perfect, a way for Sarah to earn some cash and to begin to mingle with people she liked. Soon after she began the job, Eddie showed up at our house one night and knocked on the door. He had a flower in his hand, and he thrust it towards me. "This is for Sarah. From me, not Jake." And every night after that for weeks and weeks, he showed up with another gift—a feather, a photograph, a key.

And Sarah clearly adored him in return. She always glowed with pleasure when she came home from their house. Eddie was like Dennis the Menace, the friendliest kid in the world, self-appointed mayor of Willowbank. He roamed the neighborhood selling cookies and magazines and a dozen other items—his favorite being money for annual Canada Day fireworks. No one could say no to him, and Sarah was his princess.

"He loves you, Sarah," I said.

She blushed and grinned. "It's sweet," she said. "I love him too."

"I'm sorry about the Mary Lee thing."

"I know," she said. "I know you are. I'm sorry I told my dad."

I hugged her. We made up. We always did. But most days she would start another fight, and most nights we said goodnight saying, "I love you." I loved her friends who liked to come to the house, friends like skinny Mark, all arms and legs, pale skin and golden hair, and Colette with her short cap of chocolate brown hair and her beautiful face. Frequently they came over and walked together out to the fields, and I stood at the window and watched them, watched the wind tousling their hair and chapping their skin. I felt hopeful for Sarah. I felt the pleasure she was taking in their company. They may have been smoking pot—they probably did, at least sometimes. But I knew they were also high on each other and on the river-scented air and on their friendship, and I always felt a deep desire inside to wrap Sarah in my arms. I wanted her to stay with me forever. Laura's constant pleadings for her to come home worked sometimes, and Sarah would go up to visit for a few days. And every time she returned she was sullen and snotty and more 16 than ever, and I wished she were my child.

I don't remember if it happened suddenly or if I had thought about it for a while, but I decided that year that I wanted to try to have a baby. It may have been a longing to connect more deeply to Will and to his family; it may have been the fact that my brother's wife and my sister Rachel had new babies and when, on occasion, I did talk to Mom or Dad, they crooned about their new beautiful grandchildren. Or maybe it was the pull that arose from the love I was feeling towards Sarah. I suspect it was a combination of all those emotions. And when I told Will, he wrapped his arms around me and said, "Yes, yes, yes." And we happily studied the dates of our possible upcoming trailers.

When I saw they wouldn't cooperate with my fertility, I decided that our only option artificial was insemination. That became our plan. The ease with which Will agreed to the idea surprised me, but it also buoyed me into action. Right away I began calling doctors, but everyone I called told me I was too old—in effect, I realized, if they did agree to treat me but I failed to get pregnant, their statistics would be ruined, and they didn't want to risk that possibility. But finally I found one doctor who agreed to see me. He said he had always admired my column, and he thought from everything he knew about me after reading about me for eight years, that I was the kind of person who would make a fine mother. He heaped praise upon me, citing my intelligence and openness and warmth, and as I drove to his office, I felt optimistic.

The doctor and I talked for a long, long time. He asked me hundreds of questions, and we talked about Sarah and Cass—about the strains of taking care of them and how my becoming a mother with their father might affect them, how taking care of them had affected me. Naturally I told him everything I could about Will and about both of our pasts and our present, and about this startling desire we both seemed to feel, a desire I had never felt until now, and now I was over 40. But I was healthy and strong, and in part because of Will's constant hammering home the need to be fit, I was, and so was he, at 40. I swore I would stop smoking, that this would be the final impetus. I even confessed that I hid my smoking from Will. I filled out forms. He weighed and measured me, took my blood pressure and all the other requisite tests. Everything was fine. All systems go, according to Dr. Smith.

I felt giddy with excitement—aware that it could not work out, but then, it might. And then Dr. Smith folded his hands in his lap and leaned back in his chair and said, "The only thing left to do is to have Will come to the office. I need to talk to the father to make sure he's fully onboard, and to take semen samples, of course."

I had told him everything. He knew that was impossible. I repeated the truth. "Dr. Smith, you do understand Will is in prison, right?"

"Yes, I do, of course." He shrugged. "But I'll have to look him in the eye and have a talk. It's the only way. It's fine if he comes with an escort on a pass. They give prisoners passes, don't they?"

I explained that Will wasn't yet eligible for passes. I told him it could be another year, or two, before he was. But he just shrugged again and said, "I'm sorry, Amy. See what you're able to work out. I'm sure if you tell the authorities why you need the pass, they'll cooperate with you. There's no reason they wouldn't do that."

His assumption was reasonable, of course. It was an assumption that acknowledged human needs, and it was obvious, but it was also obvious to me that he would not be granted a pass for such a visit, and that day I drove home feeling such grief it was as if I had been pregnant and had lost a child. I think it may have been the first time that I understood I would never have a baby, but I stuffed that disappointment inside, and I poured my mother-love into the girls forever after.

But Sarah was also a teenager with all the attendant hormonal angst and outbursts, and by spring break we both needed time away from each other. On a beautiful mid-March morning, I put her on the bus to Molly's house. The bus station had become almost as familiar to me as the prison since I was there every week, often twice, picking up or dropping off either Sarah or Cass, hugging one goodbye and one hello. That day when I dropped her off, she was all affection, so excited was she to be having a chance to spend a whole week with her Granny.

During that week Molly and I talked several times and agreed to meet on Saturday halfway between our houses to have lunch and exchange Sarah. I was just about to walk out the door to go to the gym when the phone rang and Sarah whispered, "Amy, Granny's sick. She had a headache last night and I was supposed to go out, and Dad called and told me it was okay, I should go out anyway, so I did, and when I got home she was sleeping, but she's still sleeping, and she never sleeps this late…"

"Slow down, Sarah, it's okay, honey. I'm sure she's fine," I said although it did sound odd. It was almost 9, and Molly always woke at 5. But I wasn't worried. I told her to call her Aunt Nora, and I let her know I would drive up after my workout.

I reached Molly's a little after one and found a note from Sarah and Nora tacked to the back door. "We're at the hospital."

I found Molly in the ER, behind a curtain, lying in a narrow bed. She was tiny and pale, and her features were compressed in pain. Her arm was in a cast. Nora came around the corner and put a hand on my shoulder. "Her blood pressure is soaring and her arm keeps swelling. We're waiting for the doctor. We don't know what's wrong."

Sarah and her cousin Jennifer were pressed against the wall, their faces drained of color. This was the hospital where Molly had worked for 40 years, the hospital where Nora still worked as a nurse. It was the hospital in a little town where nearly everyone knew and loved Molly, and so nurses hovered all around, whispering, going to her side to ask what they could do. But no one seemed able to find the doctor. "Can you reach him?" one nurse would ask another, and another would race

219

down the hall only to return shaking her head. "He said to move her to a room. He'll be here."

So they wheeled her to a room, but agonizing pain was shooting through her arm, and the arm was continuing to swell, the skin was hot to the touch. Machines connected to her beeped. Now Sarah and Jennifer stood against the wall of her room, and feeling helpless I stood beside her, touching her healthy arm, asking if I could do anything.

"Take it off," she said, and she began to tear wildly at the cast, unraveling it. I tried to stop her, but she snarled, "It has to come off," and I could see it must. The arm was swelling so quickly the skin at the edges of the cast was turning green, and this woman who was always so stoic was practically screaming, "Where's the damn doctor?"

There were more whispers, more panic, another hour on the clock, and at long last the doctor into her room. He waved dismissively at Jennifer and Sarah. "Get those minors out of here. Out..." he shooed the girls, and as they walked into the hall, they cursed him under their breath.

But he did nothing to help, and another hour passed. Finally, as it was growing dark outside, Nora and I and another nurse demanded that Molly be transferred to Ottawa General, and I sent the girls to Molly's house to answer phone calls. We called Emma and told her what was going on, and she and Keith promised to drive to Ottawa right away, a five-hour journey.

Nora climbed into the back of the ambulance and held her mother's healthy hand and I drove my car as fast as I could after the ambulance. Nora and I met in ER where a voice over an intercom called to us. We hurried over to a doctor who led us to Molly lying in a stretcher in a curtained cubicle, looking even smaller and in more agony.

"We'll need your signature to approve immediate surgery," the doctor told us. "Your mother has what's called Necrotizing fasciitis, a rare infection of the subcutaneous tissues, a monomicrobial infection of the *Staphylococcus aureaus*. I'm afraid the only remedy at this juncture is immediate surgery."

He lowered his voice, half turned us away from Molly's bed. "I have to caution you, it is possible she may lose her arm."

I'm certain Molly heard him, and Nora was too. I could see the way she looked at me, and we both saw the look in Molly's eye as she called us to move in closer to her. "Here," she said as she pulled rings off her healthy hand. Molly had a passion for rings; she collected them, and on her travels with her friend Emma, she had bought many. "I want you to have this one," she said, pressing the gold band with rubies into my hand. It matched the lion necklace Will had given me and that I had never removed. "And I want the girls to have the others...each of the girls..." she took off the opal ring, the silver band. She told us where she kept the others. "Mom, stop it, you're going to be fine," I said, and Nora nodded energetically. "You're strong, Mom. It'll be fine."

They wheeled her to the operating room, and someone led us to the Family Waiting Room. There Nora and I held each other's hands, sitting side by side on a sofa and looking out at the lights of the city. We were quiet but for occasionally telling each other she would be fine. She was a strong woman, a farm-raised woman, a horseback rider, a fighter. She could handle anything. And we would start all over again, reciting again the litany of Molly's strengths. We tried to joke about the possible loss of her arm—we imagined her balancing laundry and an iron and a coffee pot in one hand.

"I wish Emma were here," Nora said. "She'd know what to do. I wish she'd been here earlier, she would have made us come here sooner..."

"She's going to be fine..." I repeated our new mantra.

And then suddenly—perhaps an hour had passed, maybe two or three—someone was standing in the doorway surrounded by the backlight from the hall. He must have coughed because we both looked up. "Mrs. Wellstone, Mrs. Dryden...?" he asked.

We nodded. "Is she okay...?"

"I'm so sorry," he bowed his head.

She had died on the operating table. Her heart failed.

I remember only that it was dark outside, and that I couldn't imagine ever sleeping again, and I couldn't imagine how I would tell Sarah, or Will, or how we would survive without her.

* * *

That night from Molly's house I called Cataraqui Bay and asked for Paula Greene, and when I gave her the news, for the first and only time, she sounded sympathetic. "I'm so sorry," she said. I begged her not to tell him, but I told her I had to see him and that I could be there in three hours. I asked her to please make sure he wasn't hassled trying to come to visits that day—the last thing we needed was a guard forgetting to call him down, or another guard deciding he needed a second strip search. Paula promised me. And then I swallowed hard and asked for the impossible. I asked her if there was any way he could be permitted to come to the funeral.

"I'll do everything I can," she promised.

And in the visiting room I held him, and I cried, and I felt him pulling me closer, and closer, and then I felt his tears on my shoulder. Right there in the visiting room, surrounded by prisoners and guards and other wives, Will wept for a long, long time.

Paula Greene kept her word, and three days later, Will stepped outside to travel to his mother's funeral. It was the first time he had been out of prison in nearly 9 years, and he was dressed in a suit that was too big and a blue tie that clashed with the suit. I had borrowed both from Clare. Two guards drove him the two-hours north, Will in the backseat, shackled and handcuffed. I had begged Warden Whelan to let me travel with them, but that was against policy. So I drove with Kate and the girls. The earth was slushy, the air chilly, and it was sunny. I remember only the cold and the pressure on my chest as I walked into Molly's house where we gathered before the funeral.

Sun flooded the sun room, but even that room felt cold because she wasn't there. Kell climbed into her big red chair, and I thought I could see even she understood nothing was ever going to be the same. The house was crowded with family and strangers, and strangers' children. I wandered around, now and then hugging Sarah or Jennifer or Cass, tousling the little girls' hair. All of a sudden someone called, "He's here," and I ran outside to watch the blue sedan pulling up to the curb. I ran down the driveway. I watched one of the guards reach in to help him out of the car. Both guards were young and tall and handsome, and although they smiled, I sensed how embarrassed they felt.

I reached the car and thanked the guards. I hugged Will. He whispered in my ear, "Bastards make a fortune doing this detail. Overtime. Per diem. The fuckers."

"Shhh," I whispered as the sandy-haired bastard looked up the driveway towards the kids standing there watching us. He turned back to us and said, "Hey, listen, we don't need to keep these shackles and handcuffs on. It's cool."

"Dad," Sarah called, and she rushed down the drive. Cassandra and Willie hung back, and Nora's little girls hid behind their mother. But Jennifer was right behind Sarah, throwing her arms around his neck, kissing his cheek. "Hi, Uncle Will!" And he smiled for the first time and shook his head at the sight of her. "Jennifer, Jennifer, what a big beautiful girl you became."

We drove to the funeral parlor where the weight in my chest grew when I looked at Molly lying in her casket, swollen and made-up, looking like a caricature of herself. She never wore makeup like that.

"My mother's here," Sarah whispered. She had rushed to my side, but she wouldn't look into the casket. "Why did she have to come?"

I turned in time to see Kate walking towards Laura. I saw her slip an arm through hers and watched as she walked her away from us, and when it was time to sit in the chapel, Kate led Laura to the back of the room and sat there with her, and I silently said a prayer of thanks for Kate.

The chapel was packed with neighbors and family and friends. From the pulpit Russell looked out at all of us and he began to speak in that familiar, comforting voice. He nodded toward the back of the room and said, "First I would like to say thank you to two gentlemen there in the back…" And everyone turned to look two at the guards sitting as far away as they could while remaining within eyesight of Will. "Mr. James and Mr. Coyne are guards at Cataraqui Bay Institution who have been good enough to bring Molly's beloved son, Will, to be with us today, to join us in saying farewell to our beloved Molly. Gentlemen, thank you…"

They nodded and looked at their feet, and for the rest of the day, they never came near us. Will had been granted a pass for six hours, and when the ceremony ended, I checked my watch and realized that if he was going to return to prison on time, they had to leave right away. People were milling about, talking softly, and the service had ended, but we had not yet driven to the graveyard, and I wished Will could come. I walked towards the guards and said, "You have to leave now, right?"

The dark-haired man, James, shook his head. "It's discretionary," he said. "We make the decision. He can go to the graveyard with everyone, and we'll just tell you when we have to go."

They let him stay for the burial where I read a poem Molly had wanted read at her funeral, one we had found in a kitchen drawer with a note and instructions about how if she happened to die she hoped someone would read this over her grave. But the sisters felt too shy to read it, and I didn't feel odd being the daughter who read over her grave. I knew she had considered me a daughter, and though we had known each other just two years, our bond had been cemented by the trials prison creates for the families.

The church women had made sandwiches and cookies and pies, and Russell led us across the swampy lawn, out of the cold air and into the steamy church hall where smiling women poured cider and hot chocolate and every imaginable kind of sandwich and salad. I glanced across the room at the guards, raised my eyebrows, questioning. James mouthed, "It's okay."

I watched Laura flirting with the sandy-haired guard. I could hear her laugh all the way across the room, saw her lean forward and press her arms close to show off more cleavage. I actually glanced to see if Will was looking at her, but he was in deep conversation with his aunt and uncle, oblivious to Laura's show, and I admit I was relieved. "My mother's a jerk," Sarah whispered and gripped my hand.

I pulled her close. "Go spend time with your dad. He has to leave soon..."

As the sun was beginning to set, Mr. James and Mr. Coyne told me they were sorry but they would have to leave, and I walked with them to the car where they handcuffed and shackled Will and drove him back to Cataraqui Bay.

A few weeks after the funeral, Molly's house was sold. When Emma called to tell me that they wanted me to join them to clean out the house and divide up her things, I rented a Ryder truck and drove up to the house where I spent hours out in the garage going through Will's belongings, things Sean had helped to store away when Will went away. Sean worked with me, and when I pulled out from behind a stack of bags two enormous stainless steel double boilers, he burst out laughing. "For the mushrooms…" Those were the days…" and I saw that Will and his brother-in-law had shared more than their love for Nora. As we worked, we found mostly junk and much of it we agreed could be thrown away, but we also loaded up his old bedroom set and my favorite red sofa, and Kell's red chair and hundreds of pounds of weights that had sat out in that garage for a decade gathering rust. At day's end, when the house was empty and all of us were silent with heartbreak, I drove the two hours home, and for hours I unloaded the truck, leaving bruises on my thighs and rust beneath my nails.

While I worked, I kept thinking about one question, but it was a question that I never asked. I was afraid to ask. I wondered about guns. I found none in the garage or anywhere else in the house; I found no bullets. But I wish now I had asked him where they were and what kind of gun he used, and when he had first held a gun, and how many he owned and where he bought them. And why he bought them. I wish I had asked him if before the night of the murder, he had ever seen anyone killed and if back then he knew anyone who had died at someone else's hand. I wish I had asked him if he ever committed crimes for which he was never caught and what he did with the drugs he smuggled into Canada and where he traveled to find his drugs and how he found them once he had reached those places. I wish I had known as much about him as I always pretended—to others and to myself—that I knew.

Molly and Will's sisters were ruthlessly honest and law-abiding. They were the kind of women who counted their change, coming and going. And there was something else I never asked. I never asked Molly or his sisters if they knew what he was up to when he turned to crime. I never asked about the years leading up to the murder, and I never asked Will if anyone in his family knew what he did with his life besides his "day job" as a builder and a carpenter. I doubt anyone would have answered me if I asked, but I wish I had. But even by then I had noticed that whenever anyone asked Will about his past, he blamed his situation on others. He blamed his hockey coach for teaching him to use his fists; his eyesight for his failed hockey career ("you can't be a great goalie with foggy glasses," he'd say); Laura for his greed.

We had already spent nearly two years talking in visiting rooms and trailers and on telephones, years with our feet sticking to linoleum floors, our backsides aching from hard chairs, our eyes stinging from smoke, our limbs aching to touch, and I had listened to countless stories and told him countless more. I imagined myself teaching him the tools to express himself more openly; I brought him new friends who were not criminals; I saw myself saving him. But even then, and especially with Molly gone, I secretly did not believe I could. And yet, with Molly gone, I thought it still more important.

I felt as if I had failed her in not bringing him home before she died. I swore I would bring him home for me and the girls.

chapter thirty-three

Kingston is a beautiful city, the Victorian waterfront buildings built of limestone, the main square, Market Square and City Hall, an actual square. Every year in late spring on the grassy waterfront lawn, the city holds a Chili Festival. All the local restaurants compete, and I usually attended. I might not have that year—everything still felt so sad. But I wanted to vote for Van's Brew Pub chili to thank him for being so kind to me and the girls.

The Chili Fest is a happy, intimate affair, the competition real but not fierce. Zal Yanofsky of Chez Piggy's might amble over to Ed Smith's Windmills booth to taste his chili, and someone from Morrison's Diner might drop by Greek restaurant Minos's tent for a long chat and a taste of Chili and Ouzo. Kingston is a friendly town. English Canadians, and Kingston is ever-so-English, are not demonstrative but they're generally kind. They're not pompous, but they boast about their fine university, their military Fort and College. They like to point out that Kingston was Canada's first capital, home to the nation's first Prime Minister, Sir John A. Macdonald. They also openly acknowledge that was a long time ago, and that Sir John A was a notorious drunk.

But that year I felt especially out of place in my grief and envious of the couples walking arm in arm. The sun glinted off the lake; masts were clanging in the wind. I stood at the waterfront and watched the Wolf Island Ferry chugging from shore toward the big island and remembered a time when I hadn't been a prisoner's wife, when I had spent weekends riding that ferry, swimming in the lake, sailing, or traveling across the border. I dodged crowds, thinking, "Will will get out and this will all still be beautiful, and he'll be here with me," and as I so often dreamed, though more and more the dream felt too far away.

Suddenly I heard someone say my name. I turned to look but saw only a figure turning away, whispering, "Hey, Amy, tell Will hey."

"Wait," I said and strained to see who he was, but I didn't recognize this man who was carrying a stack of chairs and moving towards one of the tents. When I called he didn't stop, so I kept walking. And then, a couple minutes later another guy carrying a table walked past and under his breath said, "Give Will my best." That happened again five minutes later—a different guy, another "Say hey from Danto." I'm not sure how long it took me to understand, but finally I realized these men working the grounds were prisoners. Out there in the sunshine, surrounded by tents and pots of chili, with hundreds of children waving helium balloons and riding on their fathers' shoulders, out there with those picnic baskets and bicycles and pretty moms, there were dozens of men on day passes from prison taking care of business. It was prisoners who had pitched the tents and lugged chairs out of storage and set up tables. It was prisoners who would break down those tents and tables at the end of the day. For the first time in a long time I felt smug satisfaction that I possessed this secret knowledge of how dependent on our prisoners we Kingstonians actually were, and I understood that if people knew there were prisoners amongst us, some wouldn't have cared, but many would have been appalled. Those people who wrote angry letters to the editor about how all those prisoners in town, and all their family members, were a scourge to this fair city of ours, would rail. And suddenly I felt as protected as I ever had, and I felt, keenly, the division between the two worlds—inside and out. And I felt lonely.

Ironically, our trailer visits, meant to ease the loneliness and to be blessed retreats, often left me lonelier. Whenever I think back about those 72-hour visits, I see myself either holding my breath as guards searched through my suitcase or walking away from those same guards' prying eyes, teary and nicotine starved. My lips were always stinging from long kisses goodbye. I picture myself walking alone down long, cold hallways into a world that always felt gray after those days. I can still feel the eyes I felt back then—eyes everywhere, guards watching from every corner. Will and I shared trailer visits in every season, in three different prisons, but in my memory the weather after those visits is always the same—gloomy, overcast, and heavy. And my car is always parked in the same spot, in a faraway corner, covered with snow or ice, and I'm always standing in the cold scraping the windshield clear, praying the car will start. I always stopped on the way home for cigarettes and smoked half a dozen until I was sated and sick. Cigarettes were my companions when Will wasn't there. And in my mind's eye I always see Kell standing at the top of the hill, waiting for me. I see Kate inside my house, stirring a stew on the stove. I drop onto a sofa before the woodstove fire Kate has built, relieved at having survived the long route out.

Those guards stick with me because in the earliest days, while we were still at Middle Harbor and I wasn't yet accustomed to leaving trailers, I was headed for the Sally Port to sign out when one of the meaner, harder, younger guards called out to me. I turned and noticed his brushed-back golden hair and his high cheekbones. For one brief second I wished I had fallen in love with an ordinary, good-looking guy with a regular job, someone who could walk me out to my car and scrape off the ice, someone who could come home and sleep with me every night.

The handsome young guard smiled, and I smiled back, and then he winked and said, "Think you coulda' yelled any louder? Shame you have to waste all that energy on one of them." He nodded back towards the prison behind him, and I stifled a gag and my tears and added his lewd cruelty to my reasons for hating all guards. The hardest thing, after all these years, has been letting go of that kind of hatred, returning to the person I want to be, I believe in being, the person who understands that one guard does not represent all prison guards, that each warden, each prisoner, each prisoner's wife, and so on and on, does not stand in for all the others.

* * *

After Molly died, my desire to reconnect with my parents felt suddenly more acute. I don't remember when precisely, or how, but I began to talk with them again, and I quickly had a clearer and clearer sense of what was happening to my mother. I felt a strong need to connect with her before it was too late, and although at first we were a little shy with each other and they seldom asked me anything about Will, they did ask about the girls. So I decided late that spring to take the girls with me to Ohio to meet the family. I was uneasy about my brother, still, though it was good meeting his son, and my sister's daughter. But the best part of that visit was the day the girls and I spent with my mother in the building that had once been Cleveland's train station, converted into a tall-ceilinged mall. I sensed the changes in my mother, of course. Her reflexes were slower, and the lapses in her memory were evident. Her kitchen was cluttered with notes to herself—she had to write down everything or she forgot.

But in the mall her pleasure was most evident as the four of us shopped. I saw how much she loved trying on clothes and watching the girls trying them on. She seemed excited by an opportunity to spoil them—she bought each of them dresses and anything they wanted to eat. All my siblings' children were too young for this kind of adventure, so the girls offered my mom her first opportunity to do these grandmotherly things she seemed to have been born to do, and even now I can see the light streaming down from those open windows and I can feel the pleasure all of us felt, and I'm grateful for the memory. Best of all, that visit inspired my dad to let me know he and my mother had agreed. They were going to come to Ontario to meet my husband. They wanted to sign on to his visiting list, and they would come with open minds— this, I told the girls, was one more gift. They loved their dresses, but I think I was the one who was happiest after that trip.

Not everything about the girls gave me pleasure. Every semester the school would send me "Child at Risk" reports about Sarah. Every semester I had to attend meetings with her teachers and counselors to discuss their concerns. I urged her to tell them the problems she faced in her life, but she refused to let anyone know that her father was in prison. "They'll hate me more," she always said. When her English teacher called her spacey and complained she was "copping an attitude," I tried obliquely to explain. "She has a lot more on her plate than you can imagine," I told him.

He scoffed. "I know a lot of kids from divorced families, but they pay attention in class."

I begged Sarah with my eyes to tell this smart-ass how much he did not know. She sat in stony silence. Later I pleaded with her to let people know. "No one's going to think less of you," but she knew I was wrong.

Her father had gone to prison when she was five. Even then some families had refused to let their children play with her. People had always talked behind her back about her. Now that she had some control, she wasn't letting anyone in on the secret, and she hated it when I did.

Most Sunday nights, after Cass's weekend visit, she and I drove to a crossroad off Highway 2 where the bus would stop to pick her up. After we had missed it a few times and had to make frantic drives to Ottawa while her mother howled bloody murder, we always made sure to leave the bungalow in plenty of time to wait at the side of the road, and there we would sit beside the fields of corn, letting the engine run to stay warm, listening to the thrum of the car and to music while the windows fogged. Huddled against the passenger door, Cass would test me. "Okay who's singing?" she'd ask. Alanis Morrisette was the only one I ever got right, mostly because Cass played her music night and day. But Cass recognized every singer on every song—from the Cranberries to Frank Sinatra, from The Barenaked Ladies to The Grateful Dead. Decade and genre made no difference. She also recognized the make of every car, and she tried to teach me that, too, pointing out the shape of the taillights or the trunk, but every car looked the same to me. She was a brilliant girl, but one thing drove me mad. She didn't read, and after a while I began to recognize that she was dyslexic, but Will refused to believe me when I told him, and her mother refused to have her tested. I sometimes wondered if dyslexia worked like other disabilities, if Cass had honed her sense of shapes and sounds because she could not read. When we saw the bus cruising towards us along the black highway, we would turn off the car and run outside, wildly waving our arms so the driver would pull to the side of the road. I would reach to hug her goodbye, and she let me hug her, but she seldom hugged back. "Bye thanks," she would say, and as I drove home, I would cry because I missed her, and I wished she lived with me, and I knew what was probably coming within the next day or two.

Almost every week, she called me in tears about something that was amiss—her mother was drunk, the house going to hell, her mother had checked herself into a hospital and Cass was afraid of the man she left behind to stay with the kids. Once she called because she had run away, but by the time I reached her, Laura had called the cops on her. When

Cass refused to go home, Laura insisted she stay with a near-stranger—anyone but me. That year after Molly died, I raced to Ottawa to rescue her half a dozen times, and every weekend when she visited, her father asked her if she wanted me to go to court so she could live with me. Every time she shook her head, "no."

Cass was on a ski trip near Ottawa when I got a call from one of her teachers, out of breath, "She broke her femur. She's at Ottawa General," and for the umpteenth time I sped two hours north on icy roads and at the hospital I asked for Cassandra Dryden.

The woman studied her files and shook her head. "No one here by that name."

"She's here, I know she's here," I shouted. "She broke her leg. She's just had surgery. A ski accident..." but the woman shrugged. "Sorry. She's not on the record which means she isn't here."

I ran to another desk and again found no record of Cass. At the third desk, I broke down. Where was she? I had to find her. And then it suddenly hit me. She had called me once from a police station on the outskirts of Ottawa where she was outside having a fight with Laura. When I got there to rescue her, I heard a police officer address Laura as Laura Powell, her maiden name. It was sometime around then that I discovered Laura was working a dozen scams and often used a different name.

"Powell," I said to the woman at the desk. "Do you have a patient named Cassandra Powell?"

"Surgery A," the woman said, and there was Cass in a hospital bed, post-operative pale, her broken bone swathed in a gigantic cast and raised by a pulley almost to the ceiling. And there was Laura at her bedside, wailing. "My baby, my baby ..." When Laura heard me at the door, she turned and screamed, "Why are you here?" and I turned and walked down the hall to the waiting room.

A few hours later, a doctor poked his head into the room. "Your stepdaughter was asking for you," he said and smiled. "She's doing okay."

I walked back to the room, sat beside her and took her hand. "You'll be okay, honey. I know it hurts, but you're going to be fine," I said.

"I'm never going skiing again," she said. "It hurts so much." Her eyes overflowed, and I wished I could carry her home and hold her forever.

And then suddenly, one cold spring day in the middle of her eighth grade year, after her mother and I had stood out on a school playground shouting at each other and she had had to spend the night with another stranger, she asked me to please go to court. By that evening I had hired a lawyer, he had filed papers, and two weeks later, the court granted me sole custody of twelve-year-old Cass. We arranged for her to stay in Ottawa to finish up her eighth grade year. She would bunk with the father of her half-siblings; he had also been fighting Laura for custody, and he was happy to have Cass with him until the school year ended.

Not long after that, Gabriella Halder phoned from Berlin to suggest a child-exchange. Gaby was a beloved friend who had lived with our family when she and I were seniors in high school. Though we seldom saw each other, we still felt like sisters. She had a son, Leo, who was between Sarah and Cass in age, and they were taking a two-week sailing trip in Bavaria. She wanted Sarah to join them. She brushed away my concerns about the cost. She'd pay Sarah's fare, she said. Then Leo would fly to Canada with Sarah and stay with me for two weeks. I told her it was a generous offer, but I'd have to check with Will. I promised to get back to her soon.

Sarah, it turned out, had been listening on the extension.

The minute I hung up, Sarah started a campaign—begging, pleading, threatening. At last we struck a bargain. Gaby and I would split the fare to send her to Germany. Sarah would contribute her own money from babysitting and working at Baskin Robbins. As soon as she returned she would work at Baskin Robbins again like last summer or waitress at the Gananoque Inn. She swore to both me and Will. And so June came, and away she flew. Cass finished school and moved in with me.

In mid-July, I packed Cass and her best friend, Kelly, into the car and drove to Toronto to pick up Sarah and Leo. When they walked off the plane they were smiling, glowing, blond and happy. Sarah could not stop talking about how much she loved Leo and travel and Gaby and Germany and sailing…"Gaby's the best. She's amazing. She's so beautiful…" She talked all the way to Emma's house where we all bunked that night, sleeping on Emma's 800-ply sheets under thick comforters and waking to the smell of toast and sun. I had bought tickets for a Blue Jays baseball game because Leo was a baseball fanatic, and off we all went to the stadium.

Our seats were in left field, and the dome was open, and the day was beautiful. And I wasn't in a visiting room. After the game we walked down to the Quay, ambled around and stopped in every collectible shop to find Leo cards for Ken Griffey and Cal Ripken and Joe Carter. At supper we laughed and pigged out on nachos, and I realized this was the best time I had had in longer than I could remember. It was a relief not to be in a visiting room, but I had promised Will we would visit him the next afternoon, and besides, it was time for Sarah to go home and get a job, time to introduce Leo to my world where accommodations would not be as posh as at Emma's house, but I thought he would love it. I had planned things down to the minute. If there was no traffic, the drive from Toronto to Cataraqui Bay would take 2-1/2 hours. We would leave by 8 a.m. sharp so that we could be in the visiting room no later than noon.

But the next morning at 7:45 Sarah threw a fit. "I'm not leaving Toronto. I love it here…"

"Pack your bags," I stood with my hands on my hips in the doorway of her bedroom. She mimicked me, putting her hands on her hips and insisting they must stay. "Leo needs to see the Toronto zoo. And Little Italy."

"Sarah, you have 15 minutes," I said, and fight me though she did, somehow by ten minutes past eight I had them all shoveled into the car. And Sarah hated me. As I drove I fumed quietly, exhausted by her spoiled brat attitude. It couldn't last, I intended to tell Will. He would have to let her know she had to keep up her end of the bargain. She had just been to Berlin and Bavaria, on sailboats, at a Blue Jays game, in restaurants. I pressed the gas pedal, Sarah kicked the back of my seat, and I heard her whispering, "You're going to hate it, Leo," purposefully loudly enough so I would hear.

In the visiting room, Leo grinned at Will. "Why did you kill someone?" he asked. "What is it like in here? What do you think about?" I was amazed by the innocence with which he asked all the questions no one ever asked but everyone thought. He asked with no judgment, just curiosity, and Will relaxed into his questions and smiled and tried to answer. But Sarah scowled and slipped lower and lower in her seat, while Cassandra and Kelly giggled and whispered with each other, ignoring everyone else.

Sarah cast me a glare with a look that said: "I'm never going to smile again," and when he caught her, Will said, "Sarah, smart'en up. Go home and get a job."

Too soon the visit was over, and he was walking back to the range, and I was in the car with the kids again. I actually envied him. He was going up to his cell to be alone, and I was going home with an angry, pouting, furious 17-year-old.

At home she ran into her room, pulling the phone in with her. When she shuffled back out again, she said, flatly, "I'm spending the rest of the summer with my mom. She's my mom, and I haven't seen her in a long time, and I'm turning 18, and I'll never have the chance ever again to be with her."

Suddenly I remembered what it felt like to be 18—like the end of childhood and possibilities and parents. "Sarah, we made a deal. You can spend every weekend with your mom," I said. My heart hurt, maybe because I was envious of her mother, maybe because I could see she was going to leave. Or maybe I was just exhausted from fighting—fighting prison was plenty without adding another fight.

"I'm never going to see my mom again!" she wailed. "I hate you. I hate my dad. It was stupid to leave Toronto." She turned to Leo. "This town sucks, doesn't it?" He looked at her, and then at me. I saw he adored her just the way Eddie did. "Yes," he said.

The phone rang, and when she answered, her voice turned sweet. "Hi Mom," she cooed and again disappeared into her room.

The next day I went to see Will to talk to him about our fight. He didn't want to discuss details. He wanted to let her go. "She doesn't appreciate anything. If she wants to go, let her go."

I didn't know what to do. I didn't want her to leave. I didn't think it was right for her to turn her back on her obligations. And there was Cass—I wanted them to be together. And there was me. I wanted her to stay with me. I wept to Kate who, in her wisdom, listened and let me cry. Then she said, "Let her go. And tell her the door's always open."

I did let her go. I spent the two weeks showing Leo around the town, settling Cass in, visiting Will, carrying on, but no boyfriend breakup had ever hurt the way this hurt. In the mornings I would lie in bed and stare at the ceiling wondering how this had happened, how I had fallen so hard for her, wondering why I cared that there was no longer a difficult teenager in the house. Wondering why I felt so sad. Even all these years later whenever I look at photographs of Sarah, I feel the ache I felt in those days when I thought about her. I was always a little afraid for her. She seemed too tender and crush-able for this world. Her father went to prison, her mother drank too much, her Granny, the one person she counted on, had suddenly died. Everything she loved disappeared. One evening a few weeks after she left I was in the kitchen cooking supper when I looked out the window and saw Eddie riding his bicycle past our house. There was nothing but empty field and Clare and Nesta's house beyond the curve but he kept going. Then I saw him turn around and ride past in the other direction. A few minutes later he was riding past one more time.

I walked outside, and when he saw me, his eyes opened wide. "Where'd Sarah go?" he asked.

Her departure hadn't stopped hurting, and when I saw his face, I hurt for him, too. She hadn't told him. "Oh, Eddie, Sarah had to move away," I said.

"Oh, okay," he said, he pedaled away, but I could see he wanted to cry.

A few days later I walked to their house. Jim answered my knock, and I saw Eddie hiding behind him. "I'm so sorry, I just wanted to let you guys know Sarah moved back to Ottawa, so she can't babysit. But Cass lives with me now, and she's 13."

I apologized a few different times, a few different ways, making up excuses for Sarah the way I often did for Will when he behaved badly. Jim smiled sweetly, "I understand, sorry…" but Eddie poked his head out and said, "She never said goodbye."

chapter thirty-four

When Sarah packed all her things into a friend's car, refusing to say a word to me, not even petting Kell goodbye and staring through me as I called after her, "Sarah, remember, the door's always open…" I decided to use a different tack with Cass. I wouldn't try to shape her into the young woman I wanted her to be the way I had with Sarah. Whatever she wanted to do, within limits, of course, was fine. I never suggested she not visit her mother and siblings as I had with Sarah. I stayed out of her way with teachers. I didn't pry into her private feelings, didn't offer suggestions for friends or future plans. When she decided she wanted to play on Gananoque's softball team, I was secretly overjoyed, but I kept that joy to myself out of fear that it might scare her off.

When I told Will about her game, I could see he was glad, too. "That's good, honey," he said to her. "It's good to stay in shape. It's good to be outdoors. I'm proud of you." When she grimaced I added, "and it's good to have fun."

"And stay in shape," Will pinched my arm, nodding at me when he thought Cass wasn't looking. "You can lose a few pounds, sweetie," he added.

"She's studying hard," I defended her.

One day the spring after Sarah left, Cass seemed light-hearted and happy in the visiting room. Then she broke the news. "Alanis is playing in Ottawa next month."

"Cool, she's great," Will said.

"Yeah, and I'm going. I gotta go up there this Friday to get in line to buy tickets at Ticketmaster. I need to get the first ticket."

Will shook his head. "No way, José. You're too young to stand out in some parking lot all night, and besides, you can buy your ticket in Kingston."

"They go on sale at 5," she whined.

"I'm sure Amy will take you at 5."

I nodded. Of course I would. If it was important to her, I would wake up at three a.m. I'd been through worse, and I loved seeing her so happy.

"But Daaaad," she turned it into a three-syllable word.

"No buts. End of discussion." When Will ended a conversation, it was over, and neither Cass nor I dared pretend there was any sense in going any further. We both were stubborn, but when it came to stubbornness, he was definitely king. So I thought the matter was settled and even half-looked forward to our early-morning adventure, but on the way home she began to pout. She turned up the Alanis CD full volume, and when we reached the bungalow she ran inside, dragged the phone into her room and slammed the door behind her.

I knocked to tell her it was suppertime, but she yelled, "I'm talking to my mom…"

So I ate without her, did some work, talked to Will on the phone and decided I would simply let her pout until she had worked it out of her system.

At 10:20, after Will was locked in for the night, she finally poked her head out of her room. "My mom says it's okay for me to go. Willie and Sarah'll stand in line with me so it won't be dangerous, and then they'll drive me home on Sunday and they can visit with Dad."

Sarah had been gone for 10 months and hadn't spoken to either me or her Dad. I stared at Cass, unable to speak. I knew no matter what I said now, I could be guaranteed that someone in the family, if not everyone, would be angry with me. If I refused to let her leave, she'd wear me down with fury and her mother would call endlessly. If I turned down a chance for Will to see Sarah and Willie, I risked his being angry too. But he could just as easily be angry at me for letting her go. Finally I found my voice.

"Absolutely not. You heard what your father said. You're not going to Ottawa."

"I hate you," she said.

"Then you'll just have to hate me."

"You don't even want my dad to see his own kids," she began, tears streaming from her eyes, feet stomping the floor. Some part of me hated her in return for playing such a cruel manipulative game. "That's bullshit and you know it," I said. "Your father said you couldn't go, and if Sarah and Willie want to visit, they're always welcome."

"You don't care about anyone but you," she said. Her hair was flying, her face was red, her nose and eyes dripping tears. "You're the most selfish person I know!"

It was the proverbial straw. "You know what, Cass? I don't care what you do, but I'll tell you this. You'll have to figure out on your own how to get to the bus."

"I don't need you," she screamed and ran into her room. I followed her and stood in the doorway. I wanted to talk sensibly. I had been wrong to threaten her. I wouldn't take her to the bus station, but we had to talk. I reached out, but she turned and shouted, "Get out. Now!"

"Don't you dare talk to me that way, young lady," I said, and as she reached for the door, I grabbed her hand to stop her from slamming it closed.

"Let go!" she wailed.

For one second we tussled, but I saw how foolish I'd become. I let go and slammed the door closed.

"You hit my hand!" she wailed. The sound of her voice was terrifying. I felt my knees give out. That was the closest I had ever come to hitting someone. I breathed deeply and wrapped my arms around myself. I stopped talking. I shepherded the animals into my bedroom, crawled under my covers and after some tossing and turning, fell into a deep, dark sleep. When I woke at 8 in the morning, she was gone.

I never found out how she made her way to Ottawa—maybe Laura sent a boyfriend to pick her up or maybe she stood out on the highway and flagged down the bus. She had learned to make her way in the world.

That afternoon I visited Will and told him the story. I wanted him to comfort me, but he just laughed. "Kids'll be kids," he said.

I reminded him that it was he who had forbidden her to go, but the news that his son and daughter were planning to visit had altered the whole story for him. He was just glad to know they were coming. He teased me. "Come on, it's no big deal." More than ever, more than I had even in Kingston at the Chili Fest, more than I had leaving the trailers, more than I had for a long time, I felt alone. These three people—Sarah and Cass and Will—the people I'd given my heart, seemed to be casting it aside.

Two days later, on the day the kids were to visit, I sat next door in Carole's living room crying. I couldn't bear the idea of being home when Sarah dropped Cass at the house. I didn't want to endure her snub or Willie's, and I couldn't visit Will because it was their day. Somehow, in a single moment, I had become the outsider. I had never felt so sorry for myself as I wept into Carole's pillows.

Carole nodded. "Everyone can be an asshole sometimes," she said in her droll but tender way. "Sometimes I'm an asshole, and you're still here bein' my friend…"

"Yeah," I told her, "when you're drunk you're an asshole."

She laughed. "Yeah, and now I have cancer. What kind of fucked up neighbor gets cancer and can't do anything to help her goddamn neighbor, right?"

Guilt washed over me. Carole had been diagnosed a few months earlier, and here I was feeling sorry for myself over a stupid fight when she was facing the fight of a lifetime. "I'm the asshole," I said.

"Yep," she agreed and lit a cigarette. "Here, have a smoke. At least with me you don't have to pretend you're not a smoker."

I stayed there long after sunset, long after I heard the kids arrive and depart. I stayed until I saw Cass's bedroom light go out. Then I tiptoed across the lawn, quietly slid open the door and walked inside to wait for Will's call. He'd had time to eat and shower and relax after the visit.

The minutes ticked by and no call came, and then it was 10, and I knew he wouldn't be calling that night. I walked through the damp grass back to Carole's where she sat on her sofa, cross-legged, petting her big, fat orange cat, Pumpkin. I tapped on the door. "Carole, he didn't call."

But Carole didn't want to talk about that. She looked me in the eye. "Listen, this is important. If I don't make it, I want you to look after Pumpkin." She paused and petted him a while. "He's kinda like Will, ya know. Like nobody understands him either, and he has this gruff exterior, but inside," she started to chuckle, "inside he's a pussycat."

That night I slept like the dead and woke to the phone ringing. Cass was gone. The clock said 9:30. The call was collect, from Will.

"Hey!" I said, "you won't believe this but I'm just getting up..." I almost never slept past 6, but I was glad to have let myself sleep, and I wanted him to be happy for me. Instead he snarled, "You hit my daughter." The words felt like a slap. For once I felt a surge of pure anger, anger about all the effort I had expended on all of them only to have them turn on me. I don't know why it had taken me so long to feel the anger. I can only think that it had something to do with too much grief—with the loss of Molly and now my mother, losing Sarah, and soon Carole would be gone too. When I found my voice, I said, "You are insane. I did not hit your daughter, and I am not having this discussion." And for once it was me who hung up on him.

In seconds I was dressed and driving to school, tearing into Cassandra's counselor's office. Paul knew our story. When Cass started at the school and we were introduced, I told him everything, and he boned up on the family history. He had always been kind, and the minute he saw my face he beckoned me in. "Sit down, Amy. What's wrong?" I sobbed as I told him the story.

He nodded and handed me Kleenex after Kleenex. "I'm going to call Cass in," he said.

When she saw me, she looked at the floor, and her neck flushed red. More than ever she reminded me of Will—ashamed and distant and afraid and lost.

"Cassandra," Paul said gently, "Have a seat. Your stepmother here tells me she hit you, and I have to report these things to authorities. I'd like you to show me the bruise."

Her head shot up. "No!" I saw her tears tucked beneath the fearful gaze.

"I'm sorry, Cassandra, I insist," Paul said.

Her head dropped again. Slowly she held out her hand. He reached forward and studied the miniscule circle of blue on the fleshy area beneath her thumb. "Do you think I should report this?" he asked.

"No...." The tears began to fall. "She didn't hit me, not really, but I told my sister she did, and she told Dad, but she was just pushing the door." The tears turned to a flood. "Amy would never hit me."

The three of us talked for an hour. With Paul's help we came to an agreement. She would move back to her mother's house for the summer. She missed her brothers and sisters. In August she would decide what she wanted for the next school year. No one would force her to stay or return. She was old enough to make her own decisions. She was almost 15, and a summer apart would give us both some time.

A couple of weeks later she left, and I prayed she would return, but I knew in my heart that the four siblings would lure her back to Ottawa, and ultimately she returned to live with me only when she was in her late teens. When her father was already gone.

I spent that summer planting a garden at Landon Bay campgrounds. Charlie Donevan had turned a portion of the grounds into public gardens and parceled out small plots to anyone who wished to tend them. I took one and called my garden The Freedom Garden, dedicated to all prisoners and prisoners' families. All that summer when I wasn't working for money or writing the novel with Will or visiting or working on the Prisoners' Families brief, I planted lilies and iris, anemone and daisies. Sometimes I sat there and said silent prayers I no longer remember, but I do remember the way the sun felt on my face and the pleasure I felt in watching Kell racing across the fields, happy not to be waiting for me in a prison parking lot. Maybe in some ways I was finding a way to console myself with the idea that things wouldn't turn out the way I had imagined them. I know I was learning how to find consolation in silence and solitude, and that was new for me, something that would forever stand me in good stead.

chapter thirty-five

I don't remember how or why Elton first called years earlier from Maynard, but after his first call, he often called to hear news about Will. "Guy saved my life," he told me. "Least I can do is find a way to stay in touch. And hey, if there's anything I can ever do for you, for you guys, you just say the word."

Over the years a lot of men said the same thing—Bernard, Tim, Big Bill, Joe, Elton, Alberto. Sometimes they meant this literally. People didn't mess much with Will, the guys told me. He was tough with his fists, and although I never admitted it, I think that toughness was one of the things that first attracted me. Until Will, the men in my life had been intellectual toughs, men who could out-talk and out-write and out-wit other men, but with the exception of one short-lived affair, Will was the closest I had ever come to loving a man who had lived on the mean streets. I liked the idea of having a partner who could protect me not with money and status, but with his strength. Except of course he couldn't because he was locked up, and when he did get out, he would be living under a microscope. But I'd grown good at brushing aside realities. I just glowed at the praise Elton heaped on him. "He taught me not to mix," Elton told me. "I don't mix."

Elton was from the Maritimes, from a hard-scrabble childhood that included several stints in reform schools, classic training grounds for jails and penitentiaries. Now that he had reached his 30s, he wanted to make a new life. His sister lived in Calgary and had offered him a place to live. His voice was deep and melodic with that Maritime twang, half-Irish, half uniquely its own, and he sounded especially sweet as he began to talk about his upcoming parole hearing. He was optimistic. When the hearing was canceled, twice, I began to complain on his behalf.

I complained to Claire who told me I had to learn to work these things out. I complained to Graham Stewart who made a few phone calls that went nowhere. I complained to Bill Miles who told me the stall wasn't malice, only incompetence. I complained to Will who said it was part of the game designed to frustrate inmates, a test to see which guys would explode and blow their chance for a release.

Elton never complained. "Ya know, that's how they do things," he'd say.

Then finally one day he called to say he had his release date. He had his plane ticket out of Kingston's little airport that night, but release time was 8 a.m. He wondered if I could maybe pick him up. His voice was hard to hear when he asked.

I can still feel the churning pleasure I felt as I anticipated the day of Elton's release. The idea of leading someone out, of driving someone to his freedom was the first real pleasure I'd felt in years, the first day after too many years when the possibility of a real life with Will, outside, seemed real again.

I left home extra early and drove west on Highway 2, along the river, past farmhouses and cottages and fields of wheat, then north on two-lane Maynard Road, cutting across farmland and more fields thick with grazing cattle. Early summer in Ontario is exquisite—the lilacs in bloom, alfalfa bright. Ontario light is hard, and the land is flat, so vistas are open and wide, and still whenever I think of freedom, I think of those vistas—the opposite of closed, dark space—nothing looming like those guard towers in prison yards, nothing stony or mean, just oceans of quiet.

Elton and I had never met. When I was at Maynard as a columnist, he was staying in his cell playing guitar. He wasn't political. He just wanted to "do his time." So I had no idea what he looked like—Will had had no pictures of him. I only knew he would be the only guy standing at the Sally Port not wearing a uniform.

Elton's hair gleamed black as patent leather. His muscles bulged beneath a freshly pressed shirt. I could see his street clothes felt awkward on him; he shifted from foot to foot, a suitcase in one hand, guitar case in the other.

"Hi," I said.

The guards scowled, angry at watching a convict leave prison. I understood then for the first time, it was they who had no release date.

I hugged Elton and whispered, "Let's get out of here," and like runaway kids, we made for the door, raced under the gun towers, charged across the wide gravel lot. We both thought they might try to stop us.

My tires squealed as I pulled out, and in my rearview mirror I watched Maynard recede into the distance. Elton stared out the window. "Man, oh man," he said as we sped past fields of ripening alfalfa. "Man oh man, will you look at alla this?"

When we pulled up our drive, Elton gasped. "You live right *on* the water," he said, leaping out of the car. He jogged to the riverfront, stood on the bank and stared out towards the islands a few miles away. The sun reflected off the river, Kell was rolling in the scraggly grass, daisies were flowering.

"Think I could swim?" Elton asked shyly.

"Of course. I'll show you where to change."

Minutes later he was dressed in shorts, his leg jailhouse pale, his ink black hair a stark contrast to his pasty white skin. He raced down to the water. It was shallow, waist deep for a dozen yards. He waded out, wobbling on the stones under his feet.

And then he found the fall-off point. And he dived.

I stood watching the swirling water above him, waiting. When he splashed to the surface I felt—even from a distance of 20 feet—the sigh of his release, his relief, exhaling with pleasure. Inhaling—water, air, sky, grass, sun. Space. Life outside.

"God," I heard him breathe.

Again he dived.

I could not take my eyes off the whirlpool above him. Tears began to fall, but at first I didn't notice them. I felt transported, breathless at seeing something new and innocent entering the world. I remembered how I felt when I helped to birth lambs on the farm—wonder, the heat of the ewes' womb. New birth is unspeakably good, and that is what I felt as I watched Elton emerge again and walk out of the water, a different man.

"My God," he said again as he searched the sky, the earth, the water, looking for words. Dripping wet, he glowed, more beautiful than anyone I had ever seen.

And so there it was—that small thing that offered all that big hope, that moment when the world expands. It was what I dreamed I'd see again when Will came home.

chapter thirty-six

But dreaming of Will's coming home didn't bring him home, and at Cataraqui Bay the months rolled on monotonously. Paula Greene continually revised his assessment, adding programs, fiddling with reports, while Dilshad Marshall cancelled appointments and rescheduled for weeks later. In the reports she released, Dilshad wrote, "Will's institutional behaviour is remarkably clear with two exceptions." One of those exceptions was easy to address—it was an incident at Cataraqui Bay when Will chased an inmate down the hall to stop him from stabbing another inmate, and a guard charged Will (not the knife-wielder) with "disorderly behaviour." Even Paula understood how meaningless that charge had been. But the other "exception" was Will's "conspiracy" at Maynard, a blemish that remained on his record as if it were truth and made me feel that all the effort I had poured into its expulsion had been useless.

Outside prison I was struggling to keep my life and my career on track. When Cass decided to stay on with her mother, I was half-relieved. She and I forgave each other and returned to the old custom of her frequent visits and Sunday evenings sitting by the side of the road listening to music and waiting for the bus. Meanwhile I had signed a 15-year contract with Universal Press and was working to make sure *Tell Me a Story* was great. That was the new name we called the feature when, in negotiations, *The Whig* insisted on retaining the name *The Bedtime Story* in case they decided to let me and the illustrator go. The "new" feature for Universal ran once a week instead of six, and I was the writer of every story instead of occasional writer and fulltime editor. Within a few weeks, nearly 200 newspapers around the world had picked up *Tell Me A Story*. A few months later *The Whig* let me and

Jillian go and gave the reins of their *Bedtime Story* to someone else. My nine years at *The Whig* was over, and my reasons for spending time with fellow writers grew fewer. My circle became smaller still.

The change made me feel lonely, but at least I was back in touch with my family—and my parents even came for a visit, a slightly awkward time. Everyone was civil. But I came to understand the demons my mom was fighting, and my dad, as was his wont, zeroed in closer and closer on her, pulling in more and more to the home front, reaching out to fewer people, including his kids. It didn't matter how old I was, I still longed for mothering—most of us always do—and without Molly or Mom, I leaned on Kate and Claire. It was Claire to whom I usually despaired in long letters, in phone calls, and the occasional visit about the misery and obstinacy of prison. Whenever I felt I might collapse under the weight, whenever I felt as if we were pedalling with all our strength only to stay in place, she patiently pointed out how far Will had come, how well we were doing.

"We worry Will hasn't participated in sufficient programming," Paula wrote in his file. Dilshad added, "There is little in the way of programming that can realistically address this man's problems." They felt therapy was the only answer, and I bridled at the implication. That meant more time inside, a longer wait, more prison visits. And so I

yelled at Paula, and I wrote letters, and I debated the warden and anyone else I could find. Claire tried to calm me down. What were two or three years when so many men were looking at 15 or 20 or 30? she asked—though she was also sympathetic about how miserable even a minute could be—and I tried to console myself that two was nothing compared to 20. But every month felt longer, and when Claire said, "When he does get out, don't look back. Just get the hell out and move on," in my mind's eye I kept seeing Elton and that halo of light surrounding him as he rose out of the water. Every now and then Elton called from out west—he had fallen in love; he was working; he was happy. His voice sounded light and loved while Will's sounded increasingly heavy.

Will was seeing Dilshad once or twice a month. He began to believe she might actually help him to better understand himself, but by then I saw her only as another roadblock to his life outside. He took on the role of mollifying me, encouraging me to relax when I did fight Dilshad. When Claire visited, the two of them lectured me, urging me to let the story unfold as it would. But I was on a mission, extracting and collecting letters from everyone I could, letters that expressed the support Will could expect when he got out. My Universal editors wrote letters, my agent did, an ex-boss, old boyfriends, friends and family, lawyers, doctors, artists, teachers.

If Paula ever did the paperwork to send Will to minimum security, I intended these letters to prove that Will was surrounded by people who had nothing to do with crime or drugs or trouble of any kind. I talked to Paula trying to convince her that Will's associations were mine; I talked a Hollywood producer friend into reading a script Will was writing. I pushed Will to finish a script. Paula's mention in the file the possibility that Will might be a flight risk evoked another flurry of letters. "Our business depends upon my name and contacts and my reputation," I wrote, linking not just our personal life but my entire career to his fledgling dreams to become a writer. "Because Will is my business partner and co-writer, it is highly unlikely that either of us would risk everything...." I wrote to point out the importance of Will's children to him, neglecting to mention that Sarah hadn't talked to us in over a year. I cited statistics I had gathered from John Howard Society workshops and booklets, from Claire's letters, and from books: In the category in which Will's crime fell, there was only a 1% recidivism rate to commit the same crime upon release.

Even our trailer visits became cause for a letter of complaint. Every two or three months we were able to spend three days together, but that was never enough to ease the loneliness and longing I felt. To Paula I wrote, "CSC claims to support family and community involvement, and our family visits are supposed to occur every six weeks. Overcrowding has slowed them down, thus restricting our ability to heal our family." That was true, but my obsessions deafened me to Claire's lessons— she cautioned patience; she tried to teach me to maintain my anger at injustice without letting anger wear me down or drive me to madness.

But there was a madness in me born of all those frustrations, and although I continued to write and to teach, I saw only many years later how much of my imagination revolved not around creating new ways of seeing the world, new stories and books and ideas, but around creating arguments for why Will should be, must be, freed. I worked for weeks and months on the brief for The Alliance of Prisoners' Families, with Arlene and Graham carefully outlining the ways in which families could offer a truly rehabilitative arm to Corrections. Each year we petitioned Parliament's Justice Committee to invite us to appear before them to present our brief, but the years passed with no invitation. I might have quit except that Graham and Claire cheered us on, and Will admired me for trying to help families. When he and I talked about the brief, I saw in his eyes some of that old admiration that often seemed nearly extinguished.

And every time I thought about how useless it was to fight on behalf of prisoners or their families, something stirred me up—if it wasn't watching an old woman called into a back room for a strip search or a little boy moved to tears when he and his mother were refused a visit or a little girl learning that her father was in the hospital fighting for his life, it was something like the ion scanner. The first time I saw it, I paled because I knew by then that any test we had to pass was a test we might fail, but there it was, this big machine that looked like an oversized microwave sitting beside the guard at the Sally Port. That day when I handed her my keys, she slipped on a pair of plastic gloves, picked up my belongings and placed them inside the belly of the machine. She closed the door, and a second later we both heard a high-pitched burp, and instead of opening the door and handing back my belongings, she picked up a pen and said, "Your name, please?"

I looked at her. "My name is on the ID in that box. Just take it out and look."

"I can't do that, Ma'am. Please give me your name."

"Why? What's this machine?"

"It's an ion scanner, but the beep means nothing since we're still setting the calibrations. But you'll need to give me your name since it did beep."

I knew if I gave her my name, it would be filed in some report somewhere and would be an indication that I had tried to smuggle something illegal into my visit with Will, so I refused, and in response she refused me a visit. I demanded she let me speak to her supervisor, and she picked up the phone. A minute later a man arrived, and he coolly explained that this machine was state-of-the-art, designed to measure in Nano grams—billionths of a gram—for any narcotics on our belongings. He assured me all the finest security systems in the world were using it, and Cataraqui Bay was "lucky enough," to be the first in the Canadian prison system to try it out.

Furious, all I could think about, again, were all those guards and "official visitors" sweeping in and out of every prison everywhere without the slightest hint of suspicion, and I sneered, "Test the damn wardens then." I inhaled deeply and explained, as calmly as I could, that I would not give this woman my name because she would not tell me what she planned to do with it or why, precisely, the machine had beeped. He told me the same thing she had—that it wasn't yet properly calibrated and The Bay had no intention of doing anything with the names they collected that day.

"Then don't take them," I said, and he nodded curtly and turned to the woman and told her my name. Of course he had known it all along, and she wrote it on her list and passed it to me. "Sign here," she said. But I refused to sign and I turned to the women waiting behind me in line and made a speech, telling them that now we were being tested for any debris we might be carrying, warning them not to ride the bus or take a taxi or shake a stranger's hand. The others in line bowed their heads as I went on with my stump speech. Most of them turned away, and I understood why. I was only making their wait longer. I was causing trouble. They couldn't be seen to be "associated" with a troublemaker like me.

I gave up. I signed the paper. Later that day I wrote more letters—to Paula, to Graham, to Claire, to the Solicitor General, to reporters. Only Graham investigated, and called a few weeks later to tell me that when the National Director of Correctional Services visited Cataraqui Bay and slipped his wallet into the ion scanner, the machine began to beep furiously, and he ordered the institution to get the calibrations right. Three years later, when Will finally was transferred to a minimum security and assigned a new C.O., Hughie Morrison, one day in a meeting Hughie shoved a piece of paper towards me, and I read the report that stated that one day deep into Will's incarceration, an "unnamed visitor" had come for a visit and that this individual's belongings tested positive for drug residue in the ion scanner. Hughie was smart enough to read between the lines. He just laughed and said, "I figure this must have been you, but don't worry, I know bullshit when I see it. Please just don't write me a letter about it—that only makes me have to do more work." So I didn't write another letter; the blot remained on Will's file. Instead I wrote a long story, *Bureaubabble and the Beep* and published it in *The Journal of Prisoners on Prison*, one of the only publications that seemed interested in exploring the way prisons actually worked.

This was how three years passed. After one year at Cataraqui Bay, a dozen therapy sessions, dozens of sessions postponed, a few trailer visits, more pages exchanged, Will thought our book was finished. I knew it wasn't. I sent him back to the drawing board, but he went metaphorically kicking and screaming. His resistance didn't surprise me, exactly. Many students believed their first drafts were the last. But when I told Will this draft wasn't perfect, he grew more depressed, less optimistic that our work together would ever amount to anything.

The work for the Syndicate brought in the bulk of my income, and teaching and editing added more, but I wasn't earning enough to create the kind of nest egg Will imagined we would one day have. I was barely scraping by. "We'll travel," he said. "I can't wait to spend a winter out of this cold. Somehow I'll get the parole board to give me permission to travel." I said nothing. I couldn't bear the idea of quashing yet another dream by telling him we didn't have enough for any luxuries. Whenever I did mention having had to spend money on car repairs or fixing a hole in the roof, he brooded about being unable to help me. His litany of complaints began. He was worthless, a loser. And brooding always led to depression, and depression always led to blame. "I'm a loser," led to his blaming me for being dumb enough to marry him, and that led to blaming *The Whig* for firing me because if they hadn't, he reasoned, I'd have plenty of money, and that led to blaming me again for getting myself fired by being fool enough to marry a loser like him, and the cycle would begin all over again. I tried to stop the cycle—I worried that Dilshad and Paula would see these cycles as one more reason he ought not be considered eligible for "Camp," one more reason to add one more year to his sentence. To me that only meant one more year visiting prison, one more year without his being home to help me fix that roof, one more year of this old game. I couldn't imagine how I would stand that. So I kept my complaints to myself more and more.

Graham and Kate and Claire all promised things would get easier as time passed. Camp would offer more opportunities to spend time together and to unravel the bad habits we'd created between us. At Camp we could eat meals together and have leisurely conversations; at Camp he would be eligible for escorted passes, and later for unescorted passes. Those passes would offer us a chance to spend time out in the world together instead of in those same dingy, smoky, sad rooms. Claire suggested I begin to think about places Will could go for his escorted passes—places a parole board would consider reasonable. I wanted him home, but Claire explained he had to prove himself. Parole boards, she said, like the idea of "community service." I thought of Revelations House, the group home for young offenders where I had once served on the board.

Despite having been voted off the board, I had remained close to Alan Park, the director of the house. At Revelations House everything was based on trust, and in place of punishment as existed in prison, Alan and the staff gave the boys responsibilities. If they failed, he assigned them to work with him to design a new plan that might lead to success. Eight to ten boys lived in the house at one time, under supervision by a staff of three or four, and more often than not, the boys who passed through Revelations House left there and succeeded in school and in the world. Over the years Alan had invited many speakers into the house—police and probation officers, lawyers and government officials and guards. Indeed, one of the reasons the board had tossed me from its roster was that Alan and I had begun to talk about how important it would be to invite inmates in to speak to the boys—who better to tell them the hard truths about what serving time meant. But the board members thought that sounded dangerous. Alan thought the idea of Will getting a pass to come to the house was a terrific idea. He began to write letters to that effect for Will's file.

One chilly March day, two years after Molly's death, Will came down to visits smiling. His smiles had been fewer and fewer ever since Molly died, but now there was reason to celebrate. Paula and Dilshad

had agreed to send him to a parole hearing, requesting a transfer to minimum security. Although it was coming one year later than I had hoped it would, I knew enough not to complain. And a few weeks later we both appeared before the Board. They granted the transfer.

I called Claire to thank her for not letting me give up. Without her encouragement and faith and the energy to keep up the fight, I was fairly certain neither of us would have taken him this far, but I didn't reach her. She was traveling again, off on tour to visit some of the hundreds of men and women who counted on her to help them through their dark times just as I counted on her. I was worried to hear she was traveling. Just a year earlier she had suffered a heart attack and a stroke, and at that time she had sent out a poignant message to her huge network inside and out of prison. "This will have to be my last letter to you, and that really hurts. I must stop completely and totally what I've been doing for 20 years. Damn!" She was 77, and her doctors ordered her to slow down. But true to form, she was back at it within weeks, sending out her hundreds of letters and faxes, and now she was visiting the pens again.

"Stop the world, I want to get off," Claire ended nearly every letter to me. And then, on April 30, 1996, just a few weeks after Will's move to Camp, she got her wish when her heart gave out for the last time. It was a Sunday night. She was home in Vancouver. I heard the news on the radio just before Arlene called in tears to tell me. By then I was in tears too. Arlene and I talked about our inability to imagine going on without her, and then, amazingly, Sarah called for the first time in nearly two years. She had heard about Claire's death, and she wanted to tell me how sorry she was, to let me know she was just as sad as I was. And after that conversation, things were suddenly all right between us.

"I miss you," she said, and just as Kate had promised, my offer to keep the door open proved prescient.

Sarah and I never talked about it, but Claire's death seemed to me to help her to understand that mothers do not live forever, that we must cherish them while they are with us. I am not Sarah or Cass's birth mother, and back then, and still, we have been surrounded by people eager to point out that fact. Laura, in particular, loved to say that I never would understand what it meant to be a mother. Over the years I've known many other women who sometimes, often in subtle ways, diminish the bond of those who are not biological parents—particularly mothers. I was fortunate in this respect—no matter the discomfort my marriage to Will caused my family, from early on my parents and brother and sisters and brothers- and sisters-in-law embraced both girls as family. The girls tell me they always considered me more mother than stepmother, my family, theirs. I am a second mother yes, but not a lesser one. In my heart, always in those days and to this day, they are my beloved daughters. As time passed, the fight I was waging for Will's freedom revolved not only around my desire for our connection and a chance to be together out in the world, but for theirs.

chapter thirty-seven

Both girls joined us for Will's first escorted pass to Revelations House. At the house while we waited for him to arrive, the three of us could not sit still. We nervously pulled at threads on our sweaters as we sat at the long dining room table surrounded by juvenile delinquents—pimply kids, funny kids, kids who had committed crimes, petty and serious. Bruce, one of the long-time staffers was a wise counselor who wore a ponytail and a winning grin, and he was conducting the boys as they set the table and cooked spaghetti for their upcoming visitor. Everyone was buzzing with excitement—talkative, full of questions, wanting to know from the girls what it was like to have a dad in prison, learning how uncool they thought it was.

The telephone rang, and Bruce answered it and rolled his eyes at me. He talked for a few minutes, letting me know it was the warden from Clarendon wanting to know if I was there. Bruce told him I was and added, "Why wouldn't she be here, she's one of our best friends," but I watched his smile disappear as the warden told him I was not supposed to be there. He motioned me to the phone to talk to him, and when I answered, the warden told me this was a community service pass. It wasn't an excuse for Will to spend time with his family, he said. And of course I argued. I explained that Will planned to talk about how prison affects families, and it would be ridiculous not to let me and the girls be a part of that conversation. He argued back. The evening was not meant to be fun, it was meant to be Service. I just wanted to scream and had to bite my lip and look around at the kids who were beginning to stare at me.

This much was true, though I didn't say it to the warden. This was fun. Being in a house where the mention of prison and my prisoner husband didn't inspire people to turn away from me in disgust was immense fun. Being in a house where Cass and Sarah would not have to pretend their father wasn't a prisoner was fun—where other people wanted to hear what he had to say, that was fun. But I knew I had to convince the warden to let us stay, and I knew if I let him feel my happiness, he would feel the need to quash it. I'd done my research. Prisons in the US and Canada had become, since the '70s, places for punishment, not rehabilitation—no matter what people wanted to believe. So I told him that the last thing in the world this could possibly be considered was fun, and somehow I managed to convince him to let us stay there, so we were there to watch the guards escort Will into the house shackles and handcuffs, and this time they didn't remove them.

"You wanna look like this one day?" he asked the boys when we were all seated in the living room—the girls on either side of their father, pressed in close. "I'm just an old guy in shackles and handcuffs, kids. Look at me. And understand this. Every guy in prison's a loser. Don't be a loser."

I hated hearing him say that. Although I understood he was trying to teach them, I also understood, deep down, that he meant what he was saying. Some part of me worried that his admiration for me was withering because he felt I had married a loser. Like the old Groucho Marx joke—"I don't want to belong to any club that would accept me as a member,"—as Will's mood worsened, so did his belief in me, his belief that my marrying him reflected anything but poor judgment, bad taste, a grave error.

And there was this: Now that he was in Camp, I was in effect his only jailer. "I'm doing my time for you," he often reminded me. In other words, I was the only impediment to his taking off to find real freedom somewhere over some distant border. He told me, many times, that his commitment to me, and to the girls, and to living a straight life was real. But beneath his words, I sensed his terror at that idea. I had, over the years, read massive amounts of research on the effects of incarceration—on rehabilitation versus punishment, and much of it showed that a pessimistic "nothing works" attitude toward rehabilitation that justified the US and Canadian lean towards punishment-based policies were overstated, that in truth work programs and education and psychology could ease prisoners' transition to the outside. But research, and my conversations with Will and so many other prisoners also proved the power of the prison environment to shape behavior. There was, for instance, the famous Stanford prison experiment of 1973 that proved even psychologically healthy individuals could become sadistic or depressed when placed in prison-like environments, and that was backed up over the years by many similar studies. One of the papers I read when Will transferred focused on the high levels of anxiety and depression that came upon prisoners when they were released without decompression into lower-security facilities, and although he had been "cascading" to lower security for three years, the move to Camp felt sudden and jarring.

Just a month or two before his transfer to Camp I'd received a call at home from the daughter of an old friend of Will's—a man he'd known and liked at Maynard. The young woman was calling to let me know that her father, on parole, had fled the country. We talked for a long time. She cried. She missed him, and she couldn't contact him, and she couldn't tell me where he was—she wasn't sure she knew. He hadn't wanted her to know. He only wanted her to know that he sent his regards to Will, and his farewell. While we talked I felt for her even as I wished she hadn't called. I feared that any association, even from this distance, with a parolee who had fled the country could affect Will's chances for release.

And I said nothing to anyone about this, but I also began to nurse another fear—that Will might decide he wanted to flee the country too. Everything I'd done for more than four years had been premised on his coming home, and staying home, making a life with us in the bungalow on the river. But I knew a few other men serving lifetime paroles. I saw the restrictions wore on them. I said nothing. I told no one. I was too afraid that my fear would end up in his files and set back the release date yet again.

Instead of Camp being the panacea I had imagined it, Will despised it. He hated the petty criminals. Camp was the place to which some men cascaded, but it was also the place that housed dirty cops and small-time crooks and rats. He hated the petty rules and the petty guards, and he hated most of all the dairy barns where every Clarendon inmate was assigned to work upon arrival. Before the transfer, I had imagined that his parents' farming blood might flow through his veins and being near animals and in the air would open his heart. But from the first day he complained about having to wake at the crack of dawn, about the manure, and despite the massive weights he lifted, he complained about the weight of hay bales.

This is one more way, I learned, that we were so different from each other—one more way I might have seen that our partnership might be in peril. I had loved working on Dean's sheep farm, and I stayed as long I did in part because I hadn't been able to imagine leaving all the barn cats and the lambs and the ewes and the horse and those wide open fields. Also, I was always morning person, and I loved the smells on the farm. I had never worked on a dairy farm, but I had spent hours in barns, lifting bales of hay and tending sheep, and I had loved it, and so this became one more thing I didn't discuss with anyone because in my mind's eye again I imagined his file: "Hopeless wife, sure to leave him."

The System inspired lies, but the truth is I was worried—about how and if we would make it, about whether he would stay with me once he was out, especially about how he would feel about the bungalow. Before prison he had lived an expensive life—a big house, lots of travel, many things. But we would be eking out a living, and the bungalow wasn't fancy. Indeed, it was far from perfect, and whenever he talked about how he was going to make it more beautiful, his plans both buoyed me and worried me. And once again I shifted the worries to the back of my mind and told myself I would face them when I had to.

One sunny day Emma and Keith and Gina drove in from Toronto to visit, and because they now could share a meal with us, they brought along a picnic. As Keith barbecued chicken on the wide lawn outside Clarendon, he peppered me with questions about this world that was so unfamiliar. Then, still bubbling with curiosity, he looked over to the table where Will and his sisters were huddled in conversation, and winking at me, he said, "Hey, you guys, why don't you tell us some stories about your childhood."

Emma looked up, and her face registered horror. "What's past is past," she said coldly. Will nodded, Gina half-smiled and looked down. Over the years I had been aware of Emma's deep desire for privacy and

Will's longing to shed his past. Sometimes that had seemed healthy to me; sometimes I thought denial and hope were so closely entwined that one could not exist without the other. Denial had worked beautifully for my father in surviving not just POW camp but my mother's increasing disappearance. I had begun to wonder if ignoring facts—the fact, for instance, that I was married to a prisoner who would always be on parole, the facts, for instance, of his crime—might be the thing that could assure us a happy life. I wanted to believe that. In truth, though, I never did. Rather, I believed then, but believe more deeply now, that facing even the darkest, saddest, most difficult memories can help to heal the deepest wounds.

After each ETA the guards wrote reports, and some wrote glowingly of his behavior and of his family's. Six months after the passes had begun, the Board granted him a series of Unescorted Temporary Absences (UTAs). I had dreamed of this for so long, I almost couldn't believe it was going to happen. He would be coming home for eight whole hours, Christmas Day, no guards or shackles or spies.

part three

chapter thirty-eight

As I drove to Clarendon to pick him up for the Christmas celebration—the girls and his sisters, Keith and Willie would meet us at the house—I thought about Elton, of course. It was December and cold, and there would be no diving into the icy river. Instead he would walk into the house that smelled like turkey, and he would see the house for the first time—decorated, clean and smelling like pine, surrounded by a thick blanket of snow. I must have been nervous because I have no memory of picking him up or of driving with him in the car away from those walls and towers and gates. The vivid memory that remains is the sight that greeted us when we reached the bungalow and walked in the door. All three children had arrived, and his sisters and Keith were there, and there were boxes stacked three and four feet deep beneath the tree. His sisters were giggling. They announced that they had gone on "a little shopping spree."

"You haven't had any new clothes in so long…" Gina sighed, and Keith talked about how long the girls had been shopping. Everyone urged him to try the clothes on, and he couldn't say no, so he reached for the largest box and opened it and found inside, between folds of tissue paper, the most beautiful cashmere coat I'd ever seen—the color of Red Sea Sand. The minute I saw it, I envied Emma. I hated myself for feeling envy—I thought I ought to be grateful to her. But instead I only wished I were the one who had the money to buy him something so beautiful, something that so clearly moved him. A blush of pleasure was spreading from his forehead to his neck as he unfolded the coat. He put it on over his clothes—the new uniforms prisoners were wearing then, hideous dark blue jeans and poorly-fitted golf shirts. The coat fit as if it had been tailored for him. He suddenly looked so handsome, everyone gasped.

But Emma didn't want to stop there. She picked up a stack of boxes and pushed him into the bedroom to try everything on, and so he did. Each time he stepped out of the room he was dressed in a new outfit. The sisters seemed not to have missed a single designer or color or style. There was a Hugo Boss cashmere blazer, Yves St. Laurent slacks, Calvin Klein shirts, Givenchy ties to match the shirts, Tommy Hilfiger jerseys, Ferragamo shoes and a buttery leather bomber jacket. Every pair of pants they had bought came in threes—gray and black and tan—and shirts came in colors with names like Navaho white and Naples yellow. There were belts, scarves, socks and hats, something for every occasion, for every mood, and every time he came out of the room he was smiling more broadly, and his sisters were crooning more loudly. Emma patted Keith's sloppy stomach and said something about how fun it was to have a chance to shop for someone as slim and muscular as her brother.

While he modeled, I busied myself cooking the meal and adding one more secret worry to my list. I would never have the clothes to match his. The good clothes I owned were the clothes I wore to visit prison. I had no extra money to go shopping. And where was he going to go in all these new things? We lived in a tiny town, and even when he was released, he would be restricted from traveling. So what would he do with all those outfits? But as he continued to try on things, I crooned along with everyone about how great it was going to be to have him home. I applauded the sisters for giving him one more tool to help him in his life outside.

* * *

The tools I was working on were less lovely but I hoped more practical. For instance, I had an idea of something he could do to integrate himself into our little community, and so one day to implement this plan I went to the Gananoque police department to talk to the chief of police. Will's talks at Revelations House had been successful—both in helping him to feel he had something to give and for the boys who needed to learn where the paths they were on might actually lead them if they didn't wise up. The police chief's wife, Nancy, a ponytailed powerhouse with arms like ropes, ran the local gas station/coffee house, and whenever I stopped in she was terribly friendly. She often talked to me about how much she had loved my column and how much she wished I still wrote it. So I figured her handsome husband would be happy to help in any way he could, and since I knew the local group home often brought in speakers—parole officers and cops, social workers and therapists—I thought I would talk to Gary about Will being invited in. So I told him my idea, and he said he would think about it. He'd get back to me.

When a month had passed and I hadn't heard from him, I stopped in again to ask if he'd had any time to think about my suggestion. He nodded. He told me to sit. He had thought long and hard about it, he said, and the answer was no. He was sure my neighbors didn't like this idea of an ex-con moving to town.

I laughed. I thought he was joking. Several of my neighbors had already written letters on our behalf, I told him, and I explained that the girls babysat kids in town, and I talked about Eddie and about the retired police officer down the road who had a son in prison and understood, and about Michelle and Erin and Katie who were good friends of the girls, and about Nesta and Clare and Kate and Charlie Donevan at the hardware store. He shifted as I talked. When I was done he repeated, "We don't want ex-cons in this town. And we don't want their families."

I stood up. Blood rushed to my head. "Thanks for showing me what a prick you are," I said, and I stormed out without looking back.

Three days later, as I was driving from the bungalow into town, I approached the spot where the speed limit suddenly dipped from 55 to 30. I was driving 35, and three cars in front of me were driving much faster, but I suddenly heard a siren behind me, and when I looked in my rearview mirror, the cop waved me to the curb. He didn't wave the others over. He gave me a speeding ticket.

The next week I was stopped again, in the same spot, and the week after that I was stopped a third time. I had failed to observe a cardinal lesson in any city—do not cross the mayor or the police chief. And then I made a second mistake. I told Will about the tickets, and he placed one more brick in the wall he was building around himself to protect himself from what he so firmly believed: Nobody outside was ever going to welcome or accept him. I was furious about those tickets, but to try to fight this notion that was growing stronger the closer he came to release, I invented a story. I told him everyone was being stopped lately, that it wasn't just me.

This was late December, and there was actually a parole hearing on our horizon, scheduled for March, just three months away. I told myself we needed to present to the parole board a picture of the man he could be once he'd had a chance to live outside. Inside prison he lived under the mask of uneasy, gruff, quick-to-lose-his-temper convict, but I tried to look through that. I looked at him and saw the man in the cashmere coat and the sea blue shirt that matched his eyes. I saw the man who could make me laugh. The man who had kissed me for so many hours. I saw the man who had made my shoulder burn with lust at Maynard when he touched me on the lawn, under the sun. I saw his flaws but I was certain those could be repaired, and I blamed everything wrong on prison, and everything good—his drug-free, drink-free life, his studiousness, his desire and his efforts to be a good father and husband and brother—I attributed to his desires. Only his.

On New Year's Eve, 1997, I lay on the sofa reading Norman Mailer's *Fire on the Moon* about the astronauts. I loved the book. In those days especially I loved any art of any kind that depicted a sense of being utterly alone in this vast universe. I loved the rendering of that awesomely quiet and awesomely huge and terrifying but beautiful universe around us. The view out of the windows of the bungalow felt like that to me that night—the endless swirling snow and ice, the frozen, curving river, the world that looked enormous and unfathomable. Carole and Austin had invited me over to share champagne and ring in the New Year with them, but I hadn't wanted to intrude on their last New Year's Eve together.

A few months before Carole had walked into my house, and when I saw how yellow her skin looked, I insisted she call the doctor who diagnosed liver cancer. Quickly it became apparent she didn't have long to live, and I began to spend as many afternoons as I could sitting with her, trying to be a good friend, amazed by her equanimity in the face of so much pain and sadness. When they invited me for New Year's I was touched but also embarrassed for the way I sometimes hoarded the time Will and I had. But I said no for another reason, too. I wanted to inhale the last dregs of the loneliness that had become so familiar over the last five and half years. That's how sure I was that it was nearly behind me.

And I said no because I didn't want to miss Will's call, but by 8:00, when he hadn't yet called, I decided to risk missing him so I could take Kell for a walk around the block. She and I trudged past all the houses lit up with music and popping champagne corks, and I pulled my hood tightly around my head and watched our footprints breaking crisp new snow. I was imagining our future, six weeks away, after the parole hearing. It would be spring, and Will would be living with us, and I envisioned three steps of footprints in muddy earth.

By 10 when I hadn't yet heard from him, I began to worry that I had missed his call while we were walking, or maybe something had happened at Clarendon. My imagination began to grow wild about the possibilities, and I decided to calm myself I would call and ask if anything was wrong inside. The proximity of Will's freedom carved some of the bitterness from my heart, and for one moment I felt pity for the guard working on New Year's Eve. "Everything's quiet," he said.

"No lockdown or anything?" I prodded. Surely something had happened. The guard repeated that all was quiet, and so I asked if Will was in solitary or if something had happened to him. Although I knew better than to give a guard any ammunition against us, I couldn't stop myself, adding, "...because he didn't call tonight."

"Nothin' I can do about that," he said and he hung up. My pity for him turned to pity for myself. I shivered and noticed again the draft from the poorly insulated walls that Will had pointed out on his visit home. Afterwards he decided that when he was home he would raise the whole house and install a full basement to stop those drafts. He wanted to tear down the walls and widen the rooms, to build big cedar closets and expand the number of windows. I tossed wood on the woodstove and as I did, in the puff of smoke I noticed the dog and cat hair flying around, and I wandered to the closet to make sure his cashmere coat was carefully sealed under plastic. He had mentioned all that animal hair in the house might ruin his new clothes.

I climbed into bed, but I couldn't sleep. My mind spun with all the possibilities. Was he hurt? Or had he simply decided he didn't want to talk to me? But why would he do that? At three a.m., still wide awake, I phoned Arlene. We had talked each other through more than one night of anxiety, had always helped each other through those silences spawned by lockdowns and emergency transfers and stints in segregation cells. But that night I wept, "How could he not call me on New Year's Eve?"

Anyone who hadn't had our relationship to prison would have responded—and did when I later told the story—with anger. Other people always thought that was evidence aplenty that he was not worthy of my love or of my compassion, and that there had been much proof of that. But prisoners' wives and mothers and fathers, sisters and brothers, sons and daughters, usually empathized. Arlene listened. "Amy, he's afraid," she said. "This is a tough time for him. I'm sure he's overwhelmed by the possibilities of the hearing, either way. You have to be patient and loving. It will be all right."

She searched—just as I had done silently—for explanations and excuses. Maybe he had fallen asleep early. They did that when they got scared, she said. Maybe he had lost track of the time--that happened too during these stressful times of anticipation. Maybe he was feeling guilty again—guilty at not being outside with me on a night like this. Maybe he had wanted me to feel I had the freedom to go out if I wanted to go out without worrying about what he might think if I didn't answer his call. I loved Arlene for her generosity. Her husband had served nearly 20 years by then; she understood better than anyone how wounded so many prisoners were, and she knew, like I did, too, that for most prison only inflamed those wounds.

We always listened to each other without judgment. Later I began to understand how important it had been for me to see myself as a healer, almost a savior, but I didn't understand that then. I think it is possible that Arlene and other women married to men inside also had a need to see themselves as healers, helpers, saviors, but I'm not sure. And I do know there was one big difference between Arlene and me, though

I never acknowledged it back then. It was this: She didn't keep secrets from her husband. No matter how much honesty might cost, she didn't shy from it, and I have come to believe that is why their marriage has endured all these years. It is the reason, I believe, that when he was released, they were able to tough out the hard times outside.

Even back then, but always afterwards, people asked me why I didn't walk away that night when he didn't call, why I didn't give up in those moments over the years when I saw those waving red flags. Why, people always wanted to know, did I accept his abuse. Why did I accept Dean's before his? There is no simple answer; understanding comes in increments, and only slowly, over time. But I do know this. If I had ever thought of leaving him, it could never have been that night. I had just spent nearly six years chasing a dream, and we were on the verge. I couldn't and wouldn't have given it up. Instead I vowed to pull myself up by the bootstraps. I set my jaw. I imagine this must be the way hostages feel, and survivors, and people stranded on mountaintops or out at sea. I couldn't give up before release, descent, before the cavalry arrived.

"Happy New Year," Arlene said at 5 a.m. "Happy best year of all. I'm sure he'll call later this morning."

New Year's morning was clear and bitingly cold. I sat on the couch watching the windows fog as the heat of the woodstove smacked against the chill outside. I closed my eyes and tried to envision him sitting on the sofa beside me, his hand in mine. I tried to imagine the smell of his fish stew, tried to envision him serving it on his Mom's china that lined the cabinets.

At five o'clock I called the girls at their mother's house. "Happy New Year!"

"Ame," Sarah said softly. "Hang on. I'm changing phones." I heard her fumbling, heard a click, and then she was on again. "Can I live with you and Dad when he comes home?" she asked.

My heart expanded. "Yes. Great. For sure. Let's talk about it with Dad. Soon…" I didn't tell her he hadn't called last night. Her faith in us and her desire to be with us again felt like a sign that everything would work out, and when magical thinking begins, it usually expands as far as it can. Mine certainly did—instead of thinking about his not calling,

I thought of Sarah, of her return. I thought of all of us living happily ever after.

At 6:00 I called Kate. By 7 she and her dogs were with me, watching the first day of the New Year come to an end. I sobbed into her lap and asked her everything I feared. "What if he never calls again? What if it's all been a scam? What if he never gets out? What if he never loved me?" This, she told me, wasn't the time to let my imagination run wild; when pressure mounts, she wisely advised me, the best thing to do is to be still, to wait, to be quiet, to make no decisions in the heat of sorrow or fear or answer. That behavior, she said, was what sent people to madhouses, and prisons.

"Be patient, dear. This is a test of your strength. Hop into the shower and clean yourself up. I'll cook. You need to eat something." Two days passed that way, days I barely remember beyond Kate feeding me and feeding the wood stove. And then, on the third morning, the phone rang. I raced across the room towards it, but Kate grabbed my arm and whispered, "Be calm."

When I heard the operator's voice saying the call was collect, I collapsed onto the sofa and breathed for what felt like the first time since New Year's Eve, and I do remember hearing his voice crack and that he sounded farther away than ever, out of my grasp. "Hey, you okay?" he asked.

I couldn't find any words.

And before I could speak, he was speaking again. "We gotta end this," he said, and went on telling me how he had lain in his cell on New Year's Eve thinking all night long about us. He hadn't slept, he said. He just lay there thinking about how he couldn't saddle me with his endless years of parole, with a man who was a nobody and would only be a burden. And while he talked, I saw faces swarming before me— Louise Salem and Joe Book and Dilshad and Paula, Andrew McCabe and Bernard, Pierson and Tim, Luke who had just died still locked up in Maynard. I kept thinking someone must have put him up to this. Had Big Bill told him he ought to play the field when he got out? Had the warden warned him away? Did he hate the bungalow? Did he hate the way I looked? One day just after Christmas I had confessed to envying those beautiful clothes his sisters bought him. Should I have kept that to myself? Was it the smell of wood smoke and swirling fur he despised? I choked out words. "I've spent all these years…I love you…please, give us a chance…"

Kate sat close to me, rubbing her hand up and down my arm, whispering, "It's okay, dear…" but in my other ear Will's voice was telling me that he knew best. He always knew best. "We'll bring each other down. I know it in my bones."

I gasped for air, and right away I envisioned the Parole Board. "They'll never let you out. It'll be years before you see day parole." It was suicide, I thought, to go to the Board without me, but afraid he might hang up, I didn't say that.

"I have to take my chances. You need to get on with your life."

"You are my life," I said before I could stop myself. I heard his sharp intake of breath. "That's a mistake."

I stared at the river. "Will, do you love me?" Although I can't be sure, I think if he had told me he did not, I would have said goodbye, but right away he answered, "Yes, Amy…" and I heard a catch in his throat. "I'm doing this because it's best for you to get on with your life without a weight tugging you down." And then he hung up.

I thought I was going to drown in tears, and I thought he was my lifeboat and I was his. Kate held me while I cried. She never left my side, but the next morning, in a snowstorm, I climbed in the car and drove to the John Howard Society offices. I needed to talk to Graham, and I sat in his office, telling him the story, weeping. As always, Graham listened so attentively I felt certain he could hear even the beating of my heart.

"They do this," he said when I had run out of words. And he went on. It was Graham who told me about the stupid things so many prisoners do as the possibility of parole comes close—crimes they suddenly commit, escape attempts, suicides, breakups. "They suddenly fear this thing they've craved for so long. And as you know, fear makes people crazy and stupid."

I don't remember how or when, but somehow Will called me again and I convinced him to let me visit. When I walked through the doors of Clarendon—they were closed against the cold—I found him standing beside the guards' desk where he never stood—he didn't like being out there, exposed and alone. But there he was, waiting for me. He took me in his arms and held me more tightly than I remembered him ever holding me, and I whispered, "Please don't do that again. Please don't leave me…" And he promised he would not.

chapter thirty-nine

Just before Carole died, she asked if I would look after Pumpkin when she was gone. Ever since Carole had gotten sick, I had sensed that her big ginger cat sensed the loss ahead of him. While he once had been affectionate, even cuddly, he seemed to grow bigger and surly. Neighbors complained he was attacking their cats and kittens. But whenever he was with Carole, he curled up in her lap and purred. I had trouble imagining what he would be without her, and when I saw his big, handsome body slinking through the gardens hunting mice and kittens and muskrats, I couldn't help but think of Will playing tough. I promised Carole he would not be abandoned.

When I told Will I was going to take him in, he thought I was crazy to have promised. "I know you love Carole, and I know she loves Pumpkin, but we have some important things on our plate right now. We don't need a big angry cat, and besides, the neighbors hate him. What are you going to do with a renegade cat?" I told him and I told myself that I would find some kind of solution.

Ever since New Year's Day I had become hypersensitive to Will's frailties and cruelties and sensitivities. He saw everything as a potential disaster—even another animal though he loved animals. More and more I was struck by how much Pumpkin and Will reminded me of each other, and I became tentative around both of them. I began to keep even more secrets. When I saw Pumpkin, I called, "Carole's okay!" and I didn't tell Will that I was talking to Graham every day now about the madness that came over people facing parole. I said nothing to anyone about my notion that the same twisted fear and desire fueled Pumpkin in his prowling misery.

In February, two nights before Carole died, Pumpkin ran away. I was grateful at least that she wasn't aware he was missing. She existed in a haze of morphine by then. But I was furious at Pumpkin. I couldn't believe he would abandon her at that moment, that he could leave her just when she most needed him. I was absolutely aware that I was projecting, aware that this fury I was unleashing on a cat was the fury I wouldn't unleash on Will. But it made no difference that I understood what I was doing—I couldn't stop myself.

After Carole's funeral, I came home and began to set out lures for Pumpkin, hoping against hope he would come home. Now and then I caught a glimpse of him racing past, hiding in a bush, but whenever I moved in close, he hissed and bared his claws and teeth and ran. When Will told me to give up, I said, "Everyone needs a good home," and I didn't tell him that's the same thing I was planning to say at his parole hearing. "Everyone needs a good home" became my mantra. I said it every night to the air—hoping Pumpkin (and the gods) might hear this prayer as I placed food outside and hung tarps from the clothesline to create protection beneath which Pumpkin might sleep.

One day I finally tricked him into a walking into a crate. I had already found him a wonderful home with Doreen, an animal trainer who lived outside of town on acres of land. Doreen had to adopt him and give him a good life. So with him yowling in the crate, I drove ten twisting, winding roads out to Doreen's farm, and air kissed him goodbye.

In the weeks leading up to the hearing, every time I visited and every night on the phone, Will reminded me I'd better not count on anything. "They'll probably say no," he would say. "Don't count on anything. Ever." And when I visited Graham, he told me more stories—there was the man who jumped the fence the night before his hearing and another who took a hostage two nights before; there were the men who, at the eleventh hour, turned down their chance to attend their hearing. Graham always added, "Anything we can do we will." That was his mantra.

Every night for two weeks before the hearing, I walked around the neighborhood with Kell and Eddie, and as we walked, Eddie told me how cool it was that Will might be coming home. Every night I ate supper with Kate who always sent me to my room after we ate to write a story or grade papers, and whenever I complained that I was too tired or anxious, she shushed me and told me to get back to work because work took my mind off the things I couldn't do anything about. Many nights I talked to Arlene, confessing my fears to her because I knew she'd never tell a soul. And I spent time with Diane and Kate and Erin who were lighting candles and saying silent prayers that everything would turn out well for us.

I didn't talk to Will about the people I was counting on for help or the people I was asking favors of. I didn't tell him that I could feel them circling their wagons around us, ready to protect us. I didn't tell him because Graham had also warned me that he was probably flooded with guilt already, fearful of the ways he might let everyone down. If I reminded him of all these supporters, his guilt might send him bolting again. So I just told him stories. I told him what Eddie had told me about the way Kell always sat at the top of the laneway watching the road when I was away. The minute she heard my car turning onto the road from the highway half a kilometer away, she began to bark, and they could hear her all the way down at his house, could hear her bark that would crescendo to a howl. I imitated Eddie's imitation for Will.

"Don't the neighbors get mad?"

I explained how much everyone liked Kell, but he didn't believe me. He didn't believe the neighbors could like any of us.

When the water heater burst and the sump pump broke and the ceiling leaked, and Austin had been drunk and missing in action since Carole died, and I paid handymen, I didn't tell Will because he was already worried we didn't have enough money, would never have enough, that he could never earn enough. Trying to allay some of his fears about money, I took on another class, but when I told him about it, he scoffed. They didn't pay enough, he said, and besides, sometimes he thought they were just excuses to socialize. When I told him that work didn't have to be misery, that it could actually be fun, he shook his head at me, probably because he saw how miserable and worn out I felt. I wasn't having fun, but I pretended harder. I couldn't let the guards catch wind of any unhappiness between us.

I feared if they did, they might write a report about it and that report would go to the board, and that might lead to their questioning his ability to make it outside, and there would be one more excuse to deny his parole.

One day Arlene was visiting, trying to talk me through these myriad worries, and suddenly we heard a meow at the door. I looked around. Jazz was on the couch. My other cat, Mitzi, was sprawled on my bed. I looked through the patio door, and there he was: Pumpkin, staring at me, paws on glass. At first I blinked. There was no way he could have found his way from Doreen's house. I'd heard of animals traveling miles and miles to find their owners, but I'd never quite believed those stories. Besides, he had come to my house, not to Carole's, and the path was 10 confusing miles that crossed streams. But it was absolutely Pumpkin, skinnier, with a bruised right eye and paws thick with snow and mud. I opened the door and he ran inside. I poured him a bowl of cream and called Doreen.

She felt terrible. He'd run away ten days earlier but she hadn't had the heart to tell me. She had thought he might come back. We both were awed at his feat. "Bring him back home," Doreen said, and the way she said home made me believe that she considered it his. "This time I'll keep him inside until he's more at ease. He'll be fine. You should be proud of him, the big bugger."

Again when I looked at him an image of Will flashed before me. Will standing on the deck, gingery and battle scarred, hoping I would keep him, angry that I couldn't bring back everything and everyone he'd ever loved. And Arlene saw it too. Will and Pumpkin were alike: warriors, bruisers and bullies, and scaredy-cats.

The next day at a visit I asked Will if he hated the bungalow. He laughed at me. "Come on," he said, "look where I've been living for 13 years…" he waved his arms around the grimy visiting room. "It'll be beautiful," he said. But I didn't believe him, and so, a few days before the hearing, I started on a spring cleaning and fixing frenzy, and just as the place was beginning to feel okay, I woke one morning to discover the toilet was clogged, so I drove to Donevan's Hardware and asked Charlie for his strongest stuff. He pointed at a bottle of hot pink liquid, but he said it was poison, and I ought to use something less radical. I lived on the river, and these lethal concoctions flowed right into the waterfront—I didn't want to be one of those rotten polluters, did I?

But I had to have the strongest stuff. He sold it to me, extracting my promise to be extra careful. I promised, sped home and poured the whole bottle into the bowl.

The water seethed and sizzled, gurgled and burped. Then water rushed through the pipe and surged into the bowl. Relieved, I was just about to turn away when I saw a stain as pink as Pepto-Bismol in the center of the white porcelain bowl. I imagined Will seeing that spot. He'd already tsk tsked me for the rotting boards under the house and the cat-clawed screens and the peeling deck. I ran into the kitchen and grabbed a bottle of bleach and poured it into the toilet. Immediately the room filled with putrid, billowing smoke.

I inhaled only once. Once was enough. I started to cough and couldn't stop. I read the bottle's warning label: DO NOT MIX WITH BLEACH. I ran around frantically opening all the doors and windows, shooing all the animals outside as the stink and smoke swirled through the place. I turned on overhead fans and waved my arms, but I couldn't stop coughing or catch my breath.

I ran outside, and in the yard surrounded by meowing cats and barking Kell, I could smell the stench as the lethal stuff poured out of my lungs. I tried to stop coughing and looked longingly at my car but I couldn't even catch my breath for one second before another cough erupted, and I couldn't see through my tears. I rushed back inside and called Diane and heaved into the phone, "I need you."

She had me in Kingston General Hospital's Emergency Room within 30 minutes, and minutes later I was lying on a cot, inhaling ventilin through a mask and she was asking, "What were you thinking?"

I shook my head. I couldn't confess that I'd been thinking that Will would be unhappy with a pink stain in our toilet bowl, so I stayed quiet, and she left me for a while. The doctor said I needed time. I lay on that hospital bed, surrounded by flimsy curtains and listening to the man on one side shrieking with DTs about doctors sticking hot needles into his toes, and from the other side a man sobbing, "It was massive," and I knew he meant a heart attack. When a nurse popped her head into my

275

cubicle to ask how I was doing, I lifted the mask and said, "I'm fine, just fine." I clearly was not.

* * *

The night before the hearing, Barbara Baker called. She had been promoted and was assigned as Will's parole officer if and when he was granted parole. She was calling to tell me that letters had just come in from members of the family of Will's victim. She was faxing them over so I would be prepared since she had to present them at the hearing. The victim's wife and his brother had written demanding that the parole board not let Will out. They wrote about their grief. They called Will a cold-blooded killer. I'd heard about the brother. He had been in Cataraqui Bay in fact when Will was there, and the guards were careful to keep them separated. Dilshad had asked Will if he ever wanted to hurt this man, and Will had told her that he thought the guy was an idiot—a drug addict and trouble—but that he wanted nothing more than to get out of prison and take care of his family. He wanted nothing to do with that life that was in the past.

I knew the parole board was likely to dismiss a convicted criminal's word. But it was the second letter that froze me and sent waves of terror through my body. The wife's letter was all about Will's having shot her and the devastation that had caused. As I read the letter I realized I couldn't pretend this hadn't happened. There was a woman out in the world who had been grievously harmed by my husband. Her injuries had required several surgeries. She wrote saying she was afraid that Will would get out of prison and come to finish her off.

I finished reading and vomited. I felt sick with grief, and sick with fear, and sick with what I had a harder time explaining—anger. I was angry at her for waiting twelve whole years to write this letter. I was angry that we hadn't heard from these people when Will was first approved for passes. I wished we had found some way to address these fears and concerns, but what and how? And now what? Now it felt to me like these letters might be the seal on his coffin. They might be enough to discourage the board from seeing anything else.

And I felt something else. I wished I could meet this woman. I wished I could talk to her. I felt sick about my own behavior—the

276

way I had pushed her existence out of my consciousness for so many years. When I read those words—and I read them again and again—I was right back inside that first trailer, lying beside Will in bed, hearing about that second shot, and I wished I could see her. I wished I could understand what had moved Will to turn and shoot again after he had already shot one person. I could imagine none of it—and I didn't want to imagine. I had to be on Will's side. It was the night before the hearing.

I wished I could change the whole system.

Over the years Arlene and I had tried many times to contact representatives from Victims' Rights organizations. We had hoped to arrange a meeting of victims' families and prisoners' families—a meeting based on restorative justice models. Crime harms everyone; so does imprisonment. We wanted all those who had been hurt to gather in one room to talk, to face each other and discuss the outcome of crime and the outcome of punishment. We thought it was possible that in this kind of coming together, there might be some healing. And that night I wished I could call this woman to ask her what she needed, what I could do, how I might be able to help allay her fears. Will would never return to hurt her again. I knew that. I knew he wished only that there were some way he could turn back the clock. He wished he hadn't been drunk that night, hadn't tucked that gun into his jeans, hadn't been a dealer, hadn't been out of his mind. But maybe if she and I and he and her brother and her parents and their friends could sit down and talk, maybe some of the anger and fear and bitterness and misunderstanding and misery could be lessened. Maybe. And wasn't that worth a try? Prison didn't work to make anyone better or smarter, kinder or less frightening. And prison didn't punish only the prisoners. Like the anguish that radiated out to so many people with one man's murder, the misery of imprisonment radiated out to dozens, hundreds, thousands, hundreds of thousands.

But there was no time for conversation now, and there was no avenue for such conversations. I called Barbara back and asked her how seriously the parole board would take the Victim Impact Statements. She couldn't say, so the next day as I drove to Clarendon;

just like Will, I felt certain we had no hope. And then we were there in one of those small stark rooms seated before a panel of three, two women and one man. I couldn't read their faces. I never could. They prided themselves on that.

A woman with the tightly woven gray curls started off with the Victim Impact Statements. She passed the papers across the table to Will and asked what he thought. I was holding his hand under the table, and his hand felt ghoulishly cold.

"What do you think about this line, for instance," she asked. "... I fear for my life so I don't want him to know where I am or what I look like. I am afraid he will come to finish the job he began twelve years ago..."

Will told her he couldn't imagine her feeling any other way and that he wished he could explain what happened that night. He told her he didn't expect her ever to forgive him and that he hadn't spent a day since then not regretting his actions that night. He told her she had nothing to fear from him. He said he didn't know what else to say.

The man in the exquisite pin-striped suit leaned towards us and began to talk about his feelings about these statements, pointing out that the victim's brother had done a good deal of time and couldn't be seen as a credible source, but Will interrupted to say there was no reason any of them ought to forgive him, and that a record shouldn't automatically discredit someone because otherwise how could anyone believe anything he had to say at this hearing.

I felt proud of him for that—and it was true, of course. I knew no one saw prisoners as credible in any way, and that was as ridiculous as perceiving someone of stature as for some reason credible, but I drifted in and out of that conversation. It was hard to hear the same questions over and over, and besides, whenever I was in those rooms I thought about Edward Greenspan, one of Canada's most well-known criminal defense lawyers who wrote so scathingly about the parole system and particularly about the hearings, who so eloquently explained that only the best actors won in parole hearings. No one can feel remorse for years—it fades over time, replaced by other emotions. But it is remorse the parole board wants to hear, and the irony is that when they do hear truth, they seldom believe it. I kept thinking of the scene in *Shawshank Redemption* when the Parole Hearing Man says to Red, "your files say you've served 40 years of a life sentence. Do you feel you've been rehabilitated?" and he answers, "... Well, now let me see...I don't have any idea what that means." "It means," says the Parole Board Man, "you're ready to rejoin society..." Red tells him he has no idea what he means, that rehabilitation is a made-up politician's word so young men can dress up and wear suits and have a job. He asks if the man really wants to know if he's sorry for what he did.

Red's speech that follows always made me weep. He said what nearly everyone I met in prison felt—that not a day went by that he didn't feel regret, but not for the reason the Parole Board men thought he should. He said he looked back on that young stupid kid who committed that terrible crime, and he thought about how much he wanted to talk some sense into him. But that kid was gone, and there was just an old man left in his place. And rehabilitation "is just a bullshit word."

I knew Will was acting. I knew he truthfully regretted what had happened that night but that just like Red he wished he could go back and talk to that stupid, drunk young man he had been, and I also knew his deepest regrets now were for his own family and for himself, not for his victims. And I knew if he said such a thing out loud, they would never let him go.

Whenever I drifted back into the dialog I heard accusations, but every one of them blurred into one big accusation: "You killed someone. That is unforgiveable. Why should we ever release you?" And then I was pulled to attention when the man began to talk about the Emergency Involuntary Transfer of five years earlier. I felt the hair on my arms rise. The damn transfer was going to haunt us forever, and I think if I had been the one on the hot seat, I would have yelled, "Goddamn you, people, that was all bullshit!" But Will was a better actor than I. He calmly tried to explain. He told them the transfer had been politically motivated, that he had been actively trying to make some changes inside, and... But the woman jumped and said, "Why were you trying to make changes? What was in it for you?"

He smiled. "As it happens, nothing," he said.

The hearing went on for three hours, and just as I began to feel hopeless, the gray-haired woman brought up drugs, and Will explained that he hadn't touched a drop of drugs or alcohol since he was arrested more than 12 years earlier. And he said, "And if I could stay clean in here..." he spread his hands and looked over at the pin-striped man who had once been a warden.

"It's easier to get drugs outside than in prison," the woman said.

That's when the pin-striped man laughed. "Oh, no, no, no. That is most definitely not true," he said, and Will squeezed my hand. One little moment of hope.

My skirt was damp with perspiration by the time my three minutes for speaking finally came up. Three minutes to sum up everything. What I loved and what I loathed. What I feared and what I craved. I have no memory of what I said except I'm sure I begged them to give him a chance. I'm sure I told them he posed no risk to society. I'm sure I spoke of the fact that a life sentence meant that parole officers and parole boards and the police would always be watching, that he would always have to behave better than your average Joe. I'm sure I said that Sarah and Cass and dozens of others were committed to helping him lead a constructive life.

And then we sat out in a chilly hallway waiting for nearly an hour until Hughie Morrison told us they were ready for us, and we walked back in and sat, and the pinstriped man announced their decision to grant Will his day parole.

Under the terms of his parole, Will was to be released to live in a halfway house in downtown Kingston. He had served 12 years of a 13 to Life sentence, and until he had served the entire 13 years and returned to the Board for consideration for full parole, he would stay there. On Friday and Saturday nights he would be permitted to sleep at home, but for the rest of the week, he was to report to the halfway house no later than 11 p.m. each night. He could leave at 6 a.m. in the morning to drive the 15 miles to the bungalow. Any other travel required pre-approval by the Board. Barbara Baker would supervise his parole, seeing him once each week. And the rest of the stipulation list was short and to the point: no drugs, no alcohol, and most startlingly to me because I hadn't thought of it, no association with anyone with a criminal record.

Two weeks later, he walked out of prison. I was overjoyed. I thought everything was going to be all right. I thought all the complaints and fears and uneasiness that had grown up around us and between us would dissipate once he had lived outside for a while. It might take months, but we would move on to the next phase of our life together. I thought he would be happy; I thought I would be too. I thought he would woo me the way he had when we first met and that he would understand how good our life could be.

chapter forty

My father sent Will a puffy, beige winter jacket because that was the one thing the sisters had forgotten to buy him, and in March and on into April the weather remained cold. Each night he drove my car to the halfway house, and each morning at 6:30 a.m. he returned wrapped in that parka. Every morning he sank into the couch, getting up only to toss another log into the woodstove and to growl and pace and complain. He complained about the bungalow—it was too cold, too small. He complained about the halfway house—he was double bunked again with a man he could only call a goof. He would flick on the TV, cross his arms over his chest and lean forward to listen to the pre-opening stock market reports

At 9:30 every morning, when New York Stock Exchange opened, he turned up the volume on the TV and moved to my computer while I slinked into the back room where we had set up his older, slower machine, the one his mother had bought him years before. He needed the newer one because he was reading stock market quotes and needed a fast internet connection, but I was only writing, and an old computer did just fine. That's what he had decided, and I didn't argue, because I was too upset with how little this scene looked like the scenes of our life as I had imagined them.

Occasionally he called Emma, and I eavesdropped on their conversations. He convinced her to invest her money through him into the stock market, and I saw that he had become addicted to it. He couldn't stop trading, but the money he was trading (and usually losing) was hers, not his. It seemed to me a waste of his time, a waste of talents, a waste of resources, a waste of everything.

If I suggested we go to a movie, he would say we were too poor for such extravagances. When I said I thought a restaurant might be nice, he burst into a tirade about my overspending. He insisted I drive 35 miles to shop for groceries at the Co-op in Kingston because there we could buy in bulk instead of driving 5 miles to the local store where he said things cost far too much. Again I didn't resist, I didn't push. Over all those years we had developed a pattern, and as always, I was waiting for things to get better, and he was certain nothing would ever be good.

Often, for respite from his bad moods and from the TV and from his rants on the phone to a broker, I drove over to Diane's house where I wept about my dream that was turning into a nightmare. She listened and reminded me how hard this had to be for him. "It must be awful to not know anyone out here," she said. Katie agreed, though she brushed my hair and told me how much she loved me. When Sarah called to say she was getting ready to make the move, I kept my complaints to myself, and Kate was always trying to keep everyone upbeat and cool. She often brought us meals and set the table with flowers, trying to create a festive mood.

April bled into May, and he agreed to join the local gym, but on the first day there, when I began to bench press, he started to laugh. "That's how you've been lifting? No wonder you're not in good shape," he said, and he demonstrated how to do proper presses and squats, lunges and flies. "You have to work harder," he said. I couldn't believe what I was hearing, and I was angry, but quietly, because I also felt like a failure. Clearly nothing I did was ever going to be right. He refused to join me in daily jogs along the waterfront, and when I suggested he play hockey again—there was a local team—he said it reminded him of the beginning of all his troubles. When I suggested a construction job, he wouldn't even go for an interview; he assured me no one would hire an ex-con. If I asked him to join me and Kell on a walk, he told me he didn't like to walk because the neighbors stared at him. Bill Miles had given me a little wooden boat, but when I suggested we take a ride on it, he said the boat would take him hours of work to make it seaworthy. "There's no such thing as free," he said. "This boat? Bill Miles just gave me another job."

In early June it was finally warm, and when Barbara Baker arrived at the house for their weekly meeting, I greeted her warmly. She and I were standing outside near my garden, and she admired it, and we began to talk about forcing bulbs and annuals versus perennials. Will walked outside and glared at me for being friendly with "one of them." She was, after all, his jailer now. I felt embarrassed for liking Barbara and thinking she might be on our side. And sometimes when we were in bed and Will turned tender, he would whisper about the icy Canadian weather and about the lure of the Caribbean, but naturally I told no one about these conversations. Instead I decided we needed to take some kind of trip to break this mood. I asked Barbara if she would approve a pass for Will to visit his sister in Toronto, but she cautioned me to take things slow, and because she turned us down, I thought maybe he was right. She was an enemy.

Then one day, out of the blue, Will came to the house wearing a big smile and announced that Willie was coming to live with us for a while. It was clear to me that he and his son had talked about it, though he had mentioned nothing to me, and I tried to sound happy at the idea—his children might soften him and help him return to the world. But Willie had a criminal record. And Willie had never much liked me—he had always seen me as his mother's rival—and I wondered if his being there wouldn't be a parole violation, among other things. When I asked Barbara Baker about it, she said family members were exluded from the rule forbidding criminal associations.

I still worried about that rule. Big Bill phoned a few times, and Elton called from Calgary, and Tim called, and Alberto who was about to be released wanted to visit us with Aurelia and their kids. Bernard and Connie wanted us at their wedding. I wished I could tell Barbara that talking to his friends, all ex-convicts, was the only thing that seemed to lift Will's mood. But I couldn't tell her that because if she knew he was talking to them, she'd have to send him back inside for violating the terms of his parole, so there was another lie of omission, and all those lies ate at me.

Then Willie moved in, and the minute he did, Will's energy returned. The two of them began to work outside together under the hot summer sun. Will had concocted a plan for fixing the house that began with building a great sea wall. I watched them mixing wheel-barrow after wheelbarrow of cement and working twelve-hour days, sweating and grunting. The wall was designed to be 60 feet long, five-feet high, so firmly planted in the earth, a tsunami couldn't have toppled it. I watched it rising higher and higher, block upon block. I watched the two of them, sunburned and exhausted, work until the sun went down when they hauled themselves inside to eat the supper I cooked. While we ate they talked about their plans for the next day. Neither of them had much to say to me.

Sometimes after Willie fell asleep, Will and I slipped into our bed-room and made love. We both had been starved for sex for so many years, and our lovemaking was intense, but I began to notice there was little tenderness between us—less and less as the months passed. We would set the alarm for 10 p.m. so he could make it back to the halfway house for curfew, and we would make love and fall asleep. When the alarm went off, he woke grumbling and without saying much he walked outside and drove away, and often I could not fall back to sleep.

In August with the sea wall almost finished, I began to think we might start spending some family time. One day I came home from teaching a class to find two trucks dumping 27 loads of topsoil into our yard, and in addition to the mess and the weeks of work this portended, I pictured my credit card bill soaring toward its limit. It was my card we were using. It was, he explained, my house, and he was working to make it worth twice as much. And when I said, "But it's our house," he would shake his head and say that I had bought it and he was just trying to put in his share.

That didn't feel right. It felt manipulative, but I couldn't explain even to myself how we had come to this. So once again I kept quiet and Will and his son transformed the hill of a front lawn into a sleek, suburban slope. When they had finished that, they began to build a second wall, this one at the side of the house, and that's when it struck me—it had taken awhile but it finally hit—the utter irony of a man getting out of prison only to come home to build walls around him, to seal him off from the world.

"We'll plant trees, too," he said. "Close off the place. Give us some privacy." And while he walled himself off from everyone, he walled himself off from me too, and whenever I gingerly suggested he needed to get a real job, he railed. Couldn't I see that he was doing the real work this place needed? Didn't I appreciate how hard they were working? Wasn't I aware that without him this house would probably have tumbled to the ground by now? He climbed under the house and came up sooty and furious about the mess he'd found beneath the house and told me it would require months of work. He wondered aloud at how I could have been dumb enough to buy such a wreck.

And I drove to Diane's house and cried.

Late in July Willie announced one morning that he was leaving. He said he had things to do, and when Will came home and heard the news, he glared at his son but said nothing, and Willie left. Will spent the afternoon in furious silence under the house, coming up once in a while to put in a trade or call the broker or stare at the television set, listening to Maria Bartiromo's stock report. I became jealous of pretty Maria Bartiromo with her perfect hair and clothes and high heels and that sexy lisp. That made me even sadder. "How can I be jealous of a woman on TV?" I wept to Diane. "I have gone mad."

But I thought Sarah's arrival in early August would change everything until, almost the day she arrived, Will began to make demands. He insisted she had to figure out what she wanted to do with her life. He imposed deadlines on her for decisions. He accused her of being lazy, and when she ignored him, he became angrier still and told her she just wanted to be like her mother, a complete failure. When I tried to mediate, he turned his anger on me. Finally, towards the end of August, I decided we had to have a party to celebrate Sarah's 20th birthday, and our 44th and 45th that had just passed.

I invited everyone who had not judged us, everyone who had asked to meet him, everyone who had been kind. Violating parole regulations, I also invited Big Bill and his new girlfriend, and Aurelia and Alberto, and Tim and a couple of other guys I'd heard who had just gotten out. The list grew long.

Sarah and I had fun cooking and cleaning and putting up balloons on the trees surrounding the lawn, and by mid-afternoon on the day of the party, people began to stream onto our new beautiful lawn. The air was already getting cool in late afternoons, but kids came wearing bathing suits, and many leaped into the river from our beautiful new cedar dock that Will had also built. When anyone complimented the dock or the wall or the lawn, I loudly praised Will, loud enough so he could hear. People mingled, chatted, ate and drank, and I moved through the crowd. "I hope I get a chance to talk to Will," Richard said, and then Lisu said the same thing, and so did Debi and Tom, but Will was sitting down at the waterfront in a cluster of chairs surrounded by his old prison buddies, and they were busy swapping stories. They looked like the old crew, like old times, like they were still inside, and they made it clear that their circle was theirs, not to be invaded.

I watched my beloved friend Richard, a fellow former columnist, as he stood just outside their circle for a long time, leaning in. He smiled. He waited. He listened. I think he must have thought they would invite him in, but after a while he seemed to give up and he walked up the lawn towards me. He took my arm and whispered, "I don't mean this to sound critical, Amy, but they're like aliens. It's like they live on another planet. No wonder he's having such a hard time adjusting out here..."

I looked at them laughing, slapping thighs, leaning in close, laughing harder still, and I realized it was the first time I had seen Will relax, and the sight broke my heart because he never looked that happy with me or with Sarah. And when the party ended, as Sarah and I were cleaning up, after he had gone to bed, she said, "Amy, this is ridiculous. He's a bastard. You should throw him out. Tell him he's the one who needs to grow up!"

"Don't be so hard on him," I told her. "He just needs time."

I couldn't even take her side against him. I was sure if we just gave him time, we could all come back to each other. But time passed, and then one day in late September Barbara finally agreed to let us take a trip to Toronto to visit Emma. Sarah agreed to look after the animals, but on the morning we were to leave, Will suddenly shouted at me from the bathroom. "Damnit, Amy. Damn this hole of a house!"

I heard gushing water and rushed into the bathroom to find him standing with the faucet in his hand and torrents of water running from the tap. "Now we can't go, damn it, because now I have another job to take care of." I didn't say a word. I reached under the sink, turned off the main water tap, got in the car and drove to Donevan's Hardware where I bought a new faucet and sealing tape. I drove back home and fixed the faucet while Will stomped angrily around the house, and when I finished, I turned on the water again. I walked into the living room and said, as coldly as I could—I was furious at him finally—"We can leave now."

"What happens if something else breaks?" he snarled at me.

"Sarah knows who to call," I said. We drove for three hours in silence. I stared at the cars passing us and invented stories for their inhabitants. I wondered if any of them had lived in cells for more than a decade, if anyone else was driving to the big city for the first time in ten years. I imagined a Woody Allen-style scene, like the moment in Annie Hall when Marshall McLuhan steps out of a movie line to offer the perfect line. I envisioned a car pulling up beside us, a man leaning out and calling, "Let me tell you how to help your husband feel at home in the world…"

No one stopped. No one offered wisdom. Emma offered luxuries—dinners at the finest restaurants in Toronto, her beautiful house, brunches on the waterfront. After three days, while we were driving home, he began to talk about our needing more money—enough money to live as well as Emma lived. He said he was going to make a fortune in the stock market, and when I hesitantly suggested again that he consider a job, he laughed and told me nobody who wanted real money just took a lousy job.

That was true. There was no job in the world that could earn him the kind of money and comforts he craved. And I understood that even if there were such a thing as rehabilitation, greed was the one thing no one could cure. And when we got back home, I discovered Sarah had packed up her things. When he had left for the halfway house, she told me she could not stay, and she said that she wished I would ask him to leave. I told her I couldn't; I had made a vow, and breaking it would feel like the end of the world, the end of too many dreams. I didn't tell her that it also felt like the end of any possibility that I could ever hope to love or be loved the way my parents had loved each other. I was watching my father look after my mother— he'd moved his whole life home to take care of her, and that was what, I thought, love had to mean. And I still had that tiny flicker of hope in my heart that over time Will was going to make his way home.

One day near Christmastime, Diane invited Will to join her out in town for coffee and conversation, and when he came home, he folded me into his arms. His eyes welled up with tears and he began to apologize for his behavior all these months. "I don't know what's wrong with me. I can't feel at ease out here. I don't know what to ask of anyone. I'm so sorry, Amy…I'm so sorry…. I know I've hurt you." I thought of all those stories I had read and heard about men who beat their wives and afterwards beg forgiveness, and I couldn't forgive him. I couldn't tell him it was all okay. It wasn't okay. He kept prodding. "I promise, Amy, I will try."

The leaves were changing color. I was dreading the coming winter when we would have to spend most of our time inside. Whenever we didn't know what to say to each other, we went to bed, made love, fell asleep. That's what we did, and when the alarm rang, he woke and said, "I promise, life will be better. I swear it will." I think I had stopped believing him.

chapter forty-one

In January the ice storm began with a simple rainstorm, except the rain did not stop. Temperatures plunged, the rain kept falling, and by morning it was falling in pellets. Power lines toppled and ice pounded trees and roofs and cars. From Montreal to Ottawa and all points south, rain battered us. The first night of the storm the trees around us started to fall, and every few moments we heard a crash and the earth quaked. By mid-afternoon the next day all circuits were still overloaded and thousands of miles of distribution lines were down. We listened to the news on radios powered by generators, but in town all the flashlights and generators were sold out and batteries were impossible to find. The neighbor kids, Eddie and Michelle, appeared at our door with D-sized batteries tucked into their shirts. "Don't ask where we got 'em," they said.

I plugged them into our radio so we could hear music and news. The largest peacetime deployment of troops in Canada's history was being called in to help, and police were patrolling the roads, warning people not to budge from home unless travel was vital. I fed the woodstove, lit candles and kerosene lanterns and drove into town for gas because I didn't want Will to have to worry about running out on his trip back to the halfway house that was powered by three generators and was light and warm. I waited for two hours because Will couldn't risk being late.

On Friday, the third day of the storm, Will announced he was taking the car to Ottawa. "I'll be home late tonight. Don't wait up," he said. But he had no pass to go to Ottawa, and the highways were full of cops. I begged him not to go, but all the sweetness dropped away, and he growled at me and accused me of acting like his mother, or his jailer. He told me he was a grownup and he had someone he had to see, and without another word he was gone, leaving me with Kate and her dogs and with Connie who had come to stay with us because they had no woodstove or generators. The three of us chopped ice out of the river so we could collect water to flush the toilet. We chopped more wood and kindling to feed the woodstove so we could heat ourselves and heat water on the stove. I worried. I worried out loud. I worried to myself. I cried. And Kate tried to talk some sense into me.

Will needed help, she told me. He was ill, and he needed help, and I had to tell Barbara about what was going on so she could get him some help. I stopped listening. If I told Barbara she would send back inside, and we would be right back where we had started—nowhere. Night fell. The storm raged on. Every tree branch creaked under the weight of ice, and Kate and Connie and I huddled beneath blankets and watched the candles melt. "He might get stopped. And arrested," I said, beginning to worry out loud again. Connie and Kate fell asleep, but I just tossed and turned, checking my watch every three minutes until finally at 2 a.m. I heard the car roll up the drive, and I squeezed my eyes closed. I wanted him to think I was asleep.

Five minutes later he was sitting on the bed beside me, pressing his hand into my back and whispering, "I brought you a present." I sat up, pretending to be just waking. I took the bag he offered and inside I found a royal blue ski jacket that wasn't unlike one I already owned. "They were on sale. I couldn't resist. I thought how great your eyes would look in this," he said, and he kissed my nose. And one week later, with our power finally restored, my credit card bill arrived and I saw he had purchased that jacket on my card. Without telling him, I gave the jacket away, but I think that was one of those straws—one of those moments when I finally began to realize there wasn't any way that I could help him. And this wasn't love.

Even Diane and Kate, the most forgiving people I knew, people who cared for him, told me I had to change things. And still I created excuses for him. It was the halfway house. When he no longer had to live there, when he began to earn a living, when he met some people he liked, when I made a little more money, when his stocks began to do better, when he got back to that old novel in the drawer, when his full parole hearing came, when he was truly free...

One day in July, a few months after he had passed the year-mark of his day parole, Barbara told us she was recommending full parole for year thirteen. The hearing would be in August, next month, six weeks away. It was the long Canada Day weekend, and we lifted glasses in celebration. He was drinking ginger ale, sweating from work building the third wall he hoped we could finish building that weekend. "You know," he said, looking out at sailboats skidding along the river, "sometimes when it's this hot, I think about how just one beer would taste so damn good."

"You deserve a beer for all this work," I said and without letting myself think about what I was doing, I drove into town and bought a six-pack, brought it home to him, and we raised another glass to toast the future. Two hours later he sent me back to town to buy six more while he put the finishing touches on the wall. While I was driving back home with the beer bouncing in the backseat, I turned up the radio so the music would drown out the voice in my head that was telling me he had just crossed a line.

He did cross that line. Once he drank those beers, there was nothing to stop him from having a drink now and then, and then four, then six, then eight or ten. He always had a reason: Stock market losses. Idiot roommates. Fears about the parole hearing. Barbara's voice. The weather. Fears about the parole hearing. Losing his mom so fast. All those years inside. Fears about the parole hearing. Not being allowed to hang out with his friends. The kids being with Laura. Fears about the upcoming parole hearing.

In August we went to the hearing, and the board granted him full parole. He moved out of the halfway house and into our home, and then it was time to celebrate with a beer or two or three. Whenever he was thirsty from all that renovation work or when it was time to mourn the passing of summer, or when it was so cold and dark only a beer could cheer him up. He drank, and when he drank he did not become any less mean and cool and distant, and all of my excuses for him began to drift away, and I spent less and less time at home because I wasn't happy there.

In January, five months after he had moved home, one Sunday afternoon we had a rousing fight. I've no idea what it was about—it could have been that I asked him to stop drinking or to get a job or to be kinder or to stop trading or to tell his sister that he needed her help, and that he had lost all her money. Outside a fierce snowstorm was raging, and I couldn't jump in my car and drive to Diane's house or to Kate's. Instead I crept into the back room and into the little single bed back there. I pulled the covers over my head. I wanted to sleep alone. Kell walked in and lay down on the floor beside me. And a few minutes later Will knocked on the door and I told him to go away.

When he tried to open the door, he accidentally nudged Kell's foot. When she yelped, instead of stopping and apologizing the way I was sure he would—he loved Kell; he loved the animals—he just pushed harder, and Kell wailed. And that was it. Somehow that was the final straw. I got out of bed, walked out of the room, picked up the phone and called Emma. I told her I was finished with her brother and she would have to come take him away. I picked her because she wouldn't turn her back on him, she wouldn't do anything to hurt him, she wouldn't tell anyone anything that might send him back.

The next day as he packed we didn't speak to each other, and by mid-afternoon when Keith arrived to pick him up, all his belongings were packed away—all but a photograph on the wall. It was a gift Cass had given him at Christmas last year. She'd spent weeks making a frame, and into the frame she'd placed a picture of herself on her father's knee. She was seven, and they were sitting on the steps at a trailer visit, and his arms were around her. It reminded me of the picture I keep of me and my dad. "Don't forget this," I said, but he walked out without taking the picture or saying goodbye. After they left, I wrapped the picture and put it in the mail to Emma's house. I couldn't bear the idea that Cass might ever see he had left it behind.

For three solid months I did little else but finish the work I had to do and lie in bed and cry. Sometimes I ventured out to see Graham or Diane or Kate. I wept to Graham about what a failure I was. And blessed Graham consoled me. "You kept your word and helped him get out," he said. "You're far from a failure. Besides, how many marriages last even seven years?" But I was inconsolable then. Somehow I knew intuitively that there was nothing to do to heal but sit and wait, stay quiet, let the tears flow. Sometimes there is nothing else to do.

* * *

One morning in late March, out of the blue I got a call from the Parliamentary Justice Committee. After more than four years of trying, they had finally decided they wished to hear our brief on behalf of the Alliance of Prisoners' Families. The man who called wanted to know if I could come to Ottawa to present the brief in mid-May. When I talked to Sarah, she told me I had to go, and even better, she wanted to join me.

May in Ontario is the month of occasional fleeting last-ditch snowstorms, but also one of summer-like wind. It is the month when the smell of soil returns full force, and that day was one of the truly beautiful days. Sarah was 21 and beautiful and happy, and we were driving together with the windows wide open. Both of us were dressed in suits and heels, and we looked ordinary and sane. And I had even begun to feel sane. Sometimes all you can do is wait and think, and I had thought about everything I knew, everything I'd learned, everything I had done right, and everything I had done wrong. I shouldn't have lied to him and to myself, but I felt proud of myself too. I had gone inside to learn about prisons. And I'd learned about prison.

As we drove I told Sarah about the brief and why I thought it was so important that families play a role in Correctional planning. We talked about how much we know and how little credit people give us. I told her I was going to talk about our needing to have a voice—not the final voice. We don't know everything, and like me, a lot of prisoners' loved ones make mistakes. But we also understand a great many things about what does and doesn't help people to heal from wounds, and I told her I wanted to talk about how much I believed justice is served best through measures that resolve conflicts and repair harm. Sarah and I agreed that it is so often innocent family members whose ever fiber seeks a means to renew, a means to restore, a means to repair.

Our brief was modest. We were requesting that representatives of families be invited to sit on boards and panels that make decisions about prisoners' lives. I described to Sarah the image I had always carried of a battalion of prisoners' children marching the streets, demanding that people listen to them and understand not only that prisoners were people but that their loved ones are, and when I finally paused for breath, Sarah said, "Okay, but I'm not talking. I just came for an excuse to spend the day with you."

When we reached the building a woman told us we could sit in the hearing room to listen to those presenting before us while we waited our turn, so we tiptoed in and settled into seats in the back of the room. The speaker was a victims' rights activist, and she was complaining. Her complaints sounded familiar—it was a litany I'd heard again and again from Victims' Rights Activists, and from many others. Prisoners got out of prison too easily, too fast; prisoners were babies, coddled; parolees were dangerous; parole had to be abolished. Her list went on and on, and I closed my eyes, only half listening as she insisted Canada reinstate the death penalty and also create longer, harsher sentences. When she began to talk about how vile it was that murderers be permitted to spend time with their families, that they had destroyed families and ought therefore to be forbidden time with theirs, I felt Sarah's body stiffen.

"She doesn't even know what she's talking about," Sarah whispered to me. "I have to tell these people what it's really like."

An hour later, we moved to our seats at the microphones. We sat at a table surrounded by eight MPs—two representatives from each of the parties and a French translator for the Parti Quebecois MP. Behind them sat technicians and scribes, and I watched as Sarah looked each one of these men and women in the eye. I introduced myself, then I introduced her.

I knew what they were thinking when they looked at her. She looked young and innocent, so like the girl next door she could not possibly be the daughter of a murderer. And then she spoke. She told them that her father had gone to prison when she was five so she knew one thing: That most people in prison were treated like they were dangerous animals. And so were their families.

"You can't expect to treat people like they're dangerous animals and then expect them to behave like human beings. I think you should listen to us and not shunt us aside and maybe that could make some difference."

epilogue

When I first decided to visit prison, I wanted to learn what happened to all those who inhabit the spaces behind those walls. I wanted to discover what about prisons was wrong and what, if anything, was right and sane and helpful to society. I wanted to convey that understanding to my readers in a medium-sized Ontario city, most of them preternaturally given to being open-minded and generous of spirit.

That was my intention, and only that.

Years later, as I read my journals and letters and notebooks, memories flooded back in a series of images. Sounds returned—especially the sound of gates forever clanging behind me. I began to realize how much energy I expended in trying to paint a picture of Will that wouldn't frighten or alarm anyone, that would explain how I could love someone who had killed a man. I was working to offer an image that would create in readers empathy for not only Will but for all those who are not psychopaths but have committed serious crimes, those who want a chance, after they serve their time, to do something good out in the world. When I read my notes about the drudgery of driving, the lines, the waiting, the tiny tables, the stink, the sitting for hours, the endless talk, I remembered that I could seldom let myself feel that drudgery; if I had I might have stopped visiting. And I couldn't stop going to see him. I was, in a sense, addicted. For so many years, in so many ways, Will was one of the only people I thought truly understood the things that I understood.

Still, even after I had broken the bonds that tied us to each other, all the sadness of those years stayed tucked deep inside of me. Even after I fell in love again and married Dennis and moved to Los Angeles and began living a life of much pleasure, I couldn't stop thinking about prison. In my dreams and my waking life I returned to that time. I felt a ball of tangled words I never expressed sitting in the pit of my belly. Until I untangled that ball and understood everything I could about what happened, I would feel an ache, unable to write or think about almost anything else.

Almost 18 years to the day after I first met Will, I was rushing home from a meeting with my writing group, needing to change clothes to head to UCLA where I was to appear on a panel of writers for Career Day. As I was driving home, I thought about what I might say about this memoir I'd been working on. Sometimes I worried about what would happen when it was published. An excerpt had recently appeared in *The New York Times*. I had asked Sarah and Cass not to tell their father about it, but Sarah had, and ever since she and I had kept our distance. I was hurt that she had done something that might jeopardize me. What if he tried to keep me from telling this story? What if he… I wasn't sure he could do anything, but I was upset that I might have to swallow my truths, again.

I had showered and changed and was ready to leave the house when my cell phone rang. The area code was 416—Toronto. That meant it was Sarah or Cass, and since they seldom called in the middle of the day and Sarah's dog had been sick, I worried that this might be the vet's, so I answered. When I heard Sarah's voice, I quickly asked, "What happened? Is Maya okay?"

"She's fine. She had the operation," she said hurriedly, "but I'm calling from Dad's. He wants to talk to you." She had handed over the phone.

He and I hadn't talked for more than two years, and even before that, we'd only talked once in a while, always about matters that pertained to the kids. I knew he had stayed out. I knew he had a girlfriend and was living in relative peace. I didn't know much else except that he didn't want me to write about him.

"How's that mutt of yours?" he laughed. When we had talked, we talked about our dogs—neutral ground.

"Fantastic," I said. I began to go on but he interrupted. "So Sarah says you wrote a book…"

I waited, my heart beginning to pound.

"Sarah's worried about it," he went on, "but I was telling her what I thought, and then I thought I ought to tell you. It's this. I wish you every success. I want you to have everything you deserve—all the things you gave me …I want you to publish whatever you want to publish."

He kept talking, but this sounded so kind, I felt half ready for another shoe to drop. To cover my ass I said, "The book isn't really about you—it's about me, and about prison and how it harms so many people…"

"It does," he said. "It destroyed me." He began to talk about how crazy he had been all those years, how if he hadn't been crazy, he wouldn't have worked to destroy everything I had tried to create. "I want you to know this, Amy, and I want Sarah to know. I loved you. I did the best I could, but I was messed up. I didn't really know how to love anyone."

I began to cry, but I didn't let on that I was. He told me he wanted Sarah to know that everything I did for him and for her and for her sister and his mother had been generous and loving. He didn't want her to be crazy the way he had been. And then he asked about my mom.

I told him she was a ghost, lying nearly comatose in a nursing home, that she hadn't spoken for five years but Dad still visited her every day. My dad still sat by her side and kissed her and held her hand and talked to her.

"That's how people should love," he said.

"You think that?"

"I know that," he said, "and if I'd been sane, I would have treated you the way your dad treats her. I'm sorry I couldn't. I'm glad you've found someone who can."

"And that story in *The Times*…"

"…I read it," he said. "I knew I could trust you anyway, but I read it and it's fine. It's good. So okay, here's Sarah…"

"Hi," she said softly.

"Wow," I said.

"Yeah, I know…"

acknowledgments

Writing is a solitary sport, but the boundless friendship and brilliant notes of Diane Botnick and Thomas Frick always spur me on. I found the courage to tell this story thanks to years of stalwart friendship from "the Canadians"—Don Akenson, Eddie, Jim and Fran Byers, Jim Cavanaugh, Therese Conway-Killen, Charlie Donevan, Maureen Garvie, Jillian Gilliland, Barb Hill, the Hopley family, Mark Lackie, Don LaFlamme, Arlene Leigh, Jane MacDonald, Jean McCall, Norris McDonald, Carole McNeeley, Anndale McTavish, Erin and Katie Merrill, Diane Smith-Merrill, Bill Miles, Kate Phillips, Carolyn Sherman, and Debi Wells. I am equally grateful to "the Americans" who always had my back: Bruce Bauman, Harriet Choice, Dan Dalton, Ken Jones, Nancy Lord, Hass Murphy, Alan McDermott, Shirley and Ian Nisbet, Richard Perry, Carlyle Poteat, the Scala family, Charles Woodroffe and Suzan Woodruff.

To those places that nurture the artistic spirit, I am thankful to the Virginia Center for the Creative Arts, with gratitude to Craig and Sheila Pleasants and to Jessie Carter especially for helping to make VCCA a second home. To Wellfleet and Montauk, and to Bill Partlo for a haven in Idyllwild.

To the powerhouse women of my writing group who read parts of this book more times than anyone ought to have to, thank you, Elizabeth Berman, Melissa Cistaro, Samantha Dunn, Hope Edelman, Mim Eichler-Rivas, Deborah Lott, Sandra Kobrin, Samantha Robson, Christine Schwab, and Amy Wallen.

I am grateful to those who offered opportunities for publishing and performing excerpts along the way: Spike Gillespie & Katherine Tanney for *5,000 Stages of Grief*, Spark Off Rose producers Mark Betancourt,

Janet Blake, Karin Gutman, Alicia Sedwick, & Jessica Tuck, Wendy Hammers for Tasty Words, Lori Ada Jaroslow & Kaz Matamura for The Secret Rose, and Amy Ferris & Hollye Dexter for *Dancing at the Shame Prom*.

I am grateful to literary agents Laurie Liss and to Jennifer Lyons for support, encouragement and guidance.

I am indebted to Joyce Mott and Melissa Roth, not only for exquisite editing but for exquisite friendship, to Laura and Gary Dumm for their artistry and generosity, and to my friends whose intellect and wisdom through every draft kept me honest—Heather Cariou, Alexandra Getov, Lesley Hyatt, Roland Tec, and Marianne Wallace.

I can never say thanks enough to my dad, Skip Friedman, devoted both to me and to the power of story. I thank my brother, Peter Friedman, for his love and legal acumen, and my sisters, Karen Friedman, Rachel Friedman, and Marina Corleto Friedman, for their generous love for me and for Sarah and Cassandra.

And to my husband, Dennis Danziger, for everything, and more.

Photo Credit: Marcus DuMouchel

Amy Friedman lives with her husband, the writer Dennis Danziger in Los Angeles where she teaches memoir at UCLA Extension, Skirball Cultural Arts Center, Idyllwild School of the Arts and PEN USA. Her essays and stories have appeared in newspapers and magazines around the world and in numerous anthologies. She writes the internationally syndicated column Tell Me a Story. Desperado's Wife is her third memoir.